ONE BILLION INDIANS
Socio-Economic Conditions—Problems and Prospects

ONE BILLION INDIANS
Socio-Economic Conditions Problems and Prospects

Gulab Sen

KALPAZ PUBLICATIONS
DELHI–110 052

ONE BILLION INDIANS : Socio-Economic Conditions Problems and Prospects

(Demography)

Rs. 890

ISBN: 81-7835-096-3

The views expressed in this publication are of the author and not of the publisher

Published in 2002 in India by
Kalpaz Publications
C-30, Satyawati Nagar
Delhi-110 052
E-mail: Kalpaz@hotmail.com

Lasertypesetting by: Varsha Graphics, Delhi
Printed at: Mehra Offset Printers, New Delhi

Dedicated to

the People of India;
My Readers

Contents

Preface

नहीं पाप का भागी केवल व्याध ।
जो तटस्थ हैं समय लिखेगा उनका भी अपराध ।।

It is not only the butcher who will be responsible for the sins, all those neutral people shall also be recorded by the time for their crimes.

It is these two lines of a great poet that has accelerated this work of mine. I was sitting on these ideas for fifteen years thinking that people may come up and join their duty to sort out this mess, but I have found them self-centered and neutral if not indifferent towards the existing situation in this country. It is this neutrality of all of us that's why we are here where we belong. The time is over when we used to blame the British for our miseries or the Congress party that replaced them. It is about time that we understand our problems, the remedies and the neglect that is all around us and sort it out. Though I am not a devotee of Sri Krishna, yet I would like to quote few lines from Bhagwad Geeta:

यदा यदा हि धर्मस्य ग्लानिर्भवति भारत ।
अभ्युत्थानम धर्मस्य तदात्मनं सृजाम्यहमं ।।
परित्राणाय साधूनाम् विनाशाय च दुष्कृताम् ।
धर्मसंस्थापनार्थायः संभावामि युगेः युगेः ।।

Our normal translations and understanding of these verses have been limited until now simply to know that Sri Krishna or God get reincarnated on this earth whenever there is decline of *dharma* that is truth and to destroy the evil and preserve the good and truth, the God or Krishna comes back in reincarnation from time to time.

Many people may not believe in this, and those who believe tend to leave everything to God like our neutrality. While some others would say, even if the God comes down to the earth, He won't be able to sort out the Indian problems. They will even say and it is also true, that Sri Krishna or God Vishnu haven't got reincarnated for the past 5 thousand of years as if no sin or decline of *dharma* have taken place since the days of Mahabharata.

However, I have improved on the meaning and understanding of the above famous *slokas*. Though I have not learned Sanskrit yet it is not difficult to see the truth. It is like this, "whenever we see or do wrong a sort of revultion erupts in ourselves, it is natural, we know and become aware that I have done something wrong. The realisation that something wrong have been done manifest itself in ourselves and in the society. This is the reincarnation of God in ourselves and in the society. Therefore, the good *dharma* gets resurrected in ourselves and in the society. Further to protect this truthfulness and to destroy or punish the wrong-doers and the evilness in ourselves and in the society we have to keep remembering our duty of doing the right things from time to time means every-second. To keep it short I shall appeal to my readers to go through this book, where I have tried to understand, the chaos and the problems and I have presented to you the solutions as I have understood. It is not only for the Indian scene but for the whole world to get a grip on the new challenges facing the earth. And to break their neutrality of being an onlooker I have decided to come out.

योगः कर्मसु कौशलम

That is to do our duty very efficiently is the ultimate *yoga*. And further I would like to quote from Atharvaveda as well:

शं नौं देवीरभिष्टयं आपो भवन्तु पतियें ।
शं योरभि स्त्रंवन्तु नः ।।

O great men help the sufferers like the divine rain that comes to quench the thirst of the drought-ridden earth that helps to grow things for the comfort of the people and life and protects them from all kinds of diseases.

Similarly we need today great men of promises who can lead us to get our difficulties, the men who can symbolise the proverb 'There are men and men but every stone is not a gem', The crowd of directionless hooligans is all over on the platforms, in the streets and in the Parliament. They do not pick up the gems, they simply throw stones and stones at each other. This is neither the reflection of the constitution of India, nor the wisdom of our *vedas*. It is about time that we get educated and qualified to inherit the *vedas* instead of inheriting illiteracy and sufferings of today.

I would conclude this address to you with this mantra from *Sri Samveda*.

ॐ सहस्त्रधारः पवते समुद्रो वाचमिंङ्खयः ।
सोमस्पती रयिणाम् सखेंद्रस्य दिवेः दिवेः ।।

O Lord of the whole universe, please stay with us as our protectors and friends of our lives and property every day, every hour, every minute.

May I appeal to you all to lift this country up as a prosperous country because this country has limitless treasure in its existence.

Gulab Sen

Bharat that is India

The History of Bharat Down the Ages

Various studies show that the Homosapiens attained their form about 2,60,000 years ago or more with mankind moving towards its present civilisation about ten thousand years ago. Indian civilisation, which is known as the Indus civilisation or the Gangetic civilisation or more appropriately the Hindus civilisation is the oldest living civilisation in the world. Indian civilisation is as old as history. The last and the first time the name Bharat is recorded in the *Mahabharat* episode itself. It seems that *Bharat-khand* or Indian continent was some kind of a regional confederation where there were lots of kings and princes who finally got involved in the war of Mahabharat. Prior to that in the Puranic History, the Shiva, Vishnu, Brahma period, or the Ramayana period there was some sort of a confederation in existence, but that time the Indian confederation could have been bigger as it surely had lot of Himalayan areas including Tibet and Nepal as part of this confederation. That is no basis for deciding the borders of India today. The name India in English has been ascribed to its geographic positioning. It is more likely derived from the river Indus, known as Sindh and then Hind in Arabic. So Indu, Sindhu or Hindu, they are all variations of names in different languages. People also refer to Hindukush mountain as the beginning of the Indian border and it is interesting to note that Bharat in Turkish means spice. It seems that Bharat is not named after king Bharat, but the name comes from the Sanskrit word Bharteem, which means the glowing light of the sun. Since there is plenty of sun in India around whole year. It could be that the *Bharat-khand* turned into Bharat. Bharat still sounds the most appropriate name for India and since we have over used this very name India while talking and writing in English, it should not make much difference if the name India has been used in this text as it is written in English.

The Vedic Period. The Vedic period was the most important period of the world history. Even if we assume that the Vedic period is the history of the Indian sub-continent, it is still the most important recorded system of administration and civilisation and it is still more important that the same Vedic knowledge is passed down to us and hence the Hindus civilisation becomes the oldest living civilisation on earth. Therefore, whether you call it Indus or Hindus or Indian civilisation, the fact remains that these words are synonymous. Also people either know or should know that the word Indian is not limited to present India as well. The people in Europe who were eager to discover India also discovered America. Hence they in their desperation to reach India, called it as East India and that of the Caribbean as West Indies and when Columbus landed in America they called the natives Indians. And there are these old cultures in the American continent that have some similarities with Indian cultures and civilisation. However, it is a great consolation for the Indians that we did not get annihilated by the invaders for the last two thousand years and neither we got wiped out like the Indians of America and the aboriginals of Australia and New Zealand.

Puranic Period. The Vedic period was the most glorious period of Indian history so far because we were to first get civilised and developed into a proper social system while rest-of-the-world was still in the stone age. Then came the Vedant which virtually mean end of the Vedic period. That was the beginning of Puranic period, there is no date to prove when it actually happened. But it can be said that the Vedic period was definitely prior to the Puranic period, since there is no description of the reincarnation of the Gods on earth in the Vedas. So we can assume that the Puranic period should be that of Shiva, or Brahma, Vishnu, Mahesh when people discovered the trinity of the nature. Of course, there was Naradmuni, the information and broadcasting system.

Then came the Epic Age with the Ramayana periods and then finally we have Krishna period that of the *Mahabharat.* The Krishna period is recorded five thousand years ago. We have this Krishna year. Then we have the Gupta period, of the Golden age, the Vikramadityas or the Saka years. And, of course, we have the year of Buddha and Mahavira. The Aryans came to

India and happened to be here alongwith the Cols and Doms and the Dravidians and developed the Hindu civilisation.

Foreign Invaders. The invasion of India by Alexander followed by Changis Khan, Turks, Huns, Sakas, Persians, Afghans and further down the ages by the Mughals and European colonial powers, like the British, French and the Portuguese should go down in the Indian history as the black period. In this black period, India lost first its name *Bharat* because all the invaders called this land according to their languages. Secondly, invaders like the Mongolian, Changis Khan apart from looting destroyed everything. They burnt down our cities, schools and all that was visible by their barbaric brutality. This continued through Mohamad Gauri and Gajnis till the Mughals finally established their rule when Babar settled down. By that time, most of the Indian system have been crippled. And with the establishment of this Mughal dynasty, half of India was under the Mughals. Apart from what they did to this land and its people in this black period of our history, the worst thing that happened to this country or the continent is that they destroyed our education system. That is where we have lost our strength and prosperity.

It is not for the first time that the continent has witnessed war, the history is full of wars, but those wars though destructive as they are, did not effect our social system, education and civilisation. But the invasion by foreign races and by their religious fanaticism and later on the occupation by the British of the whole sub-continent, not only made us slaves but left us without education. That can be considered the greatest harm done to us and due to which we still continue to suffer.

It is also important to realise that the damage caused to the sub-continent by the outsiders was largely due to our negligence, due to personal prejudices and intrigues of our kings, and also due to our non-violence philosophy preached by the Buddhists and the Jains. The *Rajnities* and *Kootnities* of people like Krishna and Chanakya are all contributors to the final downfall of our great civilisation. It has been a long downfall, but we are not dead and we have managed to sit on our feet again, it is about time that we stand and walk again.

Hind or India usually meant a geographic area like a sub-continent. However, as mentioned earlier, it was inhabited by many independent states. Some Kingdoms were bigger while some smaller, but India under the British was the biggest single political identity. We have seen from the times of Ramayana and Mahabharata, Ashoka, Vikramaditya, Poras, Prithviraj or Akbar and Aurangzeb, that India under the British was the biggest single political unit in size than ever before and after. But we could trace the cultural identity that spread over from Hindukush in Afghanistan to Burma and Thailand and Indonesia in the east and to Sri Lanka in the south. Before the British, there were kingdoms all over India, and during the British rule also there were princely states all over that were autonomous political units. The princes or the Maharajas were absolute powers in their kingdoms with final powers with the British. As we know it was the India of East India Company that was enlarged and transferred into the British India. Earlier India consisted of present Pakistan, Bangladesh, Sri Lanka and Burma. Sri Lanka and Burma were separated in the late 1930s and Pakistan was created in 1947. Bangladesh was born in 1971 previously known as East Pakistan.

The British were really clever. They came in as a reward to a British doctor who treated the ailing Mughal princess. The doctor when asked for reward only asked for permission for a British company to do business in India. Slowly it turned into the East India Company. The company started to interfere financially in the conflicts of local kings and chieftains and finally consolidated their power by raising a regular army and enslaved most of India. By 1857, the native Indians rose in revolt against the British to free India. It was called sepoy mutiny by the British. The Indians lost the war for various reasons and the rule of the company was taken over by the queen and government of Britain. Nearly thirty years later, the Indian National Congress was born which was founded by A.O. Hume to redress the grievances of Indians.

The movement for freedom from the British in the country started before 1857 but the war of Independence of 1857 was not to get India free as a united country. It was again a group of kings and princes who had revolted against the British. It could have been a success if they had agreed to form a confederation of India and had formed a common command. As the country was taken over directly under the control of the British government and most of the princes had accepted the British as their sovereign, it was very much difficult to overthrow the British militarily. But soon some educated people joined the Indian National Congress to highlight the Indian grievances. And in that organisation there appeared two factions of the people who were called hot heads and the cool heads like the militants and the moderates. Moderates led by Mr. Gokhale were for slow reforms under the British, while people led by Lokmanya Tilak were for self-government. The Russian revolution also inspired the introspection among the people and the *Vilayat*-returned and educated people took India on a totally different path of freedom. It was for self-rule and democracy like in England. Tilak took it to the streets through Ganesh Pooja. Hence, he emerged as a mass leader. Later on, Mahatma Gandhi returned from South Africa and joined the freedom struggle. He could take over the leadership of Congress party after Lokmanya Tilak passed away. He joined the moderates of Gokhale camp along with Moti Lal Nehru, Sarojini Naidu, etc. M.K. Gandhi followed the Ganesh pooja style of Tilak and turned it into a Ram Rajya. Total freedom had to be achieved through non-violence. So countless meetings, agitations and civil disobedience movements followed. Finally Swaraj came at midnight of 14–15 August, 1947.

If Mahatma Gandhi is called the father of the nation, Lokmanya Tilak could be easily called the grandfather of the nation. It was Tilak who visualised freedom for the country and demanded Swaraj. He was the first mass leader who made Swaraj a real mass movement, and showed to others that a mass movement could be launched in the country successfully. Swaraj can be won by the participation of the masses and not by the armchair advocacy for reforms. Bal (Tilak) along with Lal and Pal of that time created a national awakening by advocating Swaraj. He was a master tactician and a great organiser. He defeated the British legal circles by explaining that Swaraj does not mean treachery or sedition, it only meant self-government like they have in Britain. They could not prove any charges against Tilak and he succeeded in bringing home the point to the Indians that of Swaraj. Though Gandhi had said that Gokhale was a model for him, yet he was more likely succeeding Tilak as a mass leader.

India could have attained freedom in or around 1925, if Gandhi had not withdrawn the civil disobedience movement, during which some people had burnt down a police station in Chouri Chora and three policemen were killed. Gandhi later on accepted that as the Himalayan blunder of his life. Gandhi was a puritan man and he wanted to build India on certain values of life, like truth and non-violence and he wanted people to take these principles right through the freedom struggle, so that these principles become a part of their lives and society for all times to come. Therefore, he was quick to take back the movement because he thought that more violence could take place. Gandhi's principles were allright, but as he had suppressed all levels and kinds of violence, it erupted out as the communal carnage of the partition time. It was like a counter-revolution to his non-violence, but that does not make Gandhi a small man. India had supported the British in the first world war and the British promised India a dominion status and nothing like that came after the war. The 1919 Act offered nothing like that. The civil disobedience movement had been launched successfully The first general strike in England had totally paralysed the government there and the labour party had been voted to power. This could have led to India's freedom, had Gandhi not taken back the freedom movement of civil disobedience. When Gandhi did that he stood discredited and the British put all the activists and the leaders in the jails and the whole movement was paralysed till 1933. India free in 1925 could have well been the present Indian sub-continent.

As soon as the second world war started, the British government sought co-operation from the Congress party which was rightly denied. Gandhi gave the quit India notice for which he was arrested instantly and many party workers were put in jails. Gandhi's do or die call could not materialise much and, in fact, the movement was crushed by the British. The 1935 Act was also an eyewash and was nowhere near freedom. During the war one day Subhash Chandra Bose escaped from the British confinement. The escape by Subhash was a mastermind operation and was a clear insult to the British police system. Subhash made his way through Kabul to Germany. Subhash was a socialist and a revolutionary for which Gandhi and Co. had also opposed him to be the president of the party. The Russians because of their involvement in the second world war on the side of the British, probably did not want to do any business with Subhash, so did not help him. Then Subhash had to go to Germany where he met Hitler. Subhash was no admirer of Hitler but he wanted to take the help of the enemy of the enemy. Hitler helped him to go to Japan in a submarine. Subhash struck a deal with the Japanese that he be given the Indian soldiers who were captured by the Japanese as prisoners of war to make the liberation army. Then Subhash came to Singapore and founded the Indian National Army and soon many Indian soldiers of the British crossed over to INA. It was a great success and Subhash waged a war against the British. People like Nehru did not like this action and he declared that he would go to Calcutta with a sword in his hand to fight the INA and Subhash.

As Hitler and Japan lost the war and many of the INA soldiers were captured by the British and they started to put on trial the three Generals of the INA for war crimes, there erupted widespread resentment among the people and Nehru showed up as the defense counsel but the case was advocated by Bhulla Bhai Desai. Subhash had died or disappeared for ever and Nehru just wanted to make a political capital out of that. Soon the trial resulted in the rebellion by the Army and the Navy. And that was the last but decisive nail in the coffin of the British rule in India. Sensing bloodshed, the British decided to leave India as fast as possible. Second world war had ruined all the colonial powers of Europe and Britain was no longer in a position to hold India militarily. The new government of the Labour party under Attlee announced the freedom for India and then the imperialist elements saw to it that Pakistan is created. Therefore, the Leaguers started the violence.

So, there were three major factors that led to India's freedom. First, the years of struggle for freedom; second, the second world war that ruined all the colonial powers like Britain, France, Belgium, Spain, etc. As a result of that war not only India but many Afro-Asian countries got freedom and finally, the rebellion by the armed forces. And to Britain's solace it was a decision by the Labour government to announce the freedom of India. But the British did try to leave India in problems and on its fate. It was senseless to ask Mountbatton to stay in India as the head of the State till we framed the constitution. Even the country had the chief of the army staff, a British, who was meeting his Pakistani counterpart during the Kashmir tussle. People like Sardar Patel did their best to make and unite India. He got all the princely states merged with India. He even used force to merge the states of Hyderabad and Junagarh.

Two most important things that we have achieved so far, are that India got freedom and that too through non-violence with the participation of the masses. This has helped to establish and preserve democracy in India. Second, India as a country is due to the British who colonised it. It does not matter what bad things they did to this country, it also does not matter much, even if they have created Pakistan, Burma and Sri Lanka. At last whatever we have today, the British were partly responsible for it, for the making of India, because the movement for freedom became national once we had this common foreign alien ruler. British did try to leave India as truncated as before their arrival. Also it was the British Lieutenant Governor, and administration that accepted Hindi as language in 1900 in Devnagri Script.

Lieutenant Governor of United Provinces (now UP) Anthony Mac Donnell allowed the use of Devnagari in the courts of the province. The British had hesitated for forty years to accept Devnagri Hindi in place of Persian or along with the Persian as administrative language. So when Mac Donnell recommended the use of Devnagri Script he had to explain the rivalry between the Hindus and Muslims in the British administration and considered Persian a security risk and the Muslims were well entrenched in the administration due to the use of Persian later on Urdu. The British had taken most of India from the Muslim rule so they decided to encourage the use of Devnagri to win the loyalty of the Hindus. So there emerged Hindu and Muslim elites. The Muslim elites were intent on invoking the past glories of their civilisation and colonial rule and their Persian inheritance. The Hindus, on the other hand, had now a different ruler who could be approached to accept Devnagri. Though the Hindu and Muslim elites were on different paths in the manner of their relationship with the colonial British. The British had probably developed the historical policy of divide and rule since 1857. So it seems the roots of partition of the Indian sub-continent lay not in the Muslim League's Pakistan resolution of 1940 but in the Indian Council's Act of 1890. Lala Lajpat Rai was quoted by Jinnah in his Pakistan Resolution as the propounder of two nation theory. Because Lajpat Rai did not consider the Muslims worthy of joining the freedom movement. No doubt, Lajpat Rai had reservation about the Muslims that does not mean the whole country thought like that and when Jinnah passed the resolution it was two decades since Lajpat Rai had died as a result of physical assault by the British Police. Still we must thank the British for making a country like India and promoting Devnagri and not having done the forcible religious conversions on India.

When India became free from the British it had these 300 princely states apart from the provinces that were ruled by the British directly. These princely states were given a choice by the British that they could do with themselves what they wanted, they could merge with India or Pakistan or they could keep their own identity, the British just left. The British knew that they had to leave India and they did not want to leave behind a strong and united, one big country as it was emerging. Because of their international power politics they had even plans to balkanise India. First, they separated Burma and Sri Lanka and then created Pakistan. Creation of Pakistan was no concession to the two nation theory of Jinnah, the fact is that the British encouraged Jinnah to make Pakistan his dream and promised him even before he had demanded. Pakistan was created by the British for the same reasons as Devnagri was accepted by Mac Donnell as reasons of security.

The intentions of the British specially under Churchill were mischievous. They wanted to create Pakistan to counter a resurgent India. The communalisation of India had been done intentionally through various Acts that were brought by the British to reform and give more powers to the Indians as they had demanded Swaraj. Since the Hindus and Muslims had fought jointly the first war of independence in 1857 and had formed the Indian National Congress to attain independence from the British, the British had sensed another yet greater movement for independence. The people like A.O. Hume had founded the Congress to redress the grievances of the Indians, but when people like Tilak made their presence felt in the organisation and took control of it and demanded complete Swaraj, the British got alarmed and started the policy to divide the Indians as Hindus and Muslims. After the war of 1857, the British had taken over Delhi from Bahadurshah who was a Muslim. The policy started to change as early as 1905 when Tilak took over Congress party. Tilak was the real architect of Indian freedom. The British started to tilt towards the Muslims. Hence through the various Acts of British Parliament that of

1909, 1919 and 1935, they tried to divide the people as Hindus and Muslims through the separate representations, and electoral colleges and finally leave India as truncated with all problems, spreading disaffection among the people. A strong united India was the dream of the Indians only.

In the election of 1937 when elections were held in the British provinces, only one per cent Muslims were entitled to vote, and that was the rich feudal peasantry class. They had no idea what Pakistan really meant. They probably were thinking that they were voting to have Pakistan everywhere in India or it was some kind of a Muslim party. Had the Muslims been told that they would actually migrate to Pakistan and loose their lands they owned in places like UP they would have never voted for Pakistan or Muslim League. Muslim League had been routed in the elections in Punjab, but the British gave half of Punjab to Pakistan. In the Frontier province it was Gaffar Khan whose party got majority and he was for united India yet that province was also allotted to Pakistan.

Mahatma Gandhi was honestly opposed to the creation of Pakistan, but Nehru and Patel had accepted it. Jinnah rightly had asked the Indian side to exchange the population straight away. But Nehru and company did not agree to that. Hence, the Leaguers in Pakistan started the direct action day and threw out all the Hindus and Sikhs, by violent means. Killing and looting and burnings became the law in Pakistan, so almost no Hindu or Sikh was left in Pakistan. But, on the other hand, India led by Nehru and company had their compulsions, they did not want to throw out the Muslims because a lot of Muslims led by people like the Agha Khan and Maulana Azad and Kidwai were opposed to the creation of Pakistan. Therefore, after Gandhi got assassinated, the shock of his assassination saved all the Muslims in India. Today, therefore, no part of India could further be demanded by Pakistan because it is Muslim-dominated like Kashmir. The boundaries had been decided in 1947, and no further demands from Pakistan could be entertained, should any problems arise. Pakistan should be clearly told whether they would like to take all the Muslims from India into Pakistan as that is the land created for Muslims of India. Or whether they would like to return half of Pakistan land to India as more Muslims live in India than Pakistan. Surely, they will refuse and their demand for Kashmir should thereby get nullified by the whole world. The Muslims of India know it very well that there is nothing waiting for them in Pakistan but complete loss. The ethnic violence and problems in Pakistan between the Shia and Sunni and the minority migrated Muslims from India clearly shows that the demand from Pakistan to have Kashmir is nothing but to grab more land.

Pakistan was created by the British to check India. Not only the British but the Americans had also liked the idea of the formation of Pakistan as the developments have shown later on. Indian freedom movement was secular, democratic, peaceful and socialist in character. Indian leaders of freedom movement had never asked any foreign power to influence the British to free India. Americans would have liked Indians to seek their support, but World War II had given no time for the allied powers to think about the Indian freedom as they would not like to annoy the British. The Gadar Party of India had been allowed in the USA. The Americans wanted Nehru and other leaders to see Roosevelt in connection with the Indian freedom. But the idea of the Americans as always was to see that India as a free country should join the Americans side. And Russia had really no interest in India because the freedom movement in India was a bourgeoisie movement for them. And people like Gandhi were no match for Marx and Lenin. And during the war when Subhash escaped out of India, the people at the Russian embassy could offer him no help in Kabul and even refused to recognise him. So people like M.N. Roy had enough time where they stood in relation to a communist Russia.

The cold war had started during the world war itself. In it, the perception was to contain Russia. Soon after the war, the creation of Pakistan became more important for the western alliance. Hence, Pakistan was created under the pretext that Jinnah and the Muslims wanted it. The leaders of freedom movement have been in jails several times and for years but Jinnah and Co. were not even jailed for a day, speaks volumes about the fact that the British were all out to create Pakistan. This fact is reported now in some studies. The plan of the British to balkanise India was revealed to Nehru and Patel by Mountbatten. The staff of Viceroy was opposed to such revelations which Mountbatten actually did. But it was known to everybody that the British had told everybody of the princes—

that they could do with their fate as they wanted. Mountbatten could have been recalled by the British had there been a Churchill. The Labour government had inherited the conservative bureaucracy who were making all the troubles that they could. The so-called Two Nation theory of Jinnah was not the real cause of the partition of the country, it was for personal power for Mr. Jinnah. Jinnah wanted to succeed Tilak as Congress president and he was not elected as one. Jinnah had no big problem in accepting Gandhi as the leader. Mahatma Gandhi had rejected any place of power for himself. Jinnah was opposed to the Agha Khans and also his personality clash with Nehru and in the end Nehru's provocative speeches really forced the issue of partition on Jinnah. Nehru and Jinnah were simple tools in the hands of the British, Mahatma Gandhi had even proposed Jinnah the Prime Ministership to keep India united. It was not accepted by Nehru and Patel because they wanted power for themself. Because of the behaviour of his party Jinnah is reported to have been very sour on his death bed about the mistakes he had made in accepting Pakistan and had expressed a desire to go to Delhi and ask the Indians to forget about the past and be friends again, but it was too late. As the Leaguers had never participated in the mass movements, they could not sustain democracy in Pakistan.

Nehru and After

When Pakistan attacked India in Kashmir, even Gandhi had approved of the army's action to defend the country. Nehru, the then Prime Minister, stopped the army from vacating the Kashmir territory occupied by the Pakistanis by force and aggression. He took the case to UNO and could never recover it. It is as good as lost because it is under the complete control of Pakistan and they have made roads connecting it with China.

Soon Mahatma Gandhi was assassinated. It is hard to believe but true that the government of the day let the murder take place. There had been an attempt on the life of the Mahatma a week earlier, which had failed and the assailant who was captured had told everybody that the other conspirators will come back again and they did kill Gandhi a week later. Some people believe that the day Mahatma was killed, he had said that Patel would get more importance, probably the Prime Ministership. As Gandhi was assassinated this did not happen. Then Nehru had his day, he blamed Patel for the negligence and murder of Gandhi. The Iron man was seen in tears on such a wild allegation in parliament. Then the blame was shifted to RSS—the organisation that was becoming very popular and could have been a real challenge for the Congress Party. RSS was blamed for the murder. The organisation was banned and its volunteers and workers were put in jails. Its public image was made to suffer. This paved the way of powers going into Nehru's hands. For his luck and India's bad luck Patel died two years later. Subhash already disappeared and Prasad being the President, Nehru had no real challenge to his leadership. People like Maulana, Tandon, Kidwai and Pant were second line leaders. They could never become rivals for Nehru. While people like S.P. Mukherjee, Lohia and J.P. Narayan got into the opposition parties. Thus started for India's misery the present legacy of creating problems for the country as the programme of the Congress party. Mahatma Gandhi had asked all the Congressmen to disband the party as its purpose had been achieved and he wanted a party-free system for the country. But the power hungry Congressmen must have felt relieved at Gandhi's death.

Nehru's big mistake was to ask Mountbatten to stay as the head of the State till we framed the new constitution for the country. His second big mistake was to stop the army from recovering the lost territory in Kashmir and throw back the Pakistanis. As a result of his inaction and stupidity, India lost the half of Kashmir to Pakistan and UNO could do nothing. There were people advising Nehru that the refugees from Pakistan could be settled down in J & K also, but he could not see the wisdom in the advice. Pakistan and China established their link by road through occupied Kashmir. Had India got back that part of Kashmir, China and Pakistan could never have made that road which is a threat to India's security. India's security has been jeopardised by Nehru's foolish policies. Having the challenge to his leadership eliminated within the party and outside he kept the army down with its low budgets and spread the view that there was no need of the army, least of all a well equipped army, to defend the country. He was fearful of an army takeover which never happened. When China attacked Tibet and grabbed it, there were people in India including President Rajendra Prasad who advised Nehru to raise the issue in the world forum so that Tibet could stay as a buffer state between India and China. He could not see any reason because Nehru neglected the defence of the country to the extent of a traitor. China finally attacked India in 1962 and not only India was humiliated Nehru himself stood a fallen man. India lost a big chunk of land to China and Nehru lost his own life prematurely, because he did not know how to deal with his friendly China.

Corruption is Nehru's legacy, he protected all those corrupt people and politicians who were charged with corruption and nepotism. Had he not protected those corrupt people and practices, a beginning could have been made to keep clean the places and offices of power and service from the worms of corruption. It is no satisfaction to say Nehru was a great democrat. India had all along fought for democracy and freedom. Nehru did not achieve self-sufficiency for India. Nehru's era is as good as closed today, we do not need to write a book about that. What we need to do is to see how we can sort our problems today.

Lal Bahadur was a weak prime minister but not a weak person. He had inherited a weak defence line from Nehru but was a brave man on the frontline. His solution for the problems were simple and practical. He was one of the leaders that came from the common people and so far the only prime minister who is from the poor people. His slogan of *Jai Jawan* and *Jai Kisan* was very wise and appealing. He could have started the recovery of India from the mess of problems but unfortunately he died a doubtful death while in Tashkent. His short span of 18 months as prime minister and the way he faced Pakistani war of aggression against India created confidence in the country.

Mention should be made about Gulzari Lal Nanda who twice became the prime minister, once after the death of Nehru and later on after the death of Shastri. Gulzari Lal Nanda was an honest person and a man of integrity. But the party of congressmen did not elect him the leader. Had he been elected the prime minister atleast after the death of Shastri, India definitely could have been a different country today, because he was a clean and honest man and he lived a long life. He died recently and people and the politicians in this country just forgot him. There were probably two reasons for his being not chosen as the leader. First, he was not from Uttar Pradesh, because he was from Punjab (now Haryana) and Uttar Pradesh sends these 85 members to Lok Sabha. Second he was an honest man and he was not a *Brahmin.* These two things weighed heavily against his candidature as prime minister. It took thirty years after independence, that in 1977 when a revolution took place through ballot, that Morarji Desai a non-UP leader was elected as prime minister. But soon he lost as well because the UP people like Charan Singh, Raj Narayan and Sanjay Gandhi plotted his overthrow. It is a shame that not only Gulzari Lal lost his place as prime minister, he could not be seen on any of the ministerial posts for good. Gulzari Lal could have been a good prime minister till today. The corruption and mafiosi that we see today in the country could have been nipped in the bud if Indira Gandhi had not become the prime minister and Gulzari Lal could have served for many years.

Arrival of Indira Gandhi as prime minister was made possible by people like Kamaraj and many others who thought that she will be easy to manipulate and handle than Desai. They thought that she will be like a puppet in their hands as they had not seen her as a powerful person. Moreover, they had much control over the party. Indira Gandhi resented it very much that she should be seen as a weak Prime Minister. So as a gift to

Mahatma Gandhi on his birth centenary, the Congress party had to split because Indira confronted the syndicate and got them defeated in the election of the president of India. And then started the 'Indira is India and India is Indira sort of campaign by her supporters which she enjoyed. Nowhere in the world hardly anybody had made such claims, least of all in a democracy. The birth of Bangladesh and the successful war of 1971 was considered as the greatest achievement of her term as prime minister. She won the mid-term poll with a convincing majority in parliament and later the assemblies in 1972. The same Indira Gandhi who as the President of the congress party in 1958 had said about the army that they were not needed at all and she had said that their salaries for Sundays should be deducted and given to the red cross. The reverses of 1962 and the war of 1965 had exposed the Indian defence policy as pursued by Nehru and accepted by his party, as most foolish. The opposition parties and the public opinion in the country had compelled the congress party to change its policy. Yet Indira Gandhi was acclaimed as the great warrior by her image makers. They could not save Mujibur Rehman and Bangladesh was so quickly lost to fundamentalist, anti-freedom and military dictatorship. What was the use of those armymen that we lost and the money that we spent to liberate Bangladesh.

Indira's desperation to hang on to power and her desire to establish dynastic rule in India led her to impose emergency in June 1975. That was very shameful and a very dark chapter in the history of Indian democracy. People did teach her a lesson in the general elections of 1977 when she even lost her own seat. It was not only a lesson and her rejection by the people, it was the first revolution in India, because from Bombay to Delhi and Delhi to Calcutta her party could not win a single seat in Parliament. The people demonstrated how mature they had become as voters.

The Janata Party which was dominated by former congresssmen did not last very long. Morarji Desai could not maintain one team together and Charan Singh and Jagjivan Ram soon started to look forward to get the prime minister's chair. In the process, the Janata government soon fell down. The people and the Janata Party had restored freedom back to the people and the country but could not sustain the revolution as the leaders quarrelled among themselves for their stupid pursuits of power. There is no need to go into details of it, but to recall that the people put Indira back to power. Such a shame for the country that the most discredited person had to be voted back to power. People forgave her in the national interest.

Indira Gandhi again like her father was a very power hungry person and wanted the power to stay with her and her son. All those corrupt practices in the country got more entrenched and like Nehru she created more problems for the country and hardly solved any. Not only she protected corrupt practices and people but herself indulged in practices of corruption, her election had been set aside by the Allahabad High Court in 1975 on the basis of corrupt activities. She damaged the institution of democracy a lot. Her personal wishes had to be carried out even at the expense of the law, parliament and the country. She could not win India after 1971 a permanent peace with Pakistan. The opportunity of the war was lost to sort out the problems and settle disputes with Pakistan with the Shimla agreement, with Bhutto. Her *garibi hatao* slogan could not be materialised by her, because it was a vote catching slogan framed to overshadow the Indira *hatao* campaign. Her mishandling of the Sikh politics made her the victim of violence. In her style of functioning she had left nobody in the party worth of any ability or quality who could succeed her when she died. There was no second man in command. In sheer desperation, a not so able President Giani Zail Singh appointed her son Rajiv as the new prime minister and then he ordered a general election which he won due to the sympathy wave.

Morarji Desai was probably the man in the Nehru cabinet who leaked to the press the details of a boundary settlement that Nehru was negotiating with China. There was public reaction and Nehru did not pursue the matter further and then we had the war with China. Apart from being a professed Gandhian, Desai was a man of arrogance and obduracy. He failed to inspire his colleagues and the country. He refused to resign as the leader of the party after he had lost the confidence of the Janata Party. Charan Singh and President Reddy and even with people like Sanjay and Indira Gandhi, they all made it sure that Jajivan Ram did not become the prime minister. The Bharatiya Janata Party that split later on from the Janata

Party was not smart enough, to choose its ally in the formation of the new government after the fall of Morarji Desai. It could have supported Charan Singh along with the Congress faction led by Y.B. Chavan and averted an election that followed due to Charan Singh dissolving the Lok Sabha. Desai's government went down as also the government. When the Russians went into Afghanistan, Desai made no effort to see if India could settle disputes with Pakistan because Desai was a known pro-USA man. Later on, when Indira Gandhi returned back to power in 1980, the opposition parties opposed Indira Gandhi from persuing any adventure into Pakistan. The opportunity to settle issues with Pakistan, was thus lost. Till today we have not bothered to solve any problem that Pakistan has created for us and with no real break through in Indian policy towards Pakistan there is speculation if anybody will even care to sort out Pakistan. The opportunity that India had in 1971 and later on when Bhutto was killed in Jail and when Jimmy Carter was the President and the Russians went in Afghanistan, was all lost to sort out Pakistan. This is the sorry tale of Indian leaders. Desai was given *Nishan-e-Pakistan* award by the dictator General Zia. That seems to be the greatest achievement of Desai, apart from his preference for *'pisky'* in place of whisky.

Choudhary Charan Singh was a former Congressman and an Arya Samajist his name will go down as the listless man alongwith Chandra Shekhar and other who ditched their own partymen to form the government with the support of those Congress people who had jailed them during the emergency, only to be prime minister for few months, causing instability in the country and providing a bad name for the opposition parties that they could never form a stable government. That truly has been the case with all the non-Congress prime ministers so far and Vajpayee the present Prime Minister has to work hard to change this trend in the present term.

And Rajiv? He started well with the anti-defection law, some people thought that it was done because he was distrustful and doubtful about the loyalty of some of his comrades and to keep all the challenge to his leadership under his control. Indeed it was a good step. There is nothing wrong about it, but to stay as head of the party without election for so many years is not democracy, it is the feudal fiefdom. Since the party broke in 1969 there have been no election in the party and there have been appointments. Like his mother he was quite authoritarian, had no sense of the country, wanted to bring in the country all the vices of the west and no virtue, he made so many stupid laws and administrative moves, and his policies lacked a vision as if that was to establish the family credentials. He indulged into personal likes and dislikes as far as the policies of the government were concerned, he hardly solved any problem of the country and initiated fresh ones. The introduction of bills like the Defamation bill smelled of his dictatorial mind. It is a shame that the freedom that this country achieved after 90 years of arduous and hard struggle was being taken away by its own government. Whereas elsewhere in the world today the people are having more freedom than before, in India it is being put in the reverse as if we have to compete with the dictators. The Rajiv government stinked of corruption and the whole country sank deep down in the garbage of corruption and poverty. We have to change it, not only the government but the whole system. Judging from the style of functioning of the Rajiv government there was only one person who was capable of doing things and that was Rajiv himself, and he lived with that allusion. There had been three and four times cabinet reshufflings every year on an average to prove this fact and if there was any person that had remained unaffected with the periodical changes apart from Rajiv it was the rootless Buta Singh. Serious corruption charges have been made against the Rajiv government and have been proved by the media and even by the government agencies like the Public Accounts and the Chief of the army staff. Instead of resigning the men in the government have called the Accountant general "that Charlie".

Towards the end of his term, many of his friends complained about his colleague V.P. Singh who was his finance minister and Rajiv Gandhi had actually initiated the economic reforms and V.P. Singh was his supporter who used to brag about taking the country and the economy to a takeoff stage into the 21st century. Nodoubt, the crooks around Rajiv made it sure that V.P. Singh got out of the finance ministry because they wanted a free hand to indulge in unlawful corrupt practices. Rajiv lost the mandate in the elections of 1989, but waited to destabilise the V.P. Singh government the same way Sanjay and Indira did to Morarji Desai and Charan Singh by installing Charan Singh and withdrawing the support soon after. As a result Chandra Shekhar ordered fresh elections, during which Rajiv got killed in a bomb blast by the LTTE of Sri Lanka. Rajiv is described by his well-wishers as the innocent calf who got slaughtered by the international crooks. However, it is relevant to admit that Indira Gandhi had initiated the LTTE problem and allowed it to operate in India. Later on, when Rajiv forced Prabhakaran to sign The Delhi agreement, and sent in the Indian army into Sri Lanka to enforce the agreement, he turned the LTTE against him and not only the Indian army paid a humiliating price, but Rajiv also lost his life in that bomb attack. It is very strange that his widow Sonia who was against his participation in politics has herself joined it.

The election results of 1989 proved that the people of the country do not approve corruption. Rajiv was thrown out and V.P. Singh installed. V.P. Singh had emerged as the crusader against corruption. V.P. Singh had a great problem to sustain his government, first of all his newly formed Janata Dal did not have a majority. He was supported by two opposite poles of Indian politics, the C.P.M. and the Bharatiya Janata Party. It was a tricky situation. But the problem for him started from within. It is ok to win an election on the anti-corruption wave but too difficult to fight corruption when you have corrupt people within your ranks, so a manipulative Chandra Shekhar and outraged Devilal over Choutala's sack, started pulling strings in different direction and a revengeful Rajiv and his clout hatched the final conspiracy to pull down V.P. Singh. Strangely enough, a lot of people forgot about their commitment to expose and eliminate corruption. BJP's cadres went along with the Congress to oppose the Mandalisation, which every party had promised in their election manifestoes and later on after the eclipse of V.P. Singh they all put it back in their programmes. So what was actually the problem. It seems that cadreless V.P. Singh was really opposed to corruption, and his rivals in power politics did not want him to rise higher, so they all brought him down, as lot of these politicians believe in cheating the people and maintaining their rotten habit of living with corruption. A sad end to a man of promise, though he should have had a better programme than Mandalisation and so-called secularism. Rajiv Gandhi's support to Chandra Shekhar and consequent withdrawal put the country through a phase of instability. The country lost sight of the real issues and the Mandal and Kamandal took over North India. Rajiv got killed and the sympathy wave retained some of the ground for the Congress, and P.V. Narasimha Rao, another man full of scandals emerged as the leader for the prime ministership. He did manage to put up for five years and his government brought some financial changes in the country but his record was nothing worthwhile like an old man without direction, he faded out.

The few months of Deve Gowda and Gujral just brought more instability in the country. Both men were men of integrity but on borrowed crutches. The Congress party served them the same coffee they gave to Charan Singh and Chandra Shekhar before. And few more cases like that we may see in future as well if we don't change the present system. The country is going to pay heavily for political instability and the black mailing as a direct result of political instability.

Political instability brings lot of problems for the country. The economy suffers without direction, the administration becomes chaotic, the country's standing on the international scene falls down, and its ability to solve problems domestic as well as international, gets crippled. And corruption by the politicians and the bureaucrats and prices of consumer goods all touch new heights. Neglected areas and people get more neglected. On the whole, the country goes further down the *nallah*.

Present State of Affairs in the Country

India's population has increased three times in the last fifty years from 350 millions in 1947 to one billion in 1998. The acute poverty in the country where 60 per cent people live below poverty line and at least 30 per cent of this country's total population live like neglected animals who have nowhere to go and on top of that we have same kind of people from the neighbouring countries who are flooding the slums of this country. No basic human rights of food, clothes and shelter are available to these people and, of course, no education or health assurance. India is home to half of the world's total population of poors below poverty line and half of the total population of the illiterates and half of the total population of blind and people suffering from serious diseases like leprosy and tuberculosis. Nobody has bothered to count the unaccounted crippled, disabled destitute and countless neglected patients suffering from all sorts of diseases. Average life expectancy is just over 40 years.

The unemployment situation is worsening everyday for the last 20 years. Seventy per cent people live in the rural areas and 90 per cent of them are underemployed. In the urban areas at least 20 per cent people are either unemployed or underemployed and if you take the housewives into consideration for the unemployed, the total population of the urban underemployed could also go up like in the rural areas. On the whole, you can easily assume that 50 per cent of India's population is either unemployed or underemployed. So it is no comparison to the developed countries where people maintain proper statistics because they provide social security benefits for the unemployed. In India 50 per cent of the people do not qualify for jobs because they are illiterate. So no employment venue registers them for employment and hence their unemployed status goes unaccounted. Economically though India is the sixth largest industrial power of the world, poverty-wise we are at number 141 as far as the per capita income of the people is concerned.

Corruption-wise India is among the top ten countries along with Pakistan and Indonesia who have the most corrupt systems in the world. Sanitation-wise the whole country is a slum and sports-wise we have hardly any medals from the Olympics. Politically for the last ten years India has been very unstable at the centre. Seven prime ministers in ten years and if you take Narasimha Rao's five years out, we have six prime ministers in four years. Nobody has any regard for the law and order situation in the country, 35 million cases are pending in the various courts in the country. Pollution-wise Delhi, Mumbai are among the top ten most polluted cities in the world. Our holy rivers are fully polluted and our industrial units have negligible pollution control. There is no guarantee of basic human rights in India. The country stinks, it stinks of poverty, it stinks of corruption and nepotism, it stinks of organised chaos, it stinks from the pollution from the industrial sector that produce the poor quality of consumer goods, the country is a hell of disease, it is the black hole of illiteracy. There is no law and order and there is no justice. Public amenities and places of service like electricity, transport, hospitals, courts, roads and schools all present a look of no return. On the whole, it is like a living hell for all its citizens, both the poor and the rich. The country is getting over, crowded every second with inefficient, characterless, powerless and directionless people on the rise. The country is fast moving towards a culture of no self-respect and continues to sink in the sea of its problems.

The students of economics start their studies with a famous question, India is a rich country inhabited by poor people explain. The students of Indian constitution start their studies with the study of fundamental rights, but how far we have brought this country on these counts, does it need to be explained or it needs to be seen? Unity in diversity, but we have problems in many corners of the country, foreign hand nodoubt. Onions are expensive because the crops failed, fruits and vegetables are full of pesticides, because we have discovered the art of growing them.

The top politicians supposed to be our leaders stink. They stink of corruption, nepotism, inefficiency and some of them could easily be traitors and criminals. They have no idea of themselves, what they should do or what they are expected to do. They do not see the real problems of the country and its people, they have no idea what can be done soon to save the country from the ticking time bomb of its problems that is going to explode and destroy the whole country. They are not worried about them, they only think of grabbing power and to use that power for personal glory and gratification. They are not simply able to see the misery of the people and themselves in the community of the nations of the world. The politicians of all the political parties have no idea why the country stinks of poverty, of diseases and ignorance. Look at the behaviour of these politicians in the state assemblies and in the parliament. Look at their election manifestoes and the programmes of their parties. There is no concrete and proper programme for the development of the country.

Ever since 1977 when Indira Gandhi was thrown out, the election which was actually a great revolution, the politicians from all the parties have never bothered to see what was the cause of the stink and how to remove that. Our leaders at their best are simply hooligans. Those guys who do not know even the ABC of politics seem to know XYZ of even the international politics. Look how selfish and seekers of personal interests our parliamentarians are, they have passed a law to give pension for all members of Lok Sabha who have just completed one year or 364 days.

Their performance in the parliament is no better. They fight physically in the house and abuse each other, and throw shoes at each other and have to be thrown out of house by the marshals. One party may choose to boycott the proceedings of the house for days, because one minister has spoken bad about them. "The parliament or state assemblies could suspend their members of the house for days. This is how our so-called leaders of hooligans function in the parliament and in the assemblies. How they can discipline the country, nobody knows. It seems that hooliganism is our culture, corruption our religion, bad quality our tradition, pollution our industrialisation, reckless littering our sanitation and cheating could be nationalism.

However, there is a reason for this stink. When the British took over India there probably were just one per cent people who could read and write in the land of the people that was known as 'Bharat', known for its Vedas, Upanishads and Puranas. The stories of *Ramayana* and *Mahabharat* and many mores. The great universities of Pataliputra and Takshila, later on all destroyed, left the people with that negligible number of one per cent literate. Few of them knowing Urdu and the other few Sanskrit. And when the British left, there were just 4 per cent people who could read and write and hardly just few of them could be called educated. Most of them were just clerks for the British. Since 1947, from the 4 per cent we have reached over 50 per cent today but that is not a great achievement in 50 years. It could have been 100 per cent and this 50 per cent are only busy in reading the gutter press and with no real education. The country stinks because we do not have an education policy that believes in cleanliness, honesty and purpose. Only those children go to school whose parents can afford. The schools are overcrowded because the ratio of students–teachers is as high as 100 students per teacher, that means there are not enough people employed as teachers. And many poor people simply do not send their children to school and most of them are girls. When people are not educated and those who are seen as educated or literate are at their best hooligans, there is apparently very little education. The reason is the culture of movies that are full of violence and vulgarity and on top of that we have these corrupt politicians who believe that the whole game of politics is to make money and enjoy power to promote their lust and that of their clan of supporters. The simple arithmetic of winning an election has become the rule of caste consideration, family dynasty, regional and religious formations. There is no national agenda but the politics of vote banks. When a politician stands for election his address to the electorate is somewhat like this, *Bhaio,* I am one of you, I have as many lice on my head as you. The crowd applauds, here is their leader. When this leader gets elected, he hardly knows the ABC of economics and administration, he talks to the bureaucrats who with their mind set on grinding their own axe in the spoils of power start pleasing the leader and in the way they pocket as much as they can and some money they throw down the drain to please the supporters of the leader. These practices have made most of the population corrupt as they expect some share in the loot of public funds. All norms and rules are sent to the gallows as long as the leader and the supporters can swallow. It is this form of leadership that gets thrown up by the masses one election after the other that have developed this nexus which has made the whole system stinky.

The political system is mainly responsible for most of our problems. The parliamentary form of government with multi-party system has brought the era of coalition form of governments and the culture of horse trading and eventual political instability in the absence of a clear majority for any party at the centre. Also in the provinces regionalism, casteism and even sedition is being propped up by vested interests to grab power. The separatist militancy is not just due to foreign hand, it gets complicated by the undue interference by the centre specially under the rule of Congress party, in the affairs of regional parties from Punjab, Kashmir and Assam. The problems had been created and complicated by the Congress governments at the centre that of Indira Gandhi and Rajiv. Foreign hands fish in because we have troubled waters. Again terrorism and violence is on the rise because we do not talk unless there is violence and allow the problems to get complicated by not acting reasonably and in time. For example, Nehru did not act to save Kashmir from the raiders and invaders when Raja Hari Singh sent his prime minister Mehar Chand Mahajan with the signed instrument of accession to India. Nehru preferred to listen to Sheikh Abdullah. It was only when Mr. Mahajan fed up with Nehru's indifference talked about going to Pakistan to negotiate that Patel and the defence minister Sardar Baldev Singh agreed to send the troops in Kashmir. Since Nehru stopped the army and went to the UNO and later on imposed or opposed Abdullah, that the Kashmir is where we find it today.

Same is the case with Punjab. No doubt the Akalis have a narrow agenda of regional and religious politics. But they were democratically holding power or going out of it. Indira Gandhi through back door manoeuvring propped up people like Bhindranwale to offset the established Akali leadership and in no time the situation went out of control. In the end, she paid the price and the people of Punjab had to suffer and paid a heavy price along with the rest of the country to wipe out the militancy. Sardar Beant Singh and K.P.S. Gill the supercop brought peace to Punjab with the support and cooperation of the people, because the people of Punjab had realised that enough was enough, and they had to rise against the barbaric violence. Similar is the case of Assam. The ULFA and Bodo outfits have been encouraged by the politicians. No doubt the Assamese have a genuine concern about the infiltrators from Bangladesh. So Assam Gana Parishad had been voted to power. To discredit Mahanta, the Congress party initiated the Bodoland agitation and now it is again complicated like any other problem. Same is the case with Nagaland and the far east where corruption and loot of central funds is never accounted. The issue of Ramjanam Bhoomi and Babari Masjid is another boiling and mishandled problem which nobody seems to bother to solve. Even the courts are sitting along the politicians. The corrupt politicians who are interested in the sectarian conflicts to win elections are the real criminals and traitors who need to be educated.

In this country of Buddha and Gandhi we have countless massacres of people. People get killed and looted by the bandits, police, terrorists and the mercenaries. People get massacred in caste wars, tribal wars and communal riots. Women get raped because they resisted eves teasing, they get burned in dowry cases, get acid thrown on their faces, children get abused and instead of being at schools they are compelled to work for nothing. People get run over by buses and trucks, trains get derailed. Organised crimes and mafia is on the rise and nobody feels safe. So what is this country heading for? Is not it the country whose head is the great Himalaya? Is not it the country of beautiful mountains, lakes, rivers, and beautiful beaches. Is not it the land of plenty, rich fertile soil, that grows everything. We have the largest mines of coals, iron and uranium. We have all the spices, oils, vegetables and the dals, wheat, basmati rice and sea foods. Such a big vast fertile country and a big coastal line with open sea on both sides is definitely a rich country. There is no need to prove that the country is one of the best places of the world by nature to live in and one of the richest countries in the world for its natural resources and the potential to grow as a great economic power. Of course, it's a land of plenty. If the draughts could be accepted as part of Tapovan.

But unfortunately it is not a secret but a great shame that the country is at its lowest ranking at number 142 as far as the per capita income is concerned. The foreign debt is at 96 billion US dollars. The country is simply not able to cope with its misfortune which is due to our mismanagement of the country whose political leaders have neither the vision nor the ability and the will to recover the country from the present chaotic state of affairs. The future is bleak, there is danger of people getting out of control and create a big mess that will lead to another Mahabharat. But it is still possible that the people realise in time what could be done soon to save the country.

India's present difficulties consist of various problems and on top of them is the lack of honest leadership. It is easy to count the problems but not so easy to choose the point from where to make a start to solve them. Should a beginning be made with the economic problems like poverty and unemployment or priority be given to national health, education, social justice or moral issues like corruption and dishonesty. Or should we solve the problem of political instability or social disregard for human dignity and ethical values, national defence and basic human rights. We have to deal with it all together. The country is a bottomless pit of wants screaming for attention in every field. It is true that so many problems cannot be solved in one day, but we can make a beginning. The tragedy of India is that the so-called politicians in their feverish pursuit of political power have made the whole country loose all sense of priorities. The people at large are as much responsible as the political leaders for creating the mess that we are in, if onions can decide the outcome of an election then it is definitely a great task to solve the problems of this country. Then we have these people who think that even if God comes down to India He won't be able to solve our problems. This is how some pessimistic people and soothsayers of doom have to offer.

If we want to change this system, improve our lot and state of this country then we have to take on a right plan and act on that without wasting time. Only then we can make this country a home of freedom, freedom because this country is yet to achieve as we have not achieved freedom from miseries like hunger, poverty and ill health. Freedom does not mean freedom to starve to death or freedom to get killed. Freedom means that the people have enough to eat, clothes to wear and a house to live in and not starve to death or die because of a cold wave or a hot wave and without medical attention. It is very simple to know what is freedom. If you have something to do, then you say you are not free. Similarly if you are preoccupied with your problems then you are not free. Therefore, you have to be free from want, disease and hunger. Any civilised society cannot be called civilised in these days unless it provides its members free medical attention and care to all, like a national health assurance and facilities free for all in matters of education and all kind of learning and the way to develop themselves the way they want to be and the freedom to live, they like to be. That is unless and until the basic human rights are guaranteed to all, there is no meaning of freedom.

In a democracy there are some problems which cannot be solved without annoying some vested interests but problems have to be identified, solutions discussed and decisions taken and implemented. There are no two opinions about the poverty of the millions, overall development of the country, the health, sanitation, education, unemployment, defence of the country, corruption backwardness, communal problems, crimes and violence of all kinds, pollution and population. Problems cannot be solved by miracles. They have to be discussed. People have to be treated as people and every individual treated as a human being and an honourable citizen and the people have to be taken into confidence and they have to be protected by the enlightened people against the vested interests. It is an over-statement to say that we are not capable of solving the problems of the country and its people and we lack something to produce quality and therefore, we need to invite foreign investment and technology or open the country for naked faceless capitalism of the west. A country that has the great Vedas, Upanishads and so many scriptures of wisdom, a country that has the creations of Ajanta, Ellora, Khajuraho, Konarak and Taj Mahal just to name a few, and a country that produces everything from a sewing needle to a satellite is definitely capable of producing quality. The country has a long history of Yoga and meditation that's how we have produced so many *Yogis, Rishis* and *Munis.* Thousands of years ago, there was great technology in this part of the world in the Mahabharat period which was destroyed in that great human tragedy, the war, and over the years it was lost. Bharat, that is India has a long history and, it is the oldest living civilisation. Therefore, we should be able to cope with the problems and see how we can move further to avoid the otherwise impending human tragedy, and chaos and make the country a place worth living in. All the political parties and their leaders have no idea neither about the problems nor about the solutions, they only talk vaguely and the only way to get out of this dark tunnel and see the light is the way of the Navrang Marg. Therefore, it is my duty as a citizen of this country to present it to the general public.

Moving to the Path of Yoga

One plus one makes the yoga of two, three plus four makes the Yoga of seven, yet the yoga of nine is the last and the top yoga. This is the ultimate yoga in arithmetics. For the practitioners of yoga, there are different kinds of Yoga to be practised in their lives. Whereas the business class like the yoga of money Ganit Yoga, some people talk of Raj Yoga, there are others who take on the paths of Dhyana Yoga, Bhakti Yoga and Gyan Yoga. But a Karam Yogi takes the path of Karama Yoga and sorts out his daily life by his toil and sweat. They characterise their lives in the light of the proverb, i.e., *Yoga Karamasu Kaushalam,* which means doing every job properly and perfectly is the yoga. These are the people who make a man, family, society and the state a strong, healthy and progressive domain. Society and the state needs these kind of Karama Yogis. Therefore, this country, i.e., Bharat expects all its citizens and all of us to be Karama Yogis. Let us move on the path of the nine colours, i.e., Navrang Marg and applaud Jai Insaan.

The Two Colours of the Bipolar World

Scientists are of the opinion that birds, animals and all these creatures on the earth cannot see all the colours. All the birds and animals see this world mostly in grey colour, and a snake seems to see the whole thing in red colour, yet the cows could see the difference between green grass and red cloth. Only the humans can see the seven colours of this world or putting it in another way the man can see only the seven colours. Only the human can see the rainbows, that is the belief of scientists. Therefore, Jai Vigyan is limited only to the seven colours. But if we see the ultimate total of Arithmetic, it is 9. Therefore, certainly the world has nine colours, which are these two colours more, this is something that we must ponder over. Sixteen arts of Mahabharat fame only make number seven, then there must be something more that will prove the number nine. It is, therefore, the two colours of the bi-polar world, the negative and the positive. Because of this negative and positive, the clouds thunder, the lightening and rain comes. Only then you could see the rainbow of seven colours. Therefore, behind the rainbow there are these two colours of negative and positive. This is, in other words, the Maya and the spirit, the bad and the good, the devil and the angel, Hell or the Heaven or putting it differently the untruth and the truth could be seen by a person as the two more colours in this world that dominate and rule this world.

The seven known colours are secondary. These most powerful colours create this whole universe. Therefore, we should bring the country and the people on the path of nine colours. Apart from the known seven colours, we must add two more colours to make it nine and find solutions to the problems. Identify the problems and solve them. This is the path of nine colours. Therefor this Nav Rang is dedicated to the country.

The Navrang Marg/The Path of Nine Colours

1. Full health assurance with regulated and planned family.
2. Compulsory free education and cultural reforms.
3. Guaranteed social security and basic human rights.
4. Direct election of the executive.
5. Reforms of the Judicial system and review of laws.
6. Economic reforms and production of quality consumer goods.
7. Provision of complete defence system and a modern foreign policy.
8. Protection of environment and eradication of corruption.
9. Making of a new India and compulsory social work.

1

Population Problem

India has just 1 per cent of the total global land and we have 17 per cent of the world population. That is why we have so many problems. The global warming will raise the sea level and countries like Bangladesh and probably 1/3 of India shall go under the sea in next 100 years and our population growth in no way is stopping. We are adding a total population of Australia every year. The population of India has tripled in last 50 years. Since there have been a wrong way of population control during the emergency period, the good for nothing politicians in the country have stopped even talking about the problem of all the problems. We are only hearing about secularism, reservation and WTO, and so on, but have become recklessly stupid. It is not only the one billion mark but so many other negative indexes that India has as its medals. Therefore, we need to have a Population Control Act and a health system to support the society and the vulnerable population that is also getting degenerated on the sex ratio. The just concluded census shows that the population of Delhi which was under 2,00,000 in 1950 has reached 1,38,00,000 in 2001, the national average ratio of women to men has gone down to 925 to 1,000 and in Punjab it has really become bad. There are 43 females to 57 males due to our great sex determining clinics and the sinless legal abortions. We hate women, homosexual marriages are in the offing. And on top of it all there is no concern in the parliament of India that has become a Kurukshetra due to the *Tehlka* tapes that shows Rs. 3,00,000 donation to two political parties or politicians but uncaring of the fact that the opposition has caused a net loss of Rs. fifty crore to the public exchequer in ten days by not allowing work and even debate.

Full Health Assurance with Regulated and Planned Family

Firstly, we should take on the most serious problem and that is the population, it is increasing rapidly and too fast virtually exploding into calamity. Population has been the main cause of our problems and to control the birth rate, we have not done much. No doubt it has been a programme of the government but is pursued half heartedly, and a lot of money has been spent and is being spent without any result of satisfaction. Therefore, to begin with, we should have a universal limit of two children per family and a law be made immediately to this effect. It will not be difficult to pass such a law and then implement it. Whoever passes such a law will face a serious opposition from various parties, religious organisations and people, etc. China has also done it, they have put one child limit on one family, also there are reports that some couples have killed their daughters to have a son and also in India there are these female foeticides facilitated through the ever increasing sex determination tests carried out by unscrupulous doctors. It can be argued by some people that their fundamental right to make children is being taken away. The opposition to such a law would not be beyond control. In reality the right to make children is not being taken away, actually people have been misusing the fundamental law of nature. It is not civilised to make large family. People make children and then they do not bother to stop as most of the people are illiterate and orthodox, they just think either its God who makes the children or they have to wait for a male child or for the second male child and in some cases for a daughter, and in the process they end up with a large family and make their lives miserable and so many miserable families make a country miserable. It is a pity that the state of affairs in India is miserable, and I do not understand why there should be so much longing for a male child.

The sex discrimination in this world is because of the stupid mentality of man, who is still uncivilised. Male chauvinism, violence, wars and the historical thinking of uncivilised men to grab the women and use them is the reason why people want to have a male child. But things have changed and are changing in the present day world. Because of science and technology and the industrial revolution the change was brought about in Europe. It is then that the woman started to work outside their family, the world wars brought a lot of women to work, because the men were fighting on the battle front. At the end of the second world war, there were millions of widows who had to work. Marxism had influenced the status of women in the industralised western world. The idea of equality at least in theory started to take root in the people. Because of the modern welfare state ideology, the government started many social welfare schemes and many women started working and slowly they are now in almost every field of activity. They are not only the bread makers at home but the breadwinner themselves. They have achieved a lot if not 100 per cent equality with men. This all happened because of the circumstances, and change in mentality and opportunity for women to get the same amount and kind of education and economic independence like men. Today, not only the women but the men as well have gained as a result of women independence. And they think of making one or two children. This has been made possible with the advent of contraceptives which have relieved the people and liberated the women. Whereas in the underdeveloped world, the people still have to achieve this.

Therefore, even if the people at large are not aware of what they should do, the leadership should realise that they should not waste time to limit the family size. This can be done by inviting all the social and political institutions and the students for consultation on this issue. Health programmes have to be geared up accordingly. Also the minimum age limit for marriage has to be fixed and pursued vigorously. Women should avoid bearing children before they are in their twenties.

It is still common in the rural areas and among the tribals and the harijans that the kids marriages take place and this is widely prevalent. The age limit that of 18 years for the girls and 21 years for the boys is hardly implemented by the government. People still go for early marriage and teenagers become parents. The child marriages still take place and they talk about going in the 21st century.

Yes, that is true. Not so long ago we did not have the health care facilities that are possible today even if you find them missing at large in India. But the fact is that we are better off than 1947. I mean we have managed to avoid the epidemics of cholera and malaria, etc., that used to wipe out families, villages and bigger areas. People used even to die of fever. That is why people did not think of birth control. But today things are different, man has achieved a great deal in medical science and now we have also the means to control the birth. In the times of *desi* ghee the women were not so fast to conceive, but now with change over to Dalda production we have to adopt family planning. Therefore, a small family should be followed. But in a country like India where we have people with such a contrast of outlook, religions and tribals, it will be quite difficult to convince them to go into such a stereotyped programme.

Well all of us eat food. But wear clothes and live in the houses or need a house to live in. But when we think of solving the problems of this country, we have to begin with such a plan. It is very simple to understand when you have a house or land, or are the owner of a factory or business, you like that it is inherited by your children, and, if they are many then it is not going to be enough. You always need more and then you will look for all kinds of possibilities to make more material gains and you want to leave behind for your children as much as possible. If you are in a job, you start to look for extra money and that comes very often from being corrupt or you have to work extra for which you have to pay in terms of health. Bigger the size of the family, bigger the problems. The rich people start to buy or grab the properties of others so that they can have enough and their children remain well established. Most of the crimes are there because people do not have enough or they are not satisfied; in their urge to have more. From begging onward to stealing, corruption, bribes, prostitution, smuggling and dacoity the main factor is family circumstances. Bigger families are even producing terrorists. These gang wars, caste wars, communal wars, class wars and wars of all kinds emanate from the thought of big family. People who have nobody to inherit do not indulge in crimes if they have enough. The others remain content if they have enough for their off-springs. People with one or two children always take care that they do not join bad company. Therefore, it is imperative that we decide for the whole country to have small families of one or two children. It is good for the ethnic balance also. Some communal minded people advocate bigger size of the families so that they can outnumber their opponents or rivals. This is a stupid and dangerous way of thinking. And if we do not decide the child limit now, it will definitely bring a civil war or violence in the country later on, because people will look for one excuse or the other to eliminate people and fascism is more likely than communism in this country.

Some people may say that the government has been doing a lot to encourage small families, people have co-operated, there have been a lot of sterilisations. It may also be true that forcing people by law would be bit too much as we are aware that during the dark days of emergency in 1975, the forced sterilisation and the outcome was the *Nasbandi* revolution that threw Mrs Indira Gandhi out like a despot gets routed by a popular revolution.

Well Mrs Gandhi was not thrown out just because of *Nasbandi*. There were so many other factors. First the freedom of the people was taken away, then she wanted to stay in power by all means and impose on the country, the dynastic rule. Prior to emergency there was this movement against corruption in Bihar and student unrest in Gujarat against the governments of those states and then there was this Allahabad High Court judgement against Mrs Indira Gandhi's election which enabled the opposition to ask for her resignation. This was all legitimate.

The excesses perpetrated by her reckless son Sanjay, his cronies and flunkeys and the thoughtless administration, are well known. All the opposition leaders were arrested alongwith thousands of workers of the opposition parties, the newspapers were compelled to make favours to the ruling regime of Delhi, under the pressure of emergency. People were kept in jails for 18 months without trial. And the whole exercise was illegal, improper and dictatorial. It was a clear attack on democracy and insult to the whole freedom movement against the British.

At present we are talking about the family size and it should be noted that the *Nasbandi* during the emergency was not adopted wisely. The idea was great but lacked the vision. They just wanted to get it done through an order. Targets were set to achieve to all the states and departments to bring in the number of sterilisations and those people serving under were suffering from the bureaucratic syphilis and did not even bother whom they were sterilising. Funny but true, the whole exercise was reckless and insulting. Police was used, labourers were brought in trucks on the days of payments to the camps and were sterilised, marriage parties were stopped and sterilised. The actions were simply mindless, unnecessary and uncivilised and even evil. And this was done under the order of extra constitutional centre of power.

The need for law is because of the failure of the family welfare programme. We have been doing this for last 35 years but the people have not cared enough, because they are not aware of the gravity of the situation. During the famine of 1905 people are reported to have eaten the dead people in Bengal. In the time to come there are these computers and robots that will drive many people jobless and one man will be able to do the job of ten or more. And you know the birth rate in this country and the sub-continent have not slowed down. People if any that have taken to birth control sterilisation have done so only after they have had half a dozen children. That is why the programme has not worked and, therefore, we need a law. The people shall have the choice of using the method of their convenience to control the births. The child limit has to be women oriented. That a woman shall not bear a child before she is 25 years of age. That married or unmarried, she will not have more than two children alive. In case she has got divorced or remarried, the limit shall remain the same. And in case of men who have already children they shall not be entitled to get children with other women in case they are divorced, widowed or remarried, after having crossed their limit. What shall be the position in case a man has more than one wife? In that case the two children limit shall be applied to that family. But this is not usually common that a man or woman has more than one spouse. It is not relevant here to find out what should be penalties for the offenders of such a law. It would be more relevant to suggest how such a law has to be accompanied by facilities for those mothers who are affected by such a law. First of all, when a woman gets pregnant she should be registered and given all the medical attention and advice and a bonus for her health in case she is poor. And child bonus after the delivery of a child. The child should be registered for medical attention in the primary health centre. Secondly, the woman should be taught the use of all kinds of contraceptives and their side effects. Actually the contraceptive courses should be provided at the high school or before the students leave high school. Then before marriage the eligible people should be obliged to take advice from the primary health centre about the sex related things in details, so that they are aware how to proceed with their lives and of how to bring up the children. All these facilities have to be provided at the primary health centre. Then along with this we have to provide old age pension for the needy people and social security for all the handicapped or disabled people, so that the expectations of the needy people do not make them think that they would have been better if they had a family to look after them. All this should be looked after well by the community. Therefore, the state just does not make law but shares the responsibility of such a law. Unless we make a law to control births, nobody could solve the problems of this country, you can have hundred Prime Ministers and a thousand point programme to solve the problems and develop the country, nothing will succeed. Any government could hesitate to make such a law as it would invite a considerable opposition. That too criticism by some ignorant people who do not understand the urgency of such a step. And any government would not like to or would be reluctant to make such a law for fear of loosing the votes and the chair. What could then be done?

First of all, the government need not worry that it will loose the votes just because of such a law. The legislation is passed by the parliament, and in the parliament and outside all the political parties and student organisations have to be consulted on such a vital issue. It cannot be a programme of one party, it is the problem of the whole country. The student power could be mobilised, they have to be taken into confidence and consulted and a movement for the enactment of such laws could be launched and sustained by the youth and the student power. It is finally them who will face the dire consequences of a population explosion when they will grow up in their middle ages from now, when they will face the problems and struggle to solve them. The present nuclear bomb of population will explode and annihilate the masses. Within two weeks of student agitation all over the country, the government could be forced to make such a law to control the birth rate. Subject of the National Health Assurance have to be pondered over, as it is going to be expensive and you know the conditions in the hospitals.

National Health Insurance

The country needs a National Health Insurance and

assurance scheme for everybody, a guarantee of medical attention, treatment and care. The poor people do not have money to buy medicines, some even do not have money to go on the bus to the hospital, and if they do get to the hospital, there are not enough medicines, sometimes the patients must even buy the bandage from outside. There are not enough doctors and nurses to look after the patients. Some of the people on duty are always playing truant and even running clinics outside. Some of the medicines from the hospital find their way to the private medical stores and clinics. Sometimes the patients may need to go to another bigger hospital as the local hospital cannot treat them. The better hospital may be hundreds of miles away and difficult to reach for the patients without money. Such patients do not have much hope of life. And, on the other hand, our rich people and leaders in the government go out of the country for medical treatment even if the treatment exists in India for those patients. A National Health Scheme has to be visualised to overcome all such problems. There is always the financial problems, but it is not unmanageable. Every family above the poverty line and everybody who is employed should be made to pay a certain amount of money regularly towards the health pool, apart from the public funds. And whatever the arrangement, everybody should be provided free medical aid. The patient should be paid even the bus fares and in case the patient is accompanied by another person if he/she is not capable of going on their own, the hospital must pay the expenses in such cases. The free food, free medicines, free treatment and everything the patient might need should be provided free by the hospitals. And if the case is referred to another hospital for treatment, the expenses should be made and arrangements be made by the lower hospital, because many people cannot afford the expenses, and people do not have to be deprived of medical care just because they are poor. Those people either suffer all their life or they die. To have this basic human right of life it is very important to have a National Health Service of the highest international standards. There should be at least one special hospital like the AIIMS in each state and even more in bigger states.

There have been instances where people are not allowed to work as volunteers in this country, and are not given visas to stay here as health workers on their own just because they are foreigners and we have so many doctors unemployed and yet there are so many people suffering for want of medical attention. Millions of people are suffering from diseases that can be cured, like leprosy, T.B., blindness, and millions are born handicapped. All this could be taken care of if the health service in the country takes care of it. The country should be open to foreign aid and agencies that want to help the suffering people in this country. It is strange that the government makes hurdles in the way of outside people that want to help the people here, while we fail to provide people the basic health treatment and care.

Apart from the medical service and attention we need to educate people about the health and how to take care of it What food to eat and what to avoid, a real knowledge about the food toxins and poisons, pollution and food poisoning. People should be told to wash all the food before they cook, and how to eat a balanced diet and what constitutes a balanced diet. And then the people should be able to buy and eat the balanced diet. Apart from the food they should know about hygiene at home and in public places. All the public places of eating should be clean up to the health standard, like boiling of the utensils before you serve the food to anybody, which should also be fresh. There should be toilets in all the restaurants. And above all, people have to be educated about the ways of living scientifically and naturally. People have to develop a habit of doing physical exercises, like yoga, sports and long walking. They should avoid bad habits like smoking and drinking and eating harmful things like sugar, masala and caffeine. People should brush their teeth twice a day and sleep enough and avoid noise and living in polluted places. They should wear only those clothes that are made of natural stuff like wool, cotton and silk. They should avoid polyester and nylon things as prevention is better than cure. People should use more Ayurvedic medicines and try to cure themselves with Ayurvedic systems. In this way we can make a country of healthy people. This is the right way to health and satisfaction, and before a mother could conceive, she should be checked for all medical fitness and then the whole pregnancy should be monitored and the health record be maintained for the new born child and that of the parents. And this all should be done at the primary health centre.

The argument of some people who may be opposed to such a law, that they can look after more children and can afford to have more children or that they belong to minority communities is no justification to have more children. Because we are all citizens of this country that is India that is Bharat it is everybody's duty, if we can claim rights, to abide by the common law. It does not mean that a rich man have more children and a poor man cannot have any. It also does not mean that a majority community could say that the minority communities cannot have any thing. Therefore, to be reasonable every body has to accept the limit, like we have the law to drive on the left. Unless and until we do this, the vague, and thoughtless politician in the country, will go on making a mess of everything. They will probably think of importing a leader to solve our problems as they think that the imported goods are so good.

Since the voluntary birth control failed to produce any tangible results in the last thirty years and the population of the country has gone up to over one billion now, population problem needs to be addressed urgently. The population has increased now three times. Therefore, our problems have increased in every sector and there is little to achieve by economic reforms and infrastructure talks. Unfortunately, the so-called corrupt politicians who are always ready to grab power have even stopped talking about birth control. The need of the hour is to enforce birth control by law, and save the country from otherwise impending human disaster. A very strict and effective law to enforce birth control and an efficient health insurance system to support such a law is needed. Provisions of such a law should cover all the areas concerned with birth control and family planning.

1. As a first step the age of marriage for girls should be raised to 21 whether it is arranged marriage or own choice.
2. That the couple be required to attain knowledge of birth control methods from primary health centres prior to marriage.
3. That the age of having children should be minimum 25 years.
4. That the pregnancy should be registered immediately

by the primary health centre and the health centre should be able to help the pregnant women during and after the pregnancy in all the matters and a health diary of every citizen should be kept right from the day of birth.

5. That no woman or man should have more than two children irrespective of the number of marriages or without marriage.
6. That abortion should be legal only in case there is danger to life of a woman due to pregnancy or the child is likely to be handicapped and it should be done in the government hospitals. A pregnancy cannot be terminated because of not wanting a girl child. Therefore, the sex determination tests should be prohibited and punishable by law.
7. The likely parents should receive a proper advice before, during and after pregnancy on how to bring up a child, how to look after a child and the complete medical care of a child and then, of course, how to bring up a child in relation to society, in relation to the country and in relation to the whole world.
8. The children be innoculated as per the medical timetable for the control of dangerous diseases.
9. That everybody be entitiled to have a health check every year.
10. That a marriage should be allowed only after the couple has shown each other the medical fitness certificate. This is necessary because of their contageous diseases and impotency. To avoid the neo-sati happening due to such infections as HIV that causes AIDS, Hepatitis and Tuberculosis, etc.

It has been a practice with all the major religions that the couple show each other their faces and agree to the marriage at the time of the marriage. This is because the couple should know whom they are getting married that also includes the physical status of the persons. Such a marriage certificate shall not prohibit any marriage, if some one wants to. But it is necessary as most marriages in India are arrange. In this case the identity cards will have to make the medical report. To conclude this chapter I would like to say that this is not an exercise to bring in more *babucracy* which we despise in our lives, but make our society a healthier society. To make our lives safe there should be also a provision for any deadbody to have police clearance or the medical clearance before the creamation so that a national record could be maintained about the causes of death and detect any faul play in the matter of such deaths. That will also help us to form our health policy and programme. We simply should improve on our health care and treatment and everything should be available at the district level.

2

Nature of Poverty and Guarantee of Basic Human Rights

As is clear and known that our country Bharat is full of poor people, it would not be a misnomer if we can interpret the Hindi word Bharaat as full of darkness or full of night as Bharteem means the opposite. More than 50 per cent of people are still illiterate and more than 80 per cent of the people are poor and 40 per cent of the people are below the poverty line. These people have either no house or they are living in jhuggis, shanties and slums. Most of them are half naked and are malnourished, don't get proper meal and have no access to education and health care. They die of everything, food poisoning, no food, epidemics, winter cold waves, hot waves, cyclones, malaria, TB, cholera and every disease on earth without medical care. They look for food like rats and other animals and the society does not care how they live. From day one of independence, the leaders and politicians have been promising to uplift the masses from the dirt of stinky poverty but the demons of poverty have been multiplying with the population graph. Not only do these poor people not have food, shelter and clothes, they do not have toilets. They do not go to school and there is no way that they can hope for the future that one day there will be a change for the better. Because of their poverty, they cannot even think for themselves. They vote for the people who can buy them off the night before the poll and then nobody cares for them. The politicians know that these people cannot think for themselves, so it is good not to bother about them. It is good for the rich and the middle class in India that they can hire these people for any jobs that they cannot do themselves or keep this class of poor people as servants class. The more servants they have, the better for them.

However, it will be better to study the problem of poverty so that if at all one day the people, who want to help the poor get rid of their poverty, they could understand and find the ways to solve the problem.

There is poverty because of our caste system in the country among the Hindus. As is known to most of the people, that there have been four main classes of our Hindu system of society—the Brahmins, the Kshatriyas and the Vaishyas were in a better position by their class and later on the caste system and the Shudras always have been the servant class and the poor caste by all means. So before independence though the poverty was even more acute, the poorest of the poor were from among the Shudras. And after independence, there have been a special programme of positive discrimination to uplift the downtrodden shudras. Not only the Shudras but the other tribal people as well whose lot was not better than the Shudras. So, as a matter of policy, the low castes and tribal people were provided reservation in all the fields from education, jobs and seats in the legislature and other representative bodies. This has helped a great lot of these people and now a creamy layer of new Brahmins has emerged among these reserved class people and still this class of Shudras and tribal people and lots of Muslims constitute the major chunk of the poorest of the poor people in the country. There is no doubt that the poverty is not limited to one or particular communities. The poverty has engulfed all castes and religions and now we can say that the people below poverty line should be declared as one class. It is silly to divide this class further into Shudras, Muslims or backwards. There is now only one class of poor people, that should be the one below poverty line and further up the poor people who are just little bit better than the poorest.

The cause of the new poverty after independence could be seen because of the rise in uncontrolled population growth. Even though India was the first country that thought of population control way back in 1952, its population has multiplied three times in fifty years. Now the first and foremost cause of poverty is the population growth. In the country the area is limited and in the rural areas on the same piece of land we have four times more people than we had in 1950. So the land cannot support all these people. In 1950 even those less people were as poor as they are today. Thanks to the development and progress in the country that the poor people have not become four times more poor than they were in 1950. But in future if we do not control population it is possible that the people may become poorer than today.

Today poverty is in every caste, religion and region and the state of schooling in the country is becoming worse everyday for the poor people, the job situation more worse and the social amenities going down everyday and nobody even talks about the poor any more. Indira Gandhi at least used to talk about removing poverty, but today we hear only about globalisation and liberalisation, market economy and economic reforms all for the betterment of the rich people and rich countries. Nobody is worried about the poor and poverty. There is only one very-very small group in Andhra Pradesh—the Peoples, War Group (PWG) that is perhaps the only group of people who want to carry on the fight against the rich and, on the other hand, the communists seem to have lost their revolutionary zeal and have not only become power hunters and brokers in the country, they have compromised on the communist theory as well specially after the collapse of the Soviet Union. There is another group of politicians in the country that are now busy not to talk and remove poverty but to become the creamy layer. They enjoy the reservation system for the harijans and other backward caste and tribal people. They only talk about their particular constituents of the caste they come from, only to grind their own axe and make a politics of vote banks and prosper on that.

The most disorganised are the poor people among the Muslims. They have only suffered as a result of partition. First, because of the partition of the country they feel guilty and do not come out as a group to highlight their problem of poverty. Second, they still are orthodox, hence get misguided and exploited by the Mullahs and they have also not joined any political party in a proper way. They voted and supported Congress party for long time after independence, first because the Muslims wanted to resolve the guilty problem of partition because they opted to stay back in India, and second, because there was the danger of the neo-fascists RSS which was cleverly used by the Congress party led by Nehru and Indira to turn the Muslims as the vote banks for the Congress party. And after the Babri incident, the Muslims shifted away from the Congress and since 90 per cent of them want to vote for anybody who is against the BJP. So it is very clear the Muslims have not cared about their poverty but more about their religion and its associated problems. Same is the case with regional parties. The people who could have been organised on the class of being the poor, further chose the regional parties who are again controlled by vested interests of some groups and families who just want to be the ruler of those provinces and promote their narrow political interests. So to sum it all, you can easily conclude that the poor people in India have further got divided into small patches. To start with the communist movement in India, was mostly headed by the Brahmins who can never be communists. Later on, the same caste led sections have made their own groups at the same time as the regional and communal forces. All in all there is no party that could be a party of poor people or some party that wanted and could work for the destruction of poverty in the country. On the top of it all it is strange but true that all, the politicians give a lip service to the poor and actually it is meant to remove their own poverty and become rich and join the creamy layer. Now with the fashionable liberalisation, nobody talks about poverty. Yet we have the largest population of poor people in this country.

It is very stupid to think that the poverty in this country will be taken care of by the liberalisation or the enhanced gross national products or the poverty will take care of itself. This is very dangerous thinking, both for the capitalists and the communists. There is every possibility that the situation in the country will go out of control and a big chaos will follow and many innocent people will pay by their lives. That is neither a way to solve our problems nor it will benefit anybody like the communists or the capitalists. But it is possible that the country will definitely pay heavily. Therefore, we have to act and act soon to make a system and be civilised. As has been already suggested we have to control the population by law, then schooling compulsory and free for everybody and provide the basic human rights to all with state guarantee.

What are basic human rights? When India framed its constitution, it only provided fundamental rights to its citizens. These fundamental rights are only political rights, though right of life is one of them, but this right to life does not include the provisions to enable people to live the life. These fundamental rights were included in the constitution as a result of political independence from the alien British colonists. The intentions of our constitution makers were noble but they did not and could not go to the depth of the problem of poverty to grant the basic human rights to the people because most of the people that framed the charters or the constitution were legal luminaries, and lawyers and not one of those people who could think of the poor people. They could not provide for basic human rights because the country was so poor, but because there were people other than these lawyers who framed the constitution, they could only incorporate the directive principles of state policy.

These directive principles of state policy were supposed to be the guidelines for the governments to use in the development of the country and end poverty and social discrimination. Dr Bhimrao Ambedkar was not chosen the head of the constitution committee, because he was a specialist on that subject, instead it was for political reasons. Mahatma Gandhi had the cause of the untouchables close to his heart and there was this man Dr. Ambedkar who could qualify for a job like that and because of the partition of the country, Ambedkar was given this position to prove that in the free India every section of the people shall have a say. No doubt, the Indian constitution is a great piece of legislation or the greatest charter ever, but the directive principles of state policy falls too short of the basic human rights. Today there is talk of the review of the constitution. It is doubtful that it is going to include the basic human rights. On the other, hand some unscrupulous people are making a noise for generating votes by saying that the constitution made by Dr. Ambedkar is being scrapped as if it was only Dr. Ambedkar who made the constitution.

The country has to develop a system where the basic human rights are guaranteed in practice by the state. India has aped the western modern system of government but are unable to rise above the poverty line. The basic human rights are not incorporated in the constitutions of the western countries but they have developed a system where a minimum state help is provided to the needy. It is not a great deal but considering the poverty in India it seams heavenly, getting back to the problem of poverty and employment, we have to develop this system now where the people could be lifted above the poverty line where prosperity and a dignified life for the common man could be achieved. The basic human rights, therefore, is a system that whenever a child is conceived the state should undertake to start the care. The state must ensure the well being of that unborn child and see that the child is not terminated by abortion or by miscarriage. The health of the child has to be monitored and the pregnant mother has to be looked after by the state if the parents cannot do that. After the child is born, the health care in the country has to look after the needs of the child, this means that everybody in the country will get full medical attention service. This is one of the basic human rights. Secondly, every child must go to school and if the parents are not able to provide the education, the state must do that and even provide food, clothing and all the basic needs of such children either at state homes for the children or help the parents having the children at home. The state must make sure that all kinds of children including the mentally retarded and handicapped are provided the basic human facility and amenities. The standard of such facilities has to be established. It is the duty of the parents as well as the state that the children are educated and looked after. They have to be trained to find employment and look after themselves and become responsible citizens of the country and possibly responsible parents in future.

Provision of public distribution shops at fair prices or low price of foodgrains is not enough. This is not the only solution to remove poverty. We have to go to the door of the poor even if he has got no door because he hasn't got a house or a room to live in. First, we have to take all these homeless people, provide them home, food and clothing. We have to make it sure that they do not run away to live on the streets, because the condition at their welfare homes is disgusting. Once we bring these poorest of the poor inside a door, we can start from that door of the poor. They have to be provided all the basic human rights of living and growing up. These rights will mean, the home, food and clothing. Home shall mean proper house with drinking water, electricity, toilets and beds and furniture and of course, the kitchen with cooking gas and sink. A normal family of four people should have at least four bed room house or flat. The children have to be in school and there have to be job for everybody after the education and in case there is no job, the person should be given unemployment allowance. There have to be a social security department in place to look after the needy people. Health-wise everybody must have a national health assurance scheme where everybody can have a right to call a doctor. If you do not have a job, the state must provide you money to look after yourself. Once a child becomes 18, the young person should not be a dependent on the parents. Basic human rights should mean a system where everybody should also feel secure in society—physically, socially and politically. That means if you need an ambulance it should be at your call, if you need police or fire brigade it should be at your door at your call within minutes at least in the cities. As already discussed in the national health assurance, everybody should be provided free health care and in time for everything at world standard.

Now many people will wonder where the money will come from. The answer is simple, where the money is coming from in the developed countries. They have developed a tax system even if they are capitalists. The state has taken the responsibility to look after the helpless people, you do not see children on the streets there. They are taken by social workers to children homes where they are looked after. Even if the parents or a single parent fails to reach in time to pickup their children from the school, the school authorities call in the social worker who will look after the children. In our great country and many other poverty stricken countries, the children are the greatest sufferers. They do not get any social care. Some of them die of lack of care, and if they survive, they do not have a childhood of care, play and education. Finally they are abused, to work as child labour, they are sexually assaulted, some of them end up in forced sex trade by the Mafia and as domestic bonded servants.

The sight of beggars everywhere, children, women and handicapped and lepers on the streets is a clear proof of our lack of social concern. Our faceless political *thugs* who unfortunately have become MPs and MLAs and ministers are not bothered, they only herd themselves up to have a shake hand with a white foreigner like president Clinton, otherwise they are busy looking after their own comforts and fixing deals. Poverty is not just these beggars on the street. It is spread all over the country, the beggars, the people who sleep on the pavements or under the bridges, the people living in the slums, in the make shift tents, jhuggies and shanties and sheds, the people who cannot send their children to school, the people who do not have proper sanitation, the people who do not have proper accommodation, the people who are unemployed, the people who do not get enough money as wages or from their little enterprise, the farming labours, the small farmer, all these people who constitute two-third of the population are poor. They do not have proper safe drinking water. Majority of them are malnourished.

Once we have a system in place for the whole country only then can we claim to belong to a civilisation. Therefore, we have to act fast and organise a better standard of living for everybody. The capitalists must realise that they can make more money if the common man gets more money. Some of them are even involved in human organs trade. The communists should realise that they need not wait for more poor people to rise in revolt, as communism has no takers and it is difficult to have a communist system, because people are selfish and corrupt and they do not care about the socialist state enterprises to succeed. Our Sangh Parivar people should realise as well that majority of the Hindus are poor, you cannot serve their cause unless you remove poverty. You should not become leaders of provocation or hooligans. You have to serve the cause of the people and people in this country are poor. You cannot live on the Ayodhya Ram Temple while the holy Ganga has become an open sewage from Hardwar to Kolkata.

Therefore, for a starving man freedom in free India means nothing, fundamental rights also means the same without basic human rights. Even life is not of much value. People die on the streets, people die in road accidents because there is lack of proper roads and driving culture. Many people drive or walk on the roads like buffaloes. The responsibility is never fixed. In the hospitals, there are hardly any free medicines or proper check ups. People simply suffer and die like neglected animals. The world declaration of universal human rights have meant nothing for the vast majority of the people in India.

The basic human rights of food, clothes and house, education and health have to be guaranteed to all. There are millions of people that are dying of starvation and hunger and suffering from privation. They cannot be free just to die. Freedom is not the freedom to die, freedom means freedom to live and the choice to live the way you want to live and you can in reality. Basic human rights have to be accompanied by fundamental rights of democratic world. Unfortunately more than half of the world does not even have democracy. Most of the countries in this world have either dictatorships of one party, or one man, that of the army or the fundamentalist religious fanatics. However, we can make a distinction between all kinds of states. For example, the communist countries with one party dictatorships do have basic human rights, but they don't have the fundamental rights of freedom that are there in other countries of the democratic world. Whereas in India our fundamental rights are being taken away and eroded by the government slowly through many anti-freedom laws though they are there in the constitution. We do not have the basic human rights for millions of the people just because they are poor. About 40 per cent of the people are below poverty line and hence no basic human rights, and they cannot enjoy the fundamental rights as well. Many countries in this world do not have either the fundamental rights of freedom or the basic human rights of life. All they have is dictatorships and these kinds of dictatorships represent only the uncivilised and barbaric concept of life. Systems like that have to be and should be denounced by everybody.

A new awareness has to be brought about the rights of the people and individuals. It has to be attained through education and the media of mass circulation. In old times people were more free from government even if they were despotic, because the king could not reach everybody. But in today's world of fast communication and control, everybody's life and the freedom of the individual is more vulnerable than ever before, even in the democratic society. Therefore, the need for the people to know and respect everybody's rights, that you can do with your rights, with your life what you want to and should not impose your views on the other people because the other should enjoy the same concept of freedom of life. For example, if you are driving a car on the road, you have to respect the traffic rules, nobody can say because he is free to do what he likes, therefore he can drive even in the middle of the road. The traffic rules in this way do not effect or control the freedom of a person on the road. The rules can only be anti-freedom if someone is allowed to drive while somebody else is not, even if he has a driving licence. Same way nobody can be allowed a noisy or smoky vehicle.

So the new awareness of human rights is to be realised in its right perspective. In modern times organisations like Amnesty International has come up with concern for human rights and their violations by the governments all over the world. It is time that the civilised world accepts its manifestoes that speak for the rights of the people and the individuals. The second world war had brought a new awareness about the human rights and it is a coincidence that the independence was followed by the universal declaration of human rights. One hundred and thirty five countries have accepted the declaration and most of them have been found guilty of violations of these rights themselves.

Today computers and the state have had an incredible invasion into the private lives of the people. The media has also over-stepped its limit in talking and commenting about the private life of some people. Therefore, proper safeguards have to be made to protect the individual from the state and an awareness of the dignity and pride of the individual and his rights have to be realised. To be more civilised is to have more freedom for people.

Freedom Today

Freedom that was attained for the people and the country in 1947 was defined by the constitution of the country. India which has the largest written constitution in the world has clearly written down the fundamental rights of the people and the directive principles of state policy were inscribed to be the guidelines of the future governments. Nehru started his term of the first prime minister of the free country with a ban on the RSS. It has not been proved that RSS was responsible for the murder of the Mahatma, the father of the nation. But because the RSS could have become and emerged as a strong challenge to the Congress party and to Nehru in times to come, it had to be damaged, so the blame of the murder and the ban. After the ban on the RSS, there was no challenge left to Nehru until 1962 when his *Hindi-Chini Bhai-Bhai* boomeranged into bye-bye. Nehru did not protest the Chinese as they violated the human rights in Tibet. The humiliation of 1962 when China attacked India, shocked the whole country and Nehru did not take any responsibility and Krishna Menon was made a scapegoat. Menon had to resign for the sake of Nehru and Nehru died two years later. Nehru was a democrat, no doubt, but the way Syama Prasad Mookerjee died in Kashmir while in detention and people like Kairon in Punjab were allowed to do things in violation of the rights of the people are such few cases of anti-freedom and violation of human rights that took place in his time. His opposition of President Prasad, as the latter wanted to attend the restoration ceremony of the Somnath temple, washing the feet of a Brahmin and attending the funeral of Sardar Patel were indications of this intolerance in matters of personal freedom of the other person is not democratic. Nehru never said or did anything about the basic human rights and its guarantee to all. He only spoke about the progress, though he was a great orator of socialism. Basic human rights are necessary for the real attainment of freedom. As there were not many agitations against Nehru, his being a freedom lover was still not tested. Though the conditions of jails in India and the police atrocities on the people remained as much the same as in the British times. Therefore, whether the freedom was achieved more for the common man under Nehru is a question that hangs in balance. Mahatma Gandhi was murdered with the negligence of Nehru's government. Thus, the great champion of freedom in India was killed just after independence.

Freedom under Indira Gandhi was attacked more and very often and many anti-freedom laws were framed and misused and are still in existence. Emergency was imposed and all the freedom and liberties of the people were snatched. The Janata did restore the freedom of the people and their dignity but did not and could not provide the basic human rights to the people though it was not possible to do so in such a short time. Rajiv Gandhi continued the legacy of his mother, with anti-freedom laws and many people were put in jails without trial. It is a shame that India has figured in the Amnesty International's record and chided for human rights violation. You can joke with the concert in Delhi organised by the *Times of India* Publications in the name of human rights the audience and the participating musicians were told that the money collected will go to the human rights organisation in India and at the end when they collected more than two crore rupees, they said that the money will go to the Indira Gandhi memorial—the person who violated human rights in a democracy. There are not many people in this country who can tell you what the term human rights really means.

Mahatma Gandhi was a great lover of freedom. That is why he was one of those great anarchists who wanted the State to go, he believed that the state represents violence and repression, against the individual and it is true. Tilak very much meant individual freedom when he said Swaraj is my birth right. M.N. Roy withdrew from communist movement because he believed in the freedom and dignity of the individual. So was J.P. Narayan later on. So all these great thinkers of modern India were all for the freedom of the Individual.

Poverty

India is at number 142 in the community of nations of the world as far as per capita income of the people and the nations is concerned. Now every sixth man in this world is an Indian, but 40 per cent of them are below poverty line. There is a very huge task in front of us if we really want to eradicate poverty. First, most of the people really do not worry about the poverty in the country. All that they like to feel is that they are better off than the others and some of them even think that it is not their problem to help the poor people to get rid of their poverty. And they also think if there are poor people, they can use them as cheap labour and even buy from them whatever they could sell. Therefore, the rich are becoming more and more rich and the poor stay where they have been. There are these sky high buildings in the cities owned by some rich people, while in front of these buildings you have people sleeping on the footpaths. Rich people who even cannot make a decision as to what they would like to eat because they have plenty of choice, while there are people that wait like crows or dogs for the food that is thrown out by the people as left over. Such a miserable society we have in this country. People even sell their children for few hundreds of rupees, there are bonded labourers who are being exploited by the owners. Girls get sold to the brothels, girls and boys that work as servants are sexually exploited, they never see the schools. Many people starve to death and there is no medical attention. There is just no match for Indian poverty, though India has many of the richest men in the world, and India is so rich naturally, but we have only managed the ugly look of poverty for its people. It is a national shame and clear proof of our indifference.

Birth control law could start the egalitarian society for India, as we have discussed earlier. You can also have Urban Property Ceiling Law like they have done with the Land Ceiling Act. No family should be allowed to have more than one house all over the country for the use of one family or one person. The housing societies should be oganised all over the country and new cities should be planned and rural development with proper housing system could be visualised. What is the fun and use of having an expensive house surrounded by slums, I wonder?

We have this slums mentality. The slums have come up because of the migration of poor people from the rural areas to the cities. These immigrants are from different parts of the country and even from our neighbouring countries. Some people even say that it is the slums on our railway stations and railway lines that makes India look like so poor. No doubt we have to shift these people from this misery and settle them properly elsewhere. We must stop this uncivilised way of living in this oldest living civilisation.

3

Free Education and Cultural Reforms

"Man is a social animal", he is man only because he is social. What differentiates a man from an animal is the vast potential of man to learn and grow continuously in the direction of constant change. No doubt it has been the history of mankind, that man did come from the animal world and it is only ten thousands years ago that man moved towards present civilisation. We have seen that none of the other animals have changed or learned any thing new like the humans have done. From barbaric animals they have turned into civilised, educated, well dressed, cultured and scientifically progressing human beings. Man has been continuously learning from the experience and passing on the same experience and knowledge to the next generation. That is how cultures and the religions and the social systems have developed. Passing on the knowledge to the next generation means education. Whether its done at home or schools or through social contact and media. It is all part of our education. It includes all the fields.

As we know the history of India, we also are aware of the history and nature of the type of education that we had in the past. India is one of those very few countries that has had a history of school and education system which dates back to more than five thousand years. Right from the days of agriculture and religious progress in the Gangetic region, the Vedic period proves that the formal education of the people in this country started thousands of years ago. We had that beautiful Vedic period long time ago. It is, however, a tragedy that the education and the civilisation which was so high at one time of history in this country, gradually perished since the days of Mahabharata. Then it all became folklores. By the time British arrived, there were only one per cent people who could read and write and that was either Urdu or Sanskrit. And when the country finally became free in 1947, there were only 4 per cent people who could read and write and in the last 54 years, we have just managed to cross this number to over 50 per cent. So it may take another twenty to fifty years before the people in this country could wipe out the illiteracy. But if we try hard, we may do this in five years.

The state of illiteracy in this country is due to many socio-economic reasons. The reasons could be traced back to the invasions of this country by the aliens for the last two thousand years. And even in the Mahabharata, Arjuna the great warrior had expressed his feelings to Krishna very clearly and intelligently that the war, "will make countless women widows and there will be many bastards afterwards, there will be limitless destruction of every thing". The war proved him right. All the great teachers, warriors and the technology perished in that war. Only few people could keep the records and knowledge with them. Later on, this class became Brahmins, who made it sure that the knowledge of Shastras remained the privilege and monopoly of the Brahmins. Then came the alien invaders from Mongolia, Central Asia and Western Europe. As usual, the invaders destroyed the temples, schools, libraries and places of learning and enterprise. The Mughals brought Persian and developed Urdu in the country The British introduced English but it all did not help the cause of education in the country. Only few people learned these languages who wanted jobs from their government and there were not many jobs and also not many schools. And even today many people who are unemployed or those people who are dropouts from the school have the opportunity to say that there is no use of getting educated or going to school and university as there are no jobs. This traditional thinking about going to school to be able to get a job needs to be amended. First of all, we should all know that it is the animals who cannot read and write. But as human beings, we not only can read and write but should do so to grow up culturally and spiritually and be able to stand up in this bigger world on a par with other people of the developed world. Education does not mean to pass the schools and university examinations and get degrees. Education should mean a cultural development and development of your personality and be able to interact with the other people of the world, and develop a scientific attitude towards living and everyday life around you. Therefore, we need a system of education where every child gets an opportunity to go to school, to get educated in a balanced useful manner to be able to become an honourable citizen of this country and the world. Hence, we need to make not only schooling for every child compulsory but we have to provide the facilities and an education policy that will bring cultural reforms in the country. To bring cultural reforms we have not only to give formal education to people but our social behaviour, set standards for sanitation, health awareness, social awareness about social evils and equality and freedom of all the citizens have to be a part of our education.

To make this society and the country a place worth living in, we need to highlight the poverty, illiteracy, status of women and untouchability and communal harmony in the country and provision of basic human rights for all to appear as a civilised people. Our concern should be about sanitation and pollution, littering and the slum mentality in this country. To respect everybody as if you want to be respected by the others should be our endeavour. So lot of things should be part of our education and for that we not only need compulsory schooling about real cultural reforms. Therefore, we discuss a few of these things in this chapter starting with education, unemployment and sanitation, etc.

First of all, we need to make a system in the country which has been partly discussed in the Chapter 1 on birth control that every pregnancy has to be registered, from then on we have to monitor the health of that child, a proper birth certificate on the national level and a health record book of every child should be maintained. Then at the age of five the child should be going to school. The education has to be free and compulsory. There has to be a minimum standard fixed for every school and there has to be a national education policy. A child should be given elementary schooling in the mother tongue of the child or at least in the nearest language to the mother tongue. The school bag and syllabus should not be so big that the child hurts his or her back. We see these days that a small child carries such a heavy bag to school and the bigger ones at the college just do not carry anything with them. There are so many difficult subjects and syllabus for the school kids that they can hardly understand and be interested in. For example, to teach children algebra or reverse counting, is hardly going to be useful.

We do not create any interest in our poorly equipped schools through paintings, knowing well that the children always like to make drawing and paintings and learn. It is, bit expensive way for people to afford where they cannot even give their children two meals a day. But the state can provide this. There have to be special education and health tax on everybody and then we can improve on the education standard in schools. There have to be proper buildings, teachers and facilities and an education policy that not only removes illiteracy but enables people to get employment to be able to develop themselves, economically and culturally into responsible and caring people and citizens of this country.

Not only do we have to provide the basic human rights to all the children, but we have to see that at school a proper record of every child is maintained. The children have to be encouraged, assessed and tackled properly. Though there are some English medium schools for the children of some middle class people and even most of these schools lack basic facilities and it is no secret that the situation at government schools is really bad. We are still at the same level like it was 50 years ago. Many villages or towns do not have enough schools, not enough teachers and not enough buildings and hardly any playgrounds, leave alone gardens or swimming pools. On top of that, the schools are full of dirt and dust. We have not introduced any modern ways of teaching and the situation about teaching has become worse than ever before. Even the school teachers do not think that they should be morally conscious about their moral duties in front of the school children. In many rural schools, the teachers even do not attend the schools for which they get paid. They do not worry which children have not attended school regularly or who is lagging behind. They come in and go out. They do not make any contact with the parents of the school children and do not give any report. There is hardly any communication between the teachers and the students and between the teacher and the parents. People generally say that the situation and conditions at these schools is much worse than what it was 30 years ago when children used to be interested in their studies even sitting under a tree Where as we see today in the developed western countries that the schooling is touching fresh standards.

Schooling is preceded by kindergarten or nursery. Where children below five and above three years go for few hours, to play with other children and interact. The children do paintings and drawings and they get introduced to the school systems but are not forced, so that when they actually join a school they are prepared for that. The people at the nursery have to be kind and caring and a child should be monitored and recorded for everything. The child has to be prepared at the nursery for the primary school and all the primary school documents should be prepared about the child and a formal identity card should be given to each child. The school syllabus and standard should be prepared with care and there should be no stress on the child.

The three language system should be implemented and the system of examinations have to be improved and changed to personal evaluation. There should be no rule that a student has to pass examination in such and such subjects. For example, many children drop out of the' schools or fail their examination at Matric level because of Mathematics or English. And their entry into the higher education gets blocked at school level. Frankly speaking, there is not much to lose in your life if you do not know the geometry or algebra or English. But there are many other things that people need to learn in their lives and to stop somebody at school because they do not understand algebra is ridiculous. And to make English compulsory at schools and colleges is another ridiculous idea. Students should be free to choose and only going to school should be compulsory. There should be separate institutions for such students who are not good at normal schools. Of course, after the schools there have to be one year social work service for every child, rich or poor, high or low. Then after school the students have to go for studies of their own choice and the systems have to be developed where people can go for employment oriented courses.

There are more than 40 million unemployed educated people in India, that is a lot, and if you take into consideration the overall unemployed people including the illiterate people as well the unemployment percentage goes very high. It is not only the unemployed but the underemployed people as well that the state of employment in the country is very bad. The education system in the country is such that it neither educates people nor it provides them employment. Above all we have so much unemployment among the so-called educated youths that they feel frustrated. They think that education means unemployment.

It is important to draw attention to the student and teacher ratio as well as the girls and boys ratio in the schools. The student and teacher ratio goes up to 100 students in one class per teacher which is bad and that is the way it is from the first class at school to the third year at college. The girls, ratio to boys in the rural areas is 10 to 100 which is shameful. Though in the cities it is more or less equal. With such a state of education in the country, there is one educated woman to three or more men. Educated in this sense means a person who can read and write. What kind of future do we see for the education in the country so that we could live in a country that have 100 per cent literacy and very few complaints.

Well when we talk about education it is a very vast and wide subject. Let us begin with the idea of giving every child the opportunity to go to school and complete at least school. That it should be the duty of the government and the state to see that all the children above the age of five should attend the school. It should not be just voluntary for the parents to send their children to school. Because some parents may be so poor that they cannot send their children to school. And some may not send the female child to school, as well. Therefore, it should not be just the responsibility of the parents to send the children to school but that of the state as well. Because the state has to provide free education, that means food, clothing and boarding for those who cannot afford it. And teachers, books, school buildings and playgrounds for all.

We have to think about free education for all the students till the students leave the school. That should be compulsory as well and free even later on where some students want to go for higher education. Well what then should be a model school and minimum facilities at school.

Model school will mean a class room for each class of not more than 30 students with a teacher at the school level. Not more than 1000 students in one school or for that reason in any institution. Playgrounds to play different kinds of games and sports. Children should not walk more than a kilometre for the school. There should be flush toilets for each class in the school or any other institution. The school buildings should be good for all weathers. That is the minimum requirement for accommodation.

Ideally a doctor should be added to each school who should maintain a health record of the students. Yoga, meditation and sports should be included as subjects at the schools as well as at the other educational institutions. Apart from this, the students should be taught some social manners. They should be taught the non-violence way of life and respect for others. Never stare at others or do harm to anybody. Be aware of their duties and rights. That democracy should be the best form of society and the state, should be taught regularly. Personality cult should not be taught at the school. To start with the social manners, we should stress the need of sanitation right from the homes. Because most of the people do not have toilets at homes. They just go out in the open area and ease themselves which not only makes it unpleasant and dirty but is a constant risk for the society. People are not aware of it. This awareness has to be taught and people be made aware to develop and practise this sense of sanitation in the country.

It is shameful that these people have no shame in squatting around in public view anywhere they can see, it can be the backyard of a temple or a house, on the bus stations or the railway stations, people just do that, even if there is a toilet nearby, no problem they say. There seems to be no law for cleanliness in this country. But if you go hand in hand with your wife in public or with your girl friend, some stupid men will whistle at you or they will be yelling at you, taunt and hassle you. Kissing your wife in public is nuisance for some people but pissing in public is not nonsense. Our problems are man-made and there is going to be a man-made solution. This sense of sanitation and cleanliness we have to start from the schools. Because most of the people live in the rural areas, where there are no toilets, and also in the towns there is no town planning and flush toilets are not fixed in every house. You see some sweepers even carrying the human excreta in baskets on their heads to dump it somewhere, only to earn a living. What can be more disgraceful for a society than this, and for those unfortunate people, that they have to do such an undignified job.

Therefore, it should be obligatory for every householder to have s toilet in the house, whether in the rural area or in the urban area, all over the country. That still would not be enough I think, all the public places like gardens, parks, restaurants, public buildings and offices should have toilets. Railway stations and bus stations, playgrounds, places of worship and for that reason all the buildings private or public, all should have proper and enough toilets. In the towns, there should be toilets for shopkeepers and the customers. People should know that toilets represent the modern educated cultured elite. Uncivilised are those that do not have the sense of sanitation. People should know that spitting out in public is worse than pissing. Because of the spitting you are going to spread the disease to others that you are suffering from. I do not suffer from any disease does not mean that I should spit out. It is just very bad manners to do so. Educated people should teach and preach only sanitation. Sanitation should be our religion. Countries that have achieved near complete sanitation, have been able to fight many a diseases just because of that and have attained a great level of health and long life. In this world of more than six billion people only two billion have proper sanitation. These Chai shops, Dhabas, restaurants are a regular source of disease and infections, they are so unclean.

And these *panwallahs* should be disbanded, sooner the better. The people not only harm their teeth and gums but spit around in the streets and even in the rooms like animals ease, at least animals do not spit. You see even the animals have better sense of sanitation, than many of us. The cats, for example, bury their shit in the ground and the goats broom the ground before they sit down. It is recommended that *pan*shops should be banned and the *chai*shops, restaurants and *dhaba*s be made aware of the health norms that they should obey. The used glasses, plates and all the utensils should be boiled cleaned and only after that be used for service. A minimum standard should be fixed for all these places of drinking and eating.

Our towns and cities are one of the most dirtiest in the world. The shopkeeper cleans his shop and throws the garbage in the street. People eating fruits, food and ice creams, just drop the rest what they cannot eat, on the street, and even in the green parks. These *rehriwallahs*, *dhabawallahs* and *panwallahs* should be sent to *dhobiwallahs*.

Everybody should learn the lesson for cleanliness and sanitation from the *Dhobiwallahs*. In the rural areas the problem of garbage is not so grave, the people there could put the garbage in the cowdung pits. But there is this plastic, rubber and tin stuff that needs to be buried or recycled. While in the urban areas people should have garbage collection service modeled. That all the householders, shopkeepers, buildings and complexes should keep the garbage in the garbage bags. There should be different colour of bags for different kind of garbage. For example, separate bags for wooden, paper and cloth things. A bag for glass products, a bag for tins and a bag for plastic things, while oil, chemicals and batteries stuff should be treated back by the said companies. Different kinds of bags are a must so that in dumping the different materials there is a proper handling. All this done, you will see less garbage and the streets more clean. Then there are stray animals that create traffic nuisance in the towns and the cities. They also shit in the streets which gives birth to flies around. The drainage and sewage system has to be good enough that there remains no scope for stinky spots. All the streets should be cleared of the encroachments and no shopkeeper should think of putting his stuff for sale outside the shop. It is a common thing in the countryside and the cities as well. When you arrive near the village or the town, the first thing that you come across is the bad smell, whether it is the smell from the human shit or from the industrial shit. Our villages and towns are just very stinky. We know sometimes people in cities find the drinking water pipes filled with toilet flush water. It is time that the people and the government in this country wake up and do something to clean this country

The sanitation aspect mentioned here has been generalised and need not necessarily be the case in posh areas. There are so many unclean practices going on in this country, which cannot be improved unless we develop the basic sense of sanitation. Now we come to the pollution aspect.

Sanitation and pollution are inter-related and pollution is as bad and even worse than bad sanitation.

No doubt that the industrial development has raised our standard of life and made us more comfortable. We could travel from one part of the world to the other part of the world in a matter of few hours. It has brought us the facility to see the man landing on the moon. You can see the Olympics at home, you can hear and talk across thousands of miles away. You can do so many things people even did not fancy before, but now it is possible. Yet there is this negative side of the life, positive otherwise, and that is the pollution. Coming from the industrial world and its things industrial. The biggest cities in India are the most polluted cities in the world. Because we have been so careless about the pollution. The factories have machines that produce three to five times more pollution than the factories in the advanced world. And the things like automobiles and other machinery that these factories make, produce the same amount of smoke and pollution more than the advanced industrial countries like Japan. Above all, we are as careless about pollution as we are about sanitation, the result is poor health.

Our cars, motorbikes, trucks, buses and trains will not pass any pollution test. Even in cities like Delhi and Mumbai, you see trucks and buses with their exhaust pipes producing smoke like the chimneys of factories. Then there are the chemical products, fertilisers and spray medicines that are playing havoc with the health in the country. There is no proper disposal of things that are pollution hazards. For example, take the batteries, people just throw them anywhere they like, they are the most dangerous stuff. Look at these automobiles service shops, hardly any care is taken to see that proper arrangements are made to disperse the disposable oils after the servicing and washing of the vehicles. The dirty things should go underground and the oils should go back to the refineries. Can we afford to be careless like this. Some people just open mechanical shops without any concern for pollution. They think it is none of their headache, how sad! There should be a license for such shops and it should be given only after the pollution control systems of the shops are verified.

Well you see some people just open their sewage pipes into the nearby streams or rivers and many factories throw their wastage and industrial effluent into the rivers or into the open fields. Results, the water in the river gets polluted and it causes damage to the river life and all those creatures that live in that water. Also there are these motor boat people that just clean their oil tanks on the rivers or on the sea. The sea water has become highly polluted, you could see the black layers of oil on the beaches. They are destroying the life. Recently one oil tank just got leaked near Mumbai and it spilt more than 5,000 tonnes of oil on the sea. Nobody could take any action against that ship, they went scottfree. Now will anybody come ahead to stop this kind of nonsense and crimes or it is nobody's concern.

It is so strange that the high ups in the country are so stupid that they are almost blind to see anything. What they can do they say, so incredible. But if they see somebody lying on the beach without clothes, it is illegal.

India is one of the leading countries in the world now that has high toxin contents in the food, fruits and vegetables. People just spray the produce before they take it out. So many a bad effects on the health of the consumers are being noticed. Farmers in their greed and irresponsibility out of ignorance are using a lot of chemicals for spray that it is becoming a health risk to eat anything.

There is no consumer protection service in this country of thugs, cheating and adulteration is the order of the day. Though there are these consumer courts but they really do not help enough. The media does not advise people that they should wash everything they cook with warm salt water, so that the toxins are removed before they get cooked with the food.

Just look at the plastic culture taking over all the cultures. People using plastic goods just throw them into the garbage places or out in the open as if it is paper that will get absorbed by the ground. People should know that these kinds of things have to be buried/recycled. Now everywhere you see huge piles of plastic, from the mountains down the streams into the rivers and on the beaches. Wherever the garbage people loiter, they spread litter. Just see how much plastic straws and plastic bottles they throw around.

Now this is all the subject of education and law. Coming back to the point of educating peoples, it is suggested that plastic goods should be banned. It is becoming a very disgusting habit with people that they ask for a plastic bag even for a box of matches. Education takes bit longer and it is not wise to educate a man to swim while he is drowning. Our job should be to rescue the person first and then if possible make him learn how to swim.

Education is not just to make people read and write, it should give people a general idea of life especially in the modern times, where people go so fast into the world. Therefore, to start at the school with sanitation and pollution awareness and Yoga and meditation along with sports is very important. We should make the students aware about the health. Therefore, a brief knowledge about the body and its needs should be imparted to everybody.

Status of Women

To understand the cultural reforms we have to start with the status of women in India. As from the days of *Manusmriti* they have been discriminated to this day. They have been historically badly treated by the men folk and today they suffer social discrimination right from the conception. People want male child and they go through ultrasound and scan and some people indulge in female foeticide. The birth of a girl is not celebrated. Malnutrition is a common problem among the poor people and malnutrition of girls is more serious. Even the girls are discriminated in the lower middle-class families. It has created a health problem in the country. The malnourished girls not only suffer health problems themselves but also pass on the health problem to the next generation. Therefore, we have to know that it is not only bad for those unfortunate women to be malnourished but for the whole society and the country. Apart from malnutrition and maltreatment from birth, a girl is discriminated in education, sex and in inheritance. To improve the lot of women we have to trace back the history of the status of women in this country and specially among the Hindus to find out how we can improve as there has been already some improvement in the status of women in this country.

We have to start with the *Sati* problem. There was this news about a woman (Roopkanwar) in Rajasthan some years ago performing *Sati*. Some people had rejoiced it and were planning to make a temple in her memory and honour, while others had criticised it and the government passed a law with heavy punishment for the offenders. This incident of *Sati* is one of the issues of human rights of women in India.

We have to start from the cruel practice of *Sati*. First of all it is not *sati* that has happened in Rajasthan in the traditional sense. It is most likely a practice called *Satidaha,* where a woman burns herself with the funeral fire of her deceased husband. Some people have called it *Suti* also and not *Sati*. The word *Sati* comes from the *Puranic* scriptures, and in those books *Sati* was not meant to make this kind of barbaric suicide, which they call *Sati* now, such a stupid explanation. Let us see it clear and hear it clear. The oldest of all those *sati* is the incidence involving Uma, the wife of Lord Shiva. Uma came to know from Narad about the Yagya and the party by her father where they were not invited. And when Uma did go to that party without invitation from her father Prajapati, her father talked badly about Shiva. He abused and insulted Lord Shiva in front of all those invitees. Because she had gone to that party (Yagya) against the advice of Lord Shiva, she could not tolerate the insults from her father so she immolated herself as a protest. Then she was born again as Parvati, daughter of Himachal and she married Shiva again. She was not known as *sati* because she immolated herself in fire but because she could recognise Shiva in her second reincarnation even when Shiva was in disguise.

Second case is of Savitri who chased *Yamdoot* to *Yamlok* and Yamraj under fear from *sati* returned her husband who could have been dead otherwise. The third case in point is that of Sita. Sita, the wife of Lord Ram, who passed the *Agnipariksha* after returning from the captivity of Ravana. And they were all called *sati,* all these three great women did not commit suicide on the funeral pyres of their husbands. Though we do not approve or appreciate the manner in which these things did take place, it is clear that *sati* does not mean killing a woman. *Sati* meant a woman living a life of virtue and truth and who was truthful to her husband. In those cases their husbands were not known for extra-marital relationships either. And these days widow burning if it is done by choice and conviction which is rare, should be called suicide otherwise most of these are forced and should be seen as most barbaric murder and heinous crime.

But some people think it is their traditional religious practice and they believe that this kind of practice brings all the kith and kin, dead or alive to heaven because of the *Shakti* of the *sati.* And to stop and punish such a practice is an insult to the pride of their community. *Sati* is more common among the Rajputs in the rural areas than any other community.

First of all it is not traditional or religious practice, as a tradition is a practice that is followed by masses over a very long time, and not through the rare cases of widow burning. It is not religious because it is not acceptable to God. Since the religious people believe in God and for them God orders the death. So if the God had decided that they should burn together, He should have ordered the death together. So it is neither a religious nor a traditional practice. And about the kith and kin story it is all superstition. To this day nobody has seen them flying to heaven and they will only pay their *Karma*. As far as the pride is concerned, it is false and stupid. It is a shame for those people who think they are brave to see a meek helpless woman under pressure, panic and pain forced to commit suicide with none of them helping her to live a life. Those kind of witnesses are just corpses. They see a destitute die so that they could live. The people who cannot protect the life and honour of a woman are no men at all, they are as good as dead.

No doubt that this widow burning is a shame for all Hindus. Many social and political organisations have voiced their opposition to such a crime. It is due to people like Raja Ram Mohun Roy who took such great effort to abolish this *satidaha* that British passed such laws of widow remarriage. It is only people like Rajaji who can convince and tell these Raiputs to stop this kind of incidences than any other people of the society. Of course, there is a law against it, but laws are nothing when people refuse to co-operate. Therefore, the move against widow burning should be started by the educated people among these communities.

This stupid practice has no religious history. The widow burning, among Rajputs of Rajasthan is not more than a thousand years old because even the word Rajputs is not that old. You will recollect that all those men that died in Mahabharat, their wives did not burn themselves and it is very important to remember the wording of Arjuna that there will be many Varnsankras after the war. It is only reported after the Moghuls invaded India, that the Rani Padmavati of Rajasthan after fighting bravely lit her own funeral after she was convinced that this was the only way to die with honour and to avoid the life of being raped and subjugated to humiliation. That is what the wars do to women. Many women followed her to the cremation to do the same. That was called *Jauhar* in those times. Continuing over hundreds of years of wars it did become a practice. Many women chose that path to avoid what Padmavati anticipated. Those circumstances do not exist today, but some people still think it is an ideal thing to do even now. The idea got stuck to the community. In most of the cases it is not voluntary, it is forced under pressure. Otherwise the women will be a liability, or a bad character if she indulges in sex. Most of the time, it is also property if the woman does not have children, that makes the other joint family is greedy to offer the widow to fire, because she was never related to them. It was only the man who died. Whatever the history or designs, the incidents like this are scars on the faces of civilised people. It is not happening these days but you have to talk about these things in details as to make people realise what was happening.

Bride Burning

There is yet another more serious matter and that is the bride burning which goes on like many other crimes. These days on an average there are two cases of bride or wife burning; in the Delhi area alone. It should be stopped before it becomes a tradition. North India is caught with this inhuman madness and the worst of all crimes. People get their daughters married in arranged marriages and give dowry with the bride. In many cases the dowry is settled and not enough means that even after marriage the grooms side ask for more and for years. Not getting more means, kill the bride by burning her in the kitchen.

And then look for another bride and in many cases they get another bride in no time. Same fate may meet the next woman too. In some cases people have become expert in bride burning, and in making fortune. What kind of society are we living in, is not it very disgusting? It is not a society, it is hell! And it is not just disgusting, it is horror of the slaughter house!

The dowry deaths are taking place in recent times when the greed of some people is going sky high. Dowry must have started with the gifts for the bride and the groom. The Kings and the Princes and the rich people might have thought to be show offs, the more they could give the more rich they would appear, and more the dowry, the groom's side will boast that they have got married in such a rich family. All this is immature thinking. Dowry is not a demand in the countryside as it is an urban problem where people are money-minded, that also does not mean that all the people in the cities are money-minded and they practise dowry. It is small number of people who harass their wives and daughters-in-law and few thousands among them who are dowry-minded can be a lot. Few thieves in a locality could be bad for the whole town just as few traitors can be a disaster for the whole country.

Though the women get their right over the property of their parents it is the son who gets it in all cases. There may be some women who do get the property of their parents but in most cases it is because there is no son. So when the daughter gets married the parents think that they should give her something in dowry, so that she has something in the new house that she could call her own. Some people even get some money in fixed deposit in the name of the girl. The whole marriage system is meant to be a security for the girl and a family alliance. The arranged marriages should be abolished so that when people do get married they have done it by their choice and thus there would not be bride burning for dowry.

The problem emanates from our attitude towards women. The *Parayadhan* and *Kanyadan* notions have been treating women as property in the modern sense as possession. The very concept of *Parayadhan* which means property or wealth of the others gives people the idea to treat women as possession. To get the girl married before twenty is like scoring a gold medal at the Olympic for many people. The girls are a liability and they can bring bad name for the family if they are found indulging in promiscuity or runs away with a boy of her choice. It is a fact that arranged marriage is not between two persons it is a family alliance. The dowry death and murders take place because the girls are never educated by the parents to defend themselves against a man that could be her husband. Whenever the harassed girls have complained to their parents, the parents instead of advising the girl to get divorced or live with them have very often tried to appease the in-laws and sent the daughter back to her in-laws where she gets burned eventually or she is supressed for the rest of her life. The women have little choice because there are not enough shelter places for a destitute woman. Some men even sell their wives to brothels where they are forced into prostitution and live a life of misery. This is happening in the land of *shaktis, bhagwatis* and *devis*. The way to help those women is to help them to support themselves by providing them jobs and shelter till they are self-dependent. There should be women organisations financed by the state to take care of women in distress, to console, guide and provide them mental support. The law of divorce should be made very simple to help the women from being harassed and raped by the husband. There is a need for single women hostels where women can go to stay in case they do not like to stay with the parents. Because many times the parents force the daughter to get married. There are many women that need protection from their men and it is only the women organisations that can help these women and not the law.

There should be a law that men who have been involved in the harassment of women and in attempt to kill their wives or who have been even named in cases of bride killing should be banned from remarriage by law and black-listed by the society. Such men should not be allowed to shift to other places as well. Their activities should be monitored and they should be sent to reform centres.

Above all, we have to educate the people about this menace and ask them to be vigilant. There should be women organisations that should keep track of such cases and accidents apart from the police. Even the arranged marriage system should be discouraged and abolished. As mentioned earlier, the education of women only can solve such problems. It is not only the man who commits this crime of bride burning but in many cases it is the women in-laws that are involved in the harassment and the burnings as well. It is not only for dowry or money but because the women in-laws feel jealous and there exists a sort of rivalry for dominance, and when the bride does not accept the dominance of the women in-laws, she is harassed and they try to put her down by criticising her in every way. Then some time she gets killed. It is no doubt illegal and people do get punished for such offences, but many time most of the cases get messed up by the police and are not even reported. This has to be stopped by all means and efforts. It is a shame that such dowry greedy people live in this country and it is even more disgraceful that they do get married again and manage to escape.

There are many wife bashers around and some men even kill their wives for adultery, while some others do the same to get another woman. It is illegal no doubt but atrocities are still going on.

This sort of things and violence is taking place all over the world, it is because the men suffer from the idea of possession and because the man is physically more strong than the woman and as the rule of the beast goes on in this world the big fish eat the small and men that still live in the world of sickness, can not do better things. All that people should do is there is no point in living that kind of life in their relationships when there is no love. There are many men that get drunken and beat their wives up, in that case the women should be able to protect themselves. Both men and women should change their traditional thinking now that they can live on their own now and can have any kind of relationship with anybody they like. The women can have children on their own and raise their family of their own they do not have to be dependent on man. So the man should think that marriage is not the only thing in this world to do. You see that there is so much pressure on the people to get married from the family, relatives and the people around that you have to leave the place to avoid all these suggestions and pressures. But the women even cannot do this, if they think to do so they are generally thought to be bad characters and the men face problems to find accommodation even. People ask you all the stupid questions, whether you are married, what is your profession and usually they do not rent their place to you cause they fear that the man might run away with his daughter or flirt with his wife. If ever they did rent their place to any single person, they tell you not to invite the friends of the opposite sex. It does not matter to them whether you are a homosexual or a lesbian. What I mean to tell you is that we do not have enough freedom in this country for the people to do with their lives what they want to do. There are many fundamental rights in this country but you cannot even check in hotels with your girl friend or boy friend though the Indians do not mind the foreigners doing the same. And if you have Western girl friend or boy friend it is hell like situation for the Indian to travel with the foreigner in the country. Firstly, it is a must to have a married status, secondly if it is not so then people can think of you in as many ways they can think of. The hooligans keep passing remarks at you and the police will check you for every thing, some people even can think that you are spy. All this kind of ignorance and attitude of the people makes the life hell for the lovers of freedom. What a shame!

No doubt we Indians have to change our attitude and thinking and become more free. People should know that everybody can do with his life what he/she wants to do. We are just no body to tell others what to do and how they should dress up and they should go around. It is all nonsense to tell others what they should do and what they should not. Repression of all kinds is against the dignity of man the sooner this society realises this the better it is. *Purdah* system also is a nonsense. This is also one of the ways to keep the Indian women down and is against the freedom of the women. Should not it be abolished by law?

Purdah system is as bad as any thing. There have been cases that some women have walked away with other men mistaking them to be their men. A woman waiting for her man in veil on a railway station could be misled by an other man. This system is not even ten per cent of what it used to be earlier, but it is still around. It should be abolished. *Purdah* did start before the advent of Muslims in India, but it was a social custom not common among the masses. But with the arrival of Muslims and their settlement, it gained religious importance as the Muslims have a religious sanction for it. Though it is no more a practice among the Hindus, there are some communities and families where *Purdah* still prevails, which is uncivilised. Also among the Muslims it is not as it used to be before. With the education of women it will disappear soon. Also it should not be allowed in public because you cannot recognise as to who is the person. In some families it is so funny sometimes that the women do not show their faces to the elder in-laws among men. Not only is it meant to paralyse women and keep them down, it is medically harmful as well.

In some of the *shastras* women are treated like Shudras. People like Manu and Tulsidas have put down women as the property of men and should be handled like pets and subjected to all kinds of social discrimination, that they could think of. They have formulated such social conduct for women that we cannot say was genuine, and not to speak of equality, we can not even claim that it was civilised. The stories of kings having thousands of women in their Harem, Dharamraj Yudhishtra even did not hesitate to stake his and the wife of five brothers Draupadi in gambling and ultimately loosing her, which resulted in the game of stripping her by the winners. Draupadi was shared like property by the five brothers by turns, even though Aijun had won her in the keen contest of archery, as his wife. Yet Yudhishtra was considered Dharamraj. Rama our historic hero made his wife Sita go through the *Agnipariksha* to prove that during her captivity by Ravana she remained untouched by him. These kind of stories work against the status of women and their identity as equal human being in our society.

Those were the social exceptions of those times and not common rule. Those Shastras that speak against women are not written by women, they do not know how the women feel like. And then those writers seem to have suffered from sexual frustrations in their lives. They forgot that they were born out of women. Without their mothers they would not have seen this world, not to speak of writing those Shastras. They have shown that they had no respect for women and their mothers, therefore no respect for life. Such ungrateful people. Those writers could have called themselves Shudras because they were born to women whom they described as Shudras. They proved their hypocrisy and such absurd things in those Shastras which need not be cared about. The Yudhishtra and Sita episodes were consequences of events, they need not be a model for people. There have been millions of kings in this world, we need not make them models. These are the times of democracy and freedom. Those were the days thousands of years ago. Not so long ago we did not have roads, railways and planes, that does not mean we should live like nomads and barbarians. We are living in the present world of mass communications, education and comfortable lifestyles, because of the scientific developments. Our outlook has to be scientific and modern. We do not have to follow the negative side of those olden and golden days of the past. Every period has had its negative side of social life. The negative side of modern scientific world is pollution. We have to control it and thousands of years later, if they read that there was lot of pollution in the year 2000 AD that would not give them an excuse to promote pollution. Like we have to avoid and control the pollution of the environment, we have to look at the society as what could be the better way of life of freedom for everybody. Today's call is the call of the freedom and freedom for everybody. The more free the people could feel, the better it is. Freedom does not mean just for the chosen few, it has to be for everybody. And women should have as much freedom as the men.

India has a history of kings having thousands of wives or women in the harems. Men were free to have as many wives they could have and apart from Draupadi there is no other woman who could have more than one husband. And history like this is anti-women, and when people take pride in such a history, unbalanced people think of nothing but treat women as sex objects.

Womanisers of the past cannot be models for today. Just as a prostitute cannot be a model for a normal woman. Sita is believed to have come out alive out of the fire trial. How many of us can do it, and who will come out alive? We have to be realistic and not allow ourselves to be misled by fairytales, cinema and imaginary things, like novels and scriptures. And that Raja Harishchandre refuses to cremate his own son when his wife brings the dead boy folded inside her hands. He demands money. Isn't he responsible towards his son like his wife.

Apart from the Hindus stories of discrimination against women like *Ramayna, Mahabharata* and other scriptures, we see that the two wars of Ramayna and Mahabharata were fought to restore the pride of women as well. In the Hindu Trinity of Brahma, Vishnu arid Mahesh we see that they are not away or above the trinity of women that of Saraswati, Laxmi and Shakti and all of them represent different aspects of life that is one. And the women in the trinity are as much worshipped as their male partners. And those guys Manu, Tulsidas and Co. should they say that these women should be treated like Shudras. How many followers you think they will have? The truth is that all these religions are political and promoted by vested interests. Spiritualism was corrupted by Maya that is what all these religions are. *Prakriti* was polluted by materialism. Man and woman are part of this *Prakriti* and this social degeneration is due to ignorance that degenerates people into beasts and violence and all sorts of crimes. Should the people realise the *Prakriti* of this planet and that of human being there will be no discrimination against anybody.

People have defined woman as *maya* and man as spirit. Many sages have cursed the Menakas of *maya* to have spoiled their *tapasya*. These kind of stories not only make fun of women but puts them down. Do you think that woman is Maya. This question of *Maya* and spirit have been debated by many people before as well. But whenever it reaches its peak there is confusion. I think woman is Maya for man only in limited sense and man is also Maya for woman. Both have the spirit in them as they have a soul. It depends on the person's ability to use both Maya and spirit the way they could manage. Spirit on its own cannot do much without Maya.

Caste and Communal Harmony

Now and then we witness caste and communal carnage in the country. The problem is political and economical. Political interest of the vested interests stay disguised for the common man but so obvious for the learned people. Needless to trace back its history, because the history is that of outdated people and faiths. The history of confrontation is always economical and that makes it political and results in carnage and wars The Indian mentality of fighting and gang wars emanates from the large size of the families. When there are three or four brothers in one family and their kith unemployed, they start to engage in crimes and these are done against the people of other castes, other religions, outsiders and strangers. And if the crimes are against the state, it could be a combination of people from all castes and religions. But then group rivalries also come up and that results in communal trouble and caste wars. Another factor is again economic like the grant of public land to the Harijans in the villages that have been used as the common grazing ground by the villagers of all castes. The clash of haves and havenots results in caste carnage, because the havenots mostly the Harijans and landless labourers belong to lower castes and because of their involvement with the extreme left they indulge in violence against the landlords, who in return must use the caste factor to protect themselves and hence all the trouble in UP and Bihar, of this kind. Sometime it is the untouchability factor at the village well or an inter-caste marriage, that erupts trouble. Of course, the local political elections like the Panchayats, and legislative elections of assembly, violence erupts or tensions prevail on the caste and religious lines.

Casteism among the Hindus comes from the Varnas system, that is the Hindu society constitutes of four major classes like the four major parts of human body, that of head, arms, abdomen and the legs. No doubt, this was a great system thought of long time ago and modalities of which exist even today around the world. Who cannot deny the existence of these four major classes that of the scholar or the scientist, defence forces and the administration, business class and the industrialist and finally the working class. These classes are there in any system of any kind of State. In the old times more than 2000 years back, there was really no untouchability among the four Varnas and there was no castes or sub castes in the society. There was also no limit on the choice of the person to assume for himself any kind of job because of his birth in a particular family and class. Thus, a Vishwamitra, a Valmiki or a Parshuram could opt for themselves any kind of a role in the society. But as we know that every good system has the inherent potential for degeneration, it has effected the Indian system as well.

The present form of untouchability started with the invaders into this country from the alien cultures and religions from across the Hindukush. Most of the Hindus do not eat meat though many of them do occassionally but they do not eat all kinds of meat. The upper castes or the religious minded people do not eat any meat and they are vegetarians. Cow is the holy animal and Hindu religion does not permit anybody to kill a cow and eat it. Therefore, when the cow eaters invaded India the people in India stayed aloof from the invaders even though they lost the power to any of these cow eaters. The people did not mix with the alien kings or invaders, hence untouchability touched India. Now you know that the Chinese eat everything on earth with its back towards the sky and imagine a holy man in India who have been vegetarian all his life and considers man like Chengis Khan a devil, how he can mix with people like Chengis Khan. So all kinds of races and religions invaded India and some of them even established their hegemony and enslaved the sub-continent. To preserve their honour the Indians just practised untouchability with the foreigners. That is why Muslims and Christians are not allowed even today in some of the temples. Even Indira Gandhi who had married a non-Hindu was not allowed in the Jagannath temple at Puri. The British though they were ruling the whole country, were never allowed into the temples and the British did respect the religious sentiments of the people. They had also known how dangerous it would be for them to offend the religious traditions in India.

The British did not attempt to convert the Indians into Christianity as the other European colonial powers did to the rest-of-the-world. Hinduism has an inherent power of survival, the Muslims before the British had tried it by force but had not succeeded to turn the country into Islamic subjugation. The British knew that whenever there was respect shown by any Mughal ruler towards thc Hindus, the ruler became popular like Akbar, and when a ruler like Aurengazeb tried to convert Hindus forcefully, he earned the hostility of everybody and dug the grave of Mughal empire in India. Therefore the British did not touch the religious beliefs of the people. The 1857 war of Independence was mainly triggered off with the stories of bullets that were being used by the army, were carrying beef tallow or pork tallow. So the British knew that they do not have to touch the religion in India.

Casteism started with the invasion of this country long time ago. The intermixing of so many races from the Dravidians, Aryans, Parthians resulted in different beliefs and faiths which created so many sections of people in this country. People doing one job for many years with generations in the same profession were branded one caste, and then if somebody get married into some other caste it became another caste. As a result today we have so many castes and the menace of casteism and communalism pervades in the country.

In the beginning when man gave names to all the animals they gave names to all the people as well. Man is known by the names and their family by the surnames. Therefore, the different caste and creeds. In the beginning there was no untouchability on the basis of castes and class because the four organs in the body are joined with each other, but because of the degeneration in the original society and the advent of people from the strange cultures and races, untouchability got rooted in the country to this day. Today our concern is not to trace back the history of untouchability but to eradicate it. Continued untouchability is a social evil and it needs an injection the type of which can stop it but it seems there is none yet. Mahatma Gandhi very much wanted to finish it. Therefore, he called the untouchables the Harijans, the children of God. He started a paper in the name of Harijan and the Congress party was made to shun all kinds of untouchability.

At present we do not have the same kind and amount of untouchability that was there a hundred years ago or 30 to 40 years ago. You can recollect that there was a time when even Mahatma Gandhi had a problem to go out of the country for education in England, because the voyage on the ships was considered against religion and eating on the ship and among the white people in England could have made him an untouchable as well because of mixing with the untouchables. At least he had to promise to his mother that he would not touch meat and alcohol. But now-a-days we find that we do not mind Harijan servants at hotels and restaurants and public places. In public jobs high officers, doctors and nurses and teachers and members of parliament and ministers, and almost in all the public jobs there are people from the lower castes working on a par with other people. There is positive discrimination in the country in services and other programmes for the upliftment of the Harijans. However, we still practise untouchability in our home, the whole village side has not stopped it, in the urban areas the situation is somewhat satisfactory. The middle and the rich classes of people do not practise untouchability but for reasons of marriages they still follow the caste lines. In the cities untouchability is expelled because many people do not care about it any more. But this is not enough, the problem is not just between the upper caste and Harijans below, but among various castes and categories of people. You know a high caste would not allow a low caste untouchable person into his house, not to speak of taking meals with them. But this is one side of it, let us come to the other side of it, and that is among the Harijans themselves. These so-called Harijans are united against the upper castes that of three Varnas of the Hindu society and fourth being themselves. What to speak of untouchability they would like to have marriages with them. At the same time, they are divided among themselves. There are so many castes and categories among the harijans mostly associated with their nature of work, like Sunars, Luhars, Kolis, Chamars, Dhobis, Nais, Tarkhans, and so many others, last being the Choorahs who call themselves Balmikis now. Now they would like to abolish untouchability while they cannot do so among themselves. They feel superior if there are two or three categories below anyone of them. They are practising untouchability as before but would like to abolish it whereas the high castes are concerned. Even the low caste among the Harijans do not accept food from the bit higher caste Harijans. How to remove it then.

The need to remove it has arisen out of the concern for social justice and social unity. The constituent assembly and the government have declared untouchability illegal and a legal offence. There have been programmes and schemes to uplift the Harijans to bring them at the equal social level with the other communities. The reservations in seats like the local bodies, state assemblies and the parliament and the reservation in the public jobs for the Harijans and many other economic favours of subsidies, scholarships for the Harijans have been initiated to bring them up. This has indeed helped them but most of them still stay poor and some of them who have availed themselves of the opportunities under reservations and many other favours have developed vested interests. Some of them have been getting these favours for three generations while many of them have not got any yet. For example, how a son of a minister could be treated as backward caste or the son of a big officer or industrialist for that reason could be given favours against the son of a poor Brahmin or another poor Harijan. But things are going on like this unchecked because of the politics of votes.

However, there have been suggestions for the Harijans that their lot as social untouchables could change if they convert themselves into other religions and faiths, like Islam, Christianity and Buddhism. The other religions do not practise social untouchability. This suggestion carries no weight, as the Hindus do not allow people from these religions to go into their temples and homes as well, so how the problem of social untouchability can be solved. The aim of the whole exercise is to destroy untouchability and maintain social harmony and unity.

Harijans can gain nothing by confrontation. Even then the case of conversions to other religions could be examined. Christianity would have gone to the grave long time ago in India if they had played this card. The people who have converted themselves into Christianity in the South still use their old family surnames like Reddy, Rao or Mathai or Krishanan, etc. The lot of the converts has not improved because whether they become Christian or not, locally their family background is known to everybody. The Christians are also divided into

Catholics and Protestants, the aim of social unity is lost here too. Moreover in the West hardly anybody goes to the Church and religion is fast disappearing from the society, so to try a religion like Christianity is simply no answer. So far as the Muslim converts are concerned, they are no better. First of all, they are not the Pak Muslims, secondly the caste system remains the same locally. Thus, there is a Choudhary in the eastern region or a Patel in the western region. The conversion does not solve the problem but further degrades them. The Muslims are also not a single unit. The fights between Shia and Sunnies is serious and the fresh converts are branded as Ahmedias and the Indian Muslims are called Indie by the others in West Asia. Sikhism also treats them as Majhabies and there is even a light infantry division in the army of these people. In Sikhism the caste structure is same as the Hindus. The Sikh do not practise untouchability. The upper caste Sikhs marry frequently among the high caste Hindus. Moreover, Sikhism is a part of Hindu society. It was developed as a force to protect the Hindus from the atrocities of the Muslim rulers of Delhi. Moreover, the conversions can create mass tensions in the country which is again harmful for the converts.

Dr. Ambedkar, a Harijan himself, who was the Chairman of the constituent assembly used to burn *Manu Smriti* in his public meetings and advocated Buddhism for the Harijans to embrace but hardly any Harijan to this day did that. So it seems that no conversion could change the lot of the Harijans and even if somebody does convert, they will loose the special favours that are given to the Harijans by the government and the law because they are no more Harijans. Therefore, from all counts conversion to some other religion is no good for them. Also conversion creates psychological problems for the people. Even if they are low caste among the Hindus which is a fact of thousands of years. They are content that their lot is changing now, it is not only them but the whole lot of the people is bound to change because of the freedom and development. Untouchability is a more than 2000 years curse, it will take some time to disappear totally, may be another fifty years but then fifty years is not a long time in the history of this world. It can not be abolished just by wishing it to be dead or like killing the Tsars of Russia. The mass education, economic well-being and modern style of living could bring the change and it is visible that the society does not have the same amount of prejudice as it had thirty years or fifty years ago. In the cities it is almost 10 per cent and in the countryside it is about 50 per cent in our social interaction that is what is left of the untouchability. One American once even asked if it is possible to recognise a Harijan from his dress or looks that he is a Harijan or what is his like in verification from his outlooks. The answer was simply no. Therefore, we shall recognise each other as human beings and as part and parcel of one society.

Lately a new threat to peace and harmony in our country has come to light. We have seen few chapels of Christian-converts being burned in Gujarat and Orissa. Also few missionaries have been attacked and even killed. The recent case of an Australian missionary Steins, getting burned to death in his van along with his two sons was the most horrendous. We should know they were neither the first nor the last to suffer such a fate. Thousands of people mostly poor suffer like that in many parts of India and the world. This is the historical hatred towards other people who belong to other caste, religion, region and race. It is, however, unwanted in a society that claims to be democratic and civilised. One thing that we need to speak clear and straight is that Christian missionaries in India should stop converting the poor tribals to Christianity. The violence against the Christian missionaries has taken place in the tribal areas only that is because the new converts are hurting the feelings and the traditions of these tribal people. We have certain laws in this country to protect the tribals, their property and culture as well. Seats are reserved for them in the legislature and in public services so that they are saved from the encroachments by other people. But the Christian missionaries think otherwise. They know these people are vulnerable, so they go around and do all sorts of things to convert the tribals. A very low percentage of people go to Churches in the western countries. And not many people could call themselves Christians in the land of Christianity, why these missionaries want to spread Christianity in the third world of poverty-stricken people. To maintain peace and harmony in India we have to tell these missionaries and other people that conversions be stopped and the Indian government and the Hindu community should remove poverty and illiteracy from among the tribal and all sections of Indian people so that nobody gets allured to conversions and we do not kill each other. The problems of untouchability and conversions will all disappear once we succeed in removing poverty and illiteracy from the society. Only then we can make this country a place worthy of living in.

Communal Harmony

The war of independence of 1857 which was nicknamed by the British as the mutiny saw both the Muslims and the Hindus fighting together for a common cause of independence from the rule of a trading company that had slowly enslaved India. As the Indians lost the war to the British forces, the British government took over the control of India from the company. Because the leader of the war was the Muslim ruler of Delhi called Bahadur Shah, the British started to make favours to the Hindus. But this did not last very long since the leadership of the Congress went into the hands of people like Tilak who or demanded complete *Swaraj* or self-government. The movement for *Swaraj* started to become a mass movement and the British sensed danger. Therefore, they started to appease the Muslims and incited them to form the Muslim League. Every now and then they tried to equate the Congress with the League, just to make it appear that the Congress represented the Hindus only which was a mischief. Since independence we have faced the problem of communal violence in the country.

Now coming back to the communal violence, we have to look back a bit. The communal violence started in India with the creation of Pakistan. As it is a part of the history, the fanatics of the direct action day in Pakistan started the mass murders, looting, arson, burning of the property belonging to the Hindus and the Sikhs, killing of children and rape of women all that they could think of doing, they did to displace the Hindus and Sikhs from Pakistan. There was nobody to stop those fanatics, there was hardly any government to protect the Hindus and the Sikhs in Pakistan. When they started to come to India with their stories of miseries and broken lives, and with just their clothes on, not knowing where their other members of the family have been lost, the people in India who were already resentful of the creation of Pakistan, became furious and they demanded blood for blood. Thus started the shameless bloody rioting in many places in the country. Violence spread everywhere mostly in Punjab and Calcutta and Delhi. Because it was the people of these parts of the country that suffered most because of the partition. Partition of the country was done by the British and they did not care about the violence. Because it was not against them so they did not care who killed whom. There must have been forces that wanted to prove Mahatma Gandhi wrong. Some people even think, that was the counter-revolution to Gandhi's non-violent revolution, as he had always suppressed the violent thinking among the people against the British. As Gandhi had described the Russian revolution a counter revolution because the revolution of 1917 did not free the people but put them under another dictatorship. Things in Pakistan were beyond Gandhi's control though he pacified the people in Calcutta, he could not go to Pakistan as he was assassinated.

There were proposals by some people in Pakistan and India that the populations of the two communities should be exchanged. That could have meant uprooting millions of the people which the Indian government with its secular ideas did not agree. There were so many Indian Muslim leaders who wanted to stay in India and who had been fighting for a united India. Though if you take the results of the elections of 1937 as guidelines, the Muslim League had almost taken all the Muslim seats in UP and the separatist Muslim League had been defeated in Sind and the Frontier Province and in Punjab it was the unionist party that had won the elections still the British gave half of Punjab, Sindh and the Frontier Province to Pakistan. They did because they wanted it like that to suit their future strategy. Had they asked those people that voted for the League in UP that they would have to go to the Pakistan of their creation after the partition they would have never voted for the League. The partition of the country left the Leagures in the country itself, because India has now the largest Muslim population in a single country in the whole world. The Muslim League remained intact in the country. It is a shame that the Muslim League that asked for Pakistan still hangs around in India and creates bad blood in the country.

The Congress party initiated the communal and religious factor of the minorities and the caste factors of the majority community into the politics of the country. Its election strategy is always based on such considerations and in the party they are represented by such groups. The family dynasty has always played them against each other, because that suits their politics. The Congress party has always accepted the unreasonable demands of the Mullahs like in the Shahbano cases to appease them and to keep them as the reserve vote bank. The equality of the Muslim women with the rest of the women in the country does not matter as long as it helps the party to remain in power. This kind of policy has proved harmful for the integrity and unity of the country. Because to show the fear of organisations like RSS to the minority and black mail them is not in thc interest of democracy and what is not in the interest of democracy is not in the interest of India. There are some other political and communal parties in the country that have not been banned. They banned RSS in 1948 for the murder of Mahatma Gandhi even though none of the murderers were men from the RSS. But the Muslim League was not banned, the League which got Pakistan out of India, the League that was responsible for the murder of the millions and uprooting and displacement of the millions and all sorts of atrocities and miseries that were inflicted on both the communities and the people because of its communal demands and policies.

It is time to examine the threat posed by the communal parties and forces of disintegration to the country. The communal parties, the regional racist parties and all kinds of forces of disintegration have to be checked and eliminated politically. The Akali Dal is another political party that has a communal programme, the Muslim League, the Jamat-e-Islami, the Hindu Sabhas and organisations like Shiv Sena all need to be rationalised or they should be banned. All those parties that are named after some religion or community, region and language or the race with particular separatist names and literature should be isolated and nipped. Only the nationalist, democratic and non-religious forces should be allowed to operate and function politically and socially. Whenever there is a dispute between the communities it should be referred to the Community Commission that should be headed by the judge of a High Court, permanently to sort out issues like the dispute over the Babri Masjid and Ram Janambhoomi, without wasting time. The longer the delay in settling the disputes and the issues, the bigger the risk of confrontations. The democratic constitution does not mean freedom to preach hatred, violence, anti-state feelings and activities. Religion is considered poisonous by the communists but religious hatred is more poisonous. In this country, religion combined with politics has done heavy damage to the democratic system. The bill to separate politics and religion did not include the provision to outlaw the political parties that are religiously oriented. Religion is no sin but it has been used and always interpreted by some stupid people as a way to fight other people. All the religions preach to set things right as they assume the way they know is right. Except Buddhism and Jainism, all the religions advocate violence to set the things right, in their own way. Religion is actually meant for the ordinary people to follow and get a sense of discipline in the life of a common man.

Making a survey will reveal that the minorities in India are more guilty of communal trouble than the majority community. It happens in the areas where the so-called minorities are in majorities, like in some cities of UP and Gujarat and areas like Kashmir. Honestly, nobody wants a communal clash anywhere in the country but the vested interests including the congress government at the centre provokes the communal trouble to distract people and serve their political interests. There are foreign agents in this country that are paid by the foreign parties to make trouble in this country so that India could not present an image of a free country and because of the communal problems The Muslim countries will feel sour with India.

Therefore, to set things right in India we have to do few things in this regard. First of all, the birth control law that makes the two children for every couple has to be framed. Discrimination on the basis of religion and regions has to be stopped. Educational institutions like schools, colleges and universities named after religious names have to be changed in names and characters. Imparting of religious education in schools and further up have to be stopped. Religion should be a private affair of the individual. All religious processions should be banned for ever, and administrative permission should be taken for a religious meeting of more than 100 persons. All provocateurs of communal tensions should be checked. effectively. A universal law of equality should be obeyed and formulated for all the people, and if possible preaching of religion and religious writings on the walls and stones and in the media should be discouraged. Broadcasting the Gurubani and Hindi Bhajans on the radio and telecasting of episodes like Ramayna of religious consequences should be discouraged. We should all accept now that the creation of Pakistan should not cast any shadow on the Muslims of today because they were not responsible for creating Pakistan. It was created by Churchill and Jinnah and the League. And today Muslims should also know that their present and future lies in India and that they are the worthy citizens of India. There are some stupid people in Kashmir some of them surely Pakistani infiltrators or agents that raise pro-Pakistani slogans some time. Whether it is a cricket match between India and Pakistan or a communal trouble elsewhere in India or the death of the Pakistani Zia, they must raise anti-India and pro-Pakistani slogans. These kind of people are few and they should be checked by the community for their own betterment. A democratic government in Pakistan and Bangladesh for a long period could help India in maintaining friendly relations with them and communal harmony in the country.

Rumours have to do more in fomenting communal trouble than the actual misconduct. It is a fact that the people that start communal riots are people from outside who could be paid by interested parties abroad. We have to sort out these elements, mere talking of foreign hands is nothing but running away from the problems. The role of the police in communal riots is another serious matter. The police take sides in communal riots. Some of them even indulge in looting and killings. The role of the PAC in Uttar Pradesh in communal riots in Meerut is just but one of the examples of the police as what it can do. It is the anti-social elements in society that have a vested interest in communal riots because such days of rioting are meant for them to loot and steal and they do not get booked for that. It is also them who get paid to make the trouble and eventually the common man believes the rumours. They just have to put a head of a dead cow in the temple or the head of a pig in the mosque. Instead of cleaning the place of worship they think of making a bloody communal riot. Even when they do not know who is actually behind it. Many times it was the Congress party in power that was responsible for the communal rioting and arrested the leaders of the opposition with their known community feelings only to create a fear among the minority.

In areas where the Christian missionaries are busy converting people in the eastern states like Nagaland, they try to provoke them to turn against the country itself. To win over these anti-national elements, the government has pumped so much money to these states that they have become so much corrupt and corruption is one of the reasons that these regional leaders always look to the Center and milk it limitlessly. The Christian missionaries are spreading a great deal of disinformation among the tribals that communal tensions are growing. These missionaries do not know that Jesus had been to India for those 13 hidden and unknown years of his life where he had become a great *yogi,* before he appeared again in Jerusalem, and that he did not die on the cross but actually escaped death and lived a life and finally died in Kashmir, is a fact that they would never like to accept. If they accept this fact, there will be no tension in India. There is also a belief that Mohamed was also a Shiva devotee, and that the black stone in Mecca is the famous Shiva Lingam. These stories may be true or may be not, but things like this can make people more tolerant about each other. There are other religions in India too, they are known as sister religions, like Buddhism, Jainism and Sikhism to Hinduism, with whom there is hardly any communal trouble. Though there have been some problems between the Sikhs and the others recently in some cases of communal fighting but that is again coming from the terrorist activities that influence the mind of the common man. The problem in Punjab was mainly due to the mishandling by Mrs. Gandhi of the Sikh politics. Her eventual murder by her Sikh security guards and the killings of Sikhs after her death in Delhi, all have generated bad blood, and of course the foreign hand likes to fish in troubled waters. There are two kinds of terrorists, one are the militants and the others are anti-social elements indulging in crimes to make money, and of course the police makes money too in these kind of situations. There was no sincere effort to defuse the volcano. Everybody was playing politics and the sincere people have been pushed to the dark walls. The whole issue of trouble has been blown off beyond control by all the sides involved to the extent that there was no person of integrity and respect left who could solve the crises in Punjab. A man or men of trust and status had to emerge out of that nightmare in Punjab to solve that problem. The politics in the country is fast getting criminalised and criminals are taking shelter in the religion only to misuse it to protect themselves. Religion is easy to misuse even with rumours so the perpetrators of violence and wars always use religion race or ism to spark violence. Violence is an old sickness among people and they have yet to get rid of it.

So it has been finally the will of the people of Punjab that they have successfully overcome the long nightmare of violence in Punjab which had been there for too long. The people of Kashmir can do the same. There is no communal violence in Punjab. There is none in Kashmir, but it has been only the terrorists paid and trained in Pakistan who had been under the control of ISI of Pakistan that have forced the Kashmiri Pandits to leave the valley.

Today it is most urgent that the population flood in the country is quickly controlled, and the people are saved from a future civil war like Mahabharata again in the name of religion and *Dharma*. It will only be because the stupid people will not find a solution to the population problem. Therefore, if you say you can claim to be civilised and bit educated, it is for you to prove that you could actually regulate and succeed in solving the population problem and give all the people the basic human rights without regard to race and religion.

The case of Babri Masjid and Ram Janambhoomi dispute is bringing India to prepartition days when communalism represented by the League not only resulted in the partition of the country, but in senseless human blood shed. Communal and political parties will never be able to reach a solution, that will be acceptable to both the sides. There is always going to be a trouble. Even if a High Court decision is made, there will be appeal against the decision of the High Court and there will be endless arguments fomenting communal trouble. Being such a delicate matter, it has become a prestige issue more than a religious one for both the communities.

Historically the case of the Hindus for the restoration of the Ram Janambhoomi is more valid, this is not because I am born in a Hindu family, but because the Muslim mosque actually exists in the name of Babar, who represented Imperialism and invasion, it could have been easy to dispose of such an imperialist name and structure had it been only such, like the Kings Road in Delhi was named as *Rajpath* and the Queens Road renamed as *Janpath*. But the case of the masjid is religious and that of a big group of people that constitute a considerable number of people that runs into millions. The Hindus too will not rest if any decision whether it is taken by the government or by the court goes against them. The question could not be decided by the courts for the last 50 years and there is a remote possibility that the two factions will reach any agreement. There may be many proposals but they will not get through because the people involved on both sides are not really religious people but politicians. They are not going to leave the things peaceful. Huge amounts have been collected in the name of religion and these collectors will not like to stop the flow of money. There are not two parties to the dispute, there are many factions now and they have their mills to grind. When an agreement is not reached, it is the duty of non-religious and non-political people to interfere, because religious clash is very dangerous, bloody-inhuman and uncivilised. It is not only a question of the two factions on the opposite sides struggling to make an ugly situation, but it is a question of peace, of the lives and property of the millions of people, of state expenditure to maintain law and order, of the existence of diverse communities and the existence of the country itself. Babar was an invader and an alien, both by origin of race and religion, whereas Ram was the beloved son of India and is even considered the reincarnation of Vishnu, one of the Gods in the Hindu trinity. Babar is not a symbol of Islam whereas Ram is the religious mantra of million's of the people. If the place is not restored as the Ramjanam Bhoomi as the politicians in the country won't be able to do, how the question is going to be solved.

It is true that the politicians will not be able to solve this problem. It is also true that Babar was not Ram, and in this, case, the mosque there was just like any other Masjid in the country, and it is also true that the Babri Masjid had been imposed on the site by force, which is not good any way, if today in free India we talk about reason the place must be restored as the birth place of Ram, even if there is no clear proof that the place is really the birth place of Ram. Already some Muslim associations have indicated that they are ready to make mosque elsewhere and a Hindu has offered the land to make a mosque. Such places in Mathura and Banaras too should be settled in good understanding by the two communities. It is not a time to fight over old and outdated religion but for the development of the people and their growth as human beings. The Indian Muslims are part and parcel of the Indian life and its history, no doubt Babar was an invader, so were many other races that have got down here and merged, though the Islamic people have kept their religion intact, we can recollect that the Muslims in India are not the descendants of the invaders, most of them could be descendants of anybody that were Indians because a lot of conversions took place by force or choice. Our concern today is not conversion but co-existence as human beings. The politics of communalism has to be buried. The common man has nothing to do with communalism. It is few anti-social elements that talk and act as communal politicians in this country and it is also true that the government also plays the communal cards when it suits them. The Muslims were not responsible for the creation of Pakistan. It was created by the British. The Muslims in India do not have to feel guilty for this, nor they have to fear that Islam is in danger in India. All they have to do is to avoid the communal politicians and live as the free citizens of India with honour and dignity The Indian tradition of freedom to everybody to live and practise faiths will stay and the threats to communal harmony have to be taken care of.

We have to show some courage to solve our problems, otherwise they will never be solved and we will stink of the mud that the politicians throw at each other. Some people can say or propose that the place of dispute should be made a national monument so that no community feels a looser.

The idea of making it a national monument is useless, because we should now spend money on the needs of human beings and not on unproductive fictitious monuments. Monuments are made in memory of great people, surely an invader cannot be a benevolent person to make a monument in memory. On the other hand, the people for Ram Janambhoomi want to make a temple with their own expenses. India is a secular state therefore, it cannot spend money to make temples. How many people follow the wishes of God today or how can they know what the wishes of God are like. Ram may be a religious symbol for the Hindus but Babar is not representing God for the Muslims, and we cannot make a national monument for the two opposing ideas, and the two persons. Looking at a monument does not help anybody, may be tourism, but a hospital or a stadium could help all the people. It may help the people and the country in producing sports people who could win for India medals at the Olympics, where we have made a big 'zero'. Because in this country positive things take a back seat while the negative things are brought in the forefront. We can make homes for the destitute, hospitals for the sick, football fields, hockey playgrounds for everybody. Modern scientific world, and the new human awareness should replace the old good for nothing ideas that have kept man as a slave to religion, and made them to fight each other. It is the right time to call a halt to such disputes and live in peace.

The days of religion should have been over by the end of last century. Religion is outdated, it does not help anybody, only psychologically weak people need beliefs, today people need freedom from all religions, they need to do *yoga* and meditate, to know themselves and the world around. The whole concept of religion is irrational. It is simply unacceptable from the point of view of the religious people and religions that God made. If God made man then he should have made everything else too, but it seems man has made the God. Therefore, he needs to make a temple or mosque for God to live in, is not it funny? Strange to make a house in the name of God who is believed to have made everything.

People need to be rational and think about the money and time and energy that people spend on making these Godly buildings, that serve no cause of mankind. Therefore, the better things for any group of people to do is to make social service centres and institutions and not the place of superstitions and disputes. As mentioned earlier that a hospital, school, playground, *yoga ashram* or a home for the destitute will serve better human cause than the cause of vanity, people in this world simply do not know how to enjoy themselves, they like to be miserable and make the life of other people also miserable. Being miserable in outlook, actions towards other people is the attitude towards life with some people, they need to change it, the sooner they do better it will be. After having said it all, it is still possible that some people may not agree to such noble ideas and we should sit down with all the parties to dispute and sort out the matters amicably. The recent Gujarat Carnage can be blamed on the justice system in the country. So people have taken law into their hands and shamefully again the politics of blame and counter-blame has surfaced.

Non-violence

The culture of violence and hooliganism is fast developing in the country. The incidents of holdups, eves teasing, rape, murder, street brawling and terrorist-attacks are all on the increase. What are the reasons for such an increase in this violent behaviour of the people. First of all, it is the movies that people watch showing lots of violence. There are no limits you see people making arguments, fighting and even killing in the movies. There are no policemen no judges and no system in the movies that the people could be assured of justice. It is always the violent hero who has to set everything right. This is being done and shown in all the movies for years and years. So this has become the culture of some people to think like that and in reality we also see that there is not much to expect from the law enforcement agencies proving it otherwise in the real life. So we see that this mentality is getting established everyday in our lives and in the country. So we have to take into consideration this aspect as one of the reasons for violence and find ways to make cultural reform in this country.

There is much violence around these days, day after day and year after year, we see more and more violence and all over the country and all over the sub-continent. There is violence in Kashmir, Jammu and Ladakh. There is violence in Punjab, Assam, Nagaland, Manipur and West Bengal. There is violence of all kinds present in Bihar, UP and Andhra Pradesh. There is the communal violence of religion, regions and ism and there is the state violence everywhere in the country. There were times after the Independence that Lathi charge used to be a big thing but now you see machine guns being fired by the police at the people. There is violence in Sri Lanka, Burma, Bangladesh and Pakistan and Afghanistan and bad relationship on the Nepal border and the whole sub-continent is full of tension, bombs, guns and people are being massacred all around, the black death is having its bloody dance everywhere with human skulls. Why have people become so crazy and why have they forgotten Mahatma Gandhi so easily and so soon?

Violence is the part of the negative side of life on this planet called earth. There are two kinds of creatures on this earth, carnivorous and herbivorous, the one living on other creatures and the other living on the vegetation. The carnivorous creatures have to attack and kill the other creatures for their food. Now the human beings the supreme creature at present have learned from both of these creatures to be vegetarian or not to be. So for his food man has been killing many other creatures by wild hunting or by farming. There are vegetarians that need not kill any creature to feed themselves. The people who kill other creatures have the mentality that they can snatch away from them anything including their life. There are people that eat only some kind of meat and only sometime, but there are people that eat meat all the time and all kind including human flesh. Now going back to the human history, we know that the human specie is about 2,60,000 years old they say and it is only in the last ten thousand years of history that man moved towards civilisation. The men have been living like any other animal before that, living from hunting and wild grass and fruits. When the stone age man started to cultivate land, he started to cultivate his head as well. He started to make fire and cook food. So the evolution of the mind of man started. The man started to grow and everything started to grow in him. The lust and aggression and spiritual quest, all started to grow. The brain became more developed and man started to experience more with the nature and the spirit. Hence some people started the concept of what is good and what is bad. This was the experience gained by man over thousands of years from their living.

There were two options if somebody would hunt, either he would eat it alone or share with others. When he shared it with others they might have felt happy or good. And when somebody tried to snatch away things from others just because he was more muscular, the others might have felt bad, like this the good and bad things got described and over the years the same small experience of man developed into religion, tradition and culture. The concept of good and bad became bigger. In the beginning it is the individual who wanted to protect himself from the other possible invaders, then he wanted to protect his family from the others and then he wanted to protect his locality, after that his country and then he might think of protecting the whole mankind, and living in a countryless and governmentless world.

While there are others who first as an individual thinks of stealing, of snatching and killing others, then forms a gang to attack others, then starts to rule a locality with the gang and expands his area into country, makes an army and invades another, loots and plunders around makes himself a king and expands his empire. His son becomes the next king who fights another king. This is how violence—the negative energy works. These kind of people who suffer from ignorance, which leads them into vanity, lust and crimes against other creatures and human beings, are those that are still uncivilised. Man with his goodness inherited over these thousands of years has reached enlightenment, while on the other side he is still the beast, and it is this kind of beast mentality people who are responsible for violence. They have not forgotten Mahatma Gandhi, because they never came to know people like him. They think that the lion is the king of the jungle and they are the lion among men. Many people in the country therefore think that they are marshal races, adding to their names propositions like Sinhs, Singh, Sinha, and so on. So many people in the north and the south call themselves lions and now you see lions clubs all over the country and so many varieties of tigers in Sri Lanka. This sort of mentality and tradition is also responsible for violence?

It is not lion who is the king of the jungle. There is no king there, no army and no law. Only the law of the nature rules. Moreover, there cannot be any law because there is no law-maker. All the creatures exist as long as they can. No doubt the lion is stronger than most of the animals and the mammals, but the elephant is more stronger and bigger and moreover it is vegetarian. Lion is not the king because nobody obeys him, only it is feared and it cannot be the king of the creatures that it eats, like we are not the kings of the vegetables. You know if you go to the jungle then the lion can eat you too, but does that make the lion your king? To me lion represents evil, evil forces are also natural just as the good force. As far as the Singhs in India are concerned, it may symbolise the traditional thinking among those people, but if you go deep into the meaning of the lion the king in the jungle, then these people just have an evil illusion. I have no intention of hurting anybody but I think I would not like to name myself after any mammal or animal. It is very cowardly to call yourself a lion. There are these lions clubs in the country or outside, they are so proud to call themselves animals and on the top of that the evil one. If ever I will appreciate any club named after any animal, it could be cows club or the society for protection of cows. Cow is so useful, it gives you milk, best manure for the fields and bulls to plough the fields. Cow looks after your life thats why cow is so important to Hindus, you do not need these tractors to plough the fields that cause pollution, you see already that the chemical fertilizers are killing the people round the world, no cow kills the people. There was one joke about these lions, one guy was drunken in the street and threatening everybody, that he is the son of the lion, "but tell me did your mother go to the jungle or the lion came to your house" somebody asked. It is true that this lion mentality is one of the reasons for violence, but it is not only these kind of people alone who could be violent. Everybody has violent ideas in their head, some like boxing, some like karate, some people like to see movies with fighting scenes, some like to hear stories about the kings and the wars, some indulge in violent talks. Even thinking bad of others is violence. We have to agree with Mahatma Gandhi that violence is in thinking, talking and actually indulging in violent actions. It is not only against fellow human beings but against all the creatures that have life, even plants. So it is not only the animals but the plants as well that have life also.

Is man vegetarian or non-vegetarian by nature? How do you differentiate the plants the merit of being a vegetarian and non vegetarian, if it is the question of life. I mean the vegetables also get killed, then the violence against plants cannot be different from the violence against animals.

Meat eating has its own quality of life that of *Tamasic,* whereas the vegetables have their quality of life *Rajasic* and *satvic.* As far as the issue of life is concerned, the animals do have a soul and they have red blood, some looking like the human blood, but the plants are not known to have soul and the plants you can eat alive or the fruits of it is also alive, like the juice and water is life, but the flesh is always dead and it has the energy of the dead. Moreover whenever the animal is killed it has agony and panic of being killed and that the meat has this energy passed on to the users. In difficult situations, the meat, eaters get more paranoia than the vegetarians and they lack moral courage. Moreover, meat eating is medically and spiritually a low diet.

It may be said here that meat eating is definitely not good for the humans. Some people say that the humans do have the canine teeth but it is not proved that it is for meat eating. Man simply cannot jump like a cat or lion on the other animals and eat them. Perhaps we should know that our intestines are made long by nature to be vegetarians. The meat-eating animals have short intestines. All the meat eating animals take water by licking while vegetarian animals suck and drink it down. Therefore, we are supposed to be vegetarian by nature. And if we believe Darwin that man came from the monkey then we know that monkey is vegetarian. All the animals walk looking towards the ground and suffer from various diseases and when you eat these animals you are only looking towards the ground, how to use and grab more ground. Whereas all the plants grow towards the light. They take the minerals, water and air and look and grow towards the Sun. And if you eat only vegetable plants you inherit the vision to grow towards light. They say as you eat so shall you behave. So if you want to grow and see the light you have to be vegetarian. Some people may say that they do see the light everyday like the vegetarians do. It is not this light that we can think about. The light that I am talking about is the third eye that we can open only through meditation and see the universal eternal light from within and that is called Enlightenment. It is good to know that the people who got Enlightenment practise a certain way of life that forbids use of *Tamasic* articles like alcohol, narcotics, meat and even garlic and onions because these create blocks in the way of meditation and enlightenment. Therefore, you see that the people who get enlightenment are opposed to violence.

Recently they had the mad cow disease in England. Some stupid people fed the cows with sheep meat and ended up with the cow disease. So it should be clear that you should not even try to feed vegetarian animals with meat products. Definitely meat eating is no good, it has been proved by spiritual experiences and medical tests as well. But I cannot say that meateaters are bad and that they are all violent. You know there are many vegetarians that are violent and cultivate hatred towards others, hatred is also violence. But it is the question of feelings and life, if you feel sympathetic with the animals and believe that you cannot take away the life of others if you cannot give it back then it will be more easy for the people to understand it. But if you think that it is not you who killed the animal and you did not see how painful the killing was, then it may be less of a burden to the eater.

The way the animals are killed also differ. There are ways these days to kill the animal with less agony and pain, while some people still give the animals real agony and pain like the Muslims way of Halal, which is very cruel. Yes they should not be cruel to animals like that. There is no reason to be cruel and it should be stopped. I simply do not like to kill animals. Cruelty against animals has to be punished and people have to be educated about it. If they follow my advice not to kill the animals, a day may come when it will become difficult problem to feed and look after so many animals and there may be no place for these animals to go around. Well there are already too many people around in this country and half of them are starving and do not have enough to eat, that does not mean we should kill them. We have to know and recognise the right of the animals to life.

How we can stop this violence that is spreading in the country? After the war of independence in 1857 had failed, there was this movement for freedom after some people had set up the Congress. When Tilak took over the Congress he made it a party for *Swaraj* meaning self-rule. From Tilak the leadership of the movement went to Mahatma Gandhi. They led the freedom movement peacefully. Violence was not adopted by the freedom struggle in any form. Even the struggle culminating into the civil disobedience movement of 1924 was called off by Mahatma Gandhi because it had become violent, just because a police station had been set on fire and three policemen had been killed. And today you see how many policemen are getting hurt and killed everyday in India.

Though there were some people during the freedom struggle that wanted an armed movement against the British, it was not accepted by the leaders of the day neither by choice and nor as a strategy. Though the peaceful struggle against the British could not be the only factor in achieving freedom for India, but it was very important the way Tilak and Gandhi led the people against the British. It made the masses aware of their freedom and never indulged in violence. Violence always results in further and counter violence and violence leads to destruction. Nothing has ever been achieved by violence. The people who think that they can achieve something by violence, die in violence. Whether it is the political, religious, economical and personal reasons that motivate some people to take to violence, it can never win the people and their co-operation. The concept of instant and distant Karma is always there to see and it works. Violence is a very low form of Karma, a low energy, that blocks the growth of the indulgent to grow higher, and directs their energy to go more lower. Have you ever met a person who has achieved spiritual high through violence. A person who is enlightened will tell you that he or she has not indulged in violence and they do not like it. People go to see such enlightened persons out of their choice and not out of fear. They win the love of the other creatures, they can even make a wild beast to sit by them just like a pet. Have you ever heard of a person who has been spiritually high that has advocated violence? We have heard of such persons, as Krishna and Arjuna, making wars to achieve justice, and Krishna is considered as reincarnation of Vishnu the God, so he must have been spiritually high when people think of him as God, who advised Arjuna to make war, I mean violence. I do not know that they were spiritually high, enlightened or Gods, but the folklore has made them so, and that is why war is considered a legitimate means to achieve justice or the goals. Whereas among the Muslims there is always this call for *Jehad,* a similar way of war and violence to achieve their goals.

If you can recollect from the *Gita* or *Mahabharata* the episode of war for justice, you will see when Arjuna saw his relatives, kith and kin and his teachers opposite him to start war, he refused and he said, "I do not want to kill them, I have no desire to live after killing them". He further said that in the war millions of people will die and there will be millions of widows after the war and millions of children without father. He did not want to fight such a bloody war. He was right, but then Krishna manipulated him to make war. He said, "If you win the war you will be the king of the earth and you will enjoy the fruits and if die fighting the war you will go to heaven. And if you refuse to fight the war you will be known as the greatest coward." Such a philosophy had legitimacy with the people of those times and even with some people these days like Hitler, Mao and Khomeni. Then you also see the outcome of Mahabharata. After the war Aijuna did not become the king of the earth, the Pandvas were ashamed of the war and the sufferings and agony of war that they left for the Himalayas to die in peace there. Neither he could enjoy the fruits of the war nor he could go to heaven because he did not die in fighting. The war destroyed every thing, the technology the knowledge, the love and charm of life for which people hope to live for. It was complete destruction. Frankly speaking it was a great human tragedy.

No doubt, it was a complete destruction and all wars are destructive and evil, but what can you do when you are attacked don't you have to defend yourself ? And that defending yourself could be a part of war. Then how can we defend ourselves, our freedom from the invaders if we do not get ready for war. They say if you want peace get ready for war.

The war of Mahabharata was a war of indulgence. It was more of a destructive football match where whistles were blown off in the form of shells and the rules and rituals were followed like matches. It was not an invasion of a sleeping country. Also the war took place between the armies of the two opposite blocks. No civilian died in the cross shooting and no body was looted or raped. But the wars are otherwise full of evil, that they are known for. Invasion of the other country is bad but if you have to defend yourself against an invading army, you have to fight such a war. Therefore, it is necessary to remain ready to defend yourself against war and aggression, and not to get ready for war. Defence preparedness cannot be called violence. If you have to defend yourself against violence specially on the borders, a limited violence is justified because you have no other choice. For internal violence you could go to court or police or the community to protect you but on the borders when they attack you, you are a loser if you do not defend. Having a muscular body and training in karate does not make you are violent and it cannot be called violence. It is the way you use your power that could be called violence and non-violence. Though Mahatma Gandhi had said that Hitler's invasion could have been faced with no violence and passive resistance, he did approve of sending of troops to Kashmir to chase away the Pakistanis. It was Nehru who stopped the army when they had cleared half of Kashmir and Nehru decided to take the matter to the UNO where it was never decided.

Almost every political agitation in the country these days is becoming violent whether it is the Tamil opposition to Hindi or Assam's anti-foreigner agitation, whether it is trouble in Kashmir and Ladakh, whether it is Nagaland, Gorkhaland or Bodoland, or the naxalites in Andhra or the caste clashes in UP and Bihar and the communal clashes all over the country, all of them becoming violent, they are taking to guns and bombs. Moreover, the Khalistanis terrorists in Punjab, the Kashmiri, ULFA and other separatists, and above all the state terrorism. The suppression by the police by brutal force and in fake encounters the police running berserk and abetting to violence many times, torturing people in police custody. It is a matter to think and ponder about as to how we can stop this violence that this country has everyday including murders by the criminals, and bandits and violence against women and weaker sections of the society.

Violence is the creed of the uncivilised. We have to make everybody know this. The peaceful agitations do not get noticed by the Kumbhkaranas of the government and the violent incidents get reported by the press. So both the government and the press are responsible for these activities of violence of some people. Every day you see that the negative news is reported on the front pages of the newspapers. So when people see these negative things on the front pages of the papers, their life gets conditioned to bad things. They even do not know what good things have been around. And our papers give lot of space to political news. Should the newspapers give one tenth of the front pages to positive things like yoga and science, the attitude of the people will change. Our radio and television have become addicted to biased news and are imitating the broadcasting agencies of the authoritarian regimes. A friend of mine was working in the Indian embassy in North Korea, he has just returned, he told me that the people in that country are only told three things, their great country, their great leader and the dear leader. The great leader and his successor who could be his wife or son is the dear leader. That is the first line and the second line in the bureaucracy. It seems we are propagating the great leader and the dear leader concepts.

The issues, of violence that we face are of regional, communal and class colours and in most of the problems it is the government at the centre that is responsible for the agitation. If you take on one issue after the other, you will clearly see that it is the government at Delhi that is squarely responsible for violence. Nehru had the fear of losing his power to the Hindu revivalist forces like the RSS. So the first thing that he did was to blame the RSS for the murder of Mahatma Gandhi and ban it. Then he wanted to appease the Muslims by showing them the danger of the RSS. He collaborated with Sheikh Abdullah and even did not give his consent for the induction of Indian army into Kashmir to vacate the Pakistani aggression and invasion. Then the Prime Minister of Jammu and Kashmir Mr Mahajan said in front of Patel that he might go to Pakistan to reach a settlement about the status of Jammu and Kashmir, because even when the Maharajah of Jammu and Kashmir had signed a blank paper of accession to the Union of India, Nehru was playing the political cards of Sheikh Abdullah, and offering no help to Jammu and Kashmir. Only then Sardar Patel told Mr Mahajan that he did not have to go to Pakistan for help and that the Indian Army was sent to Kashmir. Nehru who had studied European history and was influenced in his outlook by the European set-up, and was nicknamed in the Congress party as our Englishman, thought of a set-up of the provinces on the language basis. He decided that Hindi will not be imposed on the non-Hindi states like Tamil Nadu, then known as the state of Madras. Now is not it strange that the Tamils have a preference for English, a foreign imperialist language than the native national language Hindi. It is because Nehru never wanted a united India on the basis of Indian culture that he thought was a threat to his political career. It was due to people like Nehru that India could not be called Bharat, it remained India for the foreigners in English and for the Hindi people, Bharat. Which country has this much distortion about its name in the whole of the world. When the whole country has accepted Hindi as its national language why one state of Tamil Nadu couldn't.

And you see this Assam problem, there are many refugees from Bangladesh settled there, the local people have a problem because the outside people started to influence the political and social status of the local people, it was natural that they resented it. So you have a regional party getting to power there and that regional party does not like the Congress party in power in Delhi for understandable reasons. It was further encouraging the Bodoland agitation that became violent, to divide Assam further, thus, they have created Nagaland out of Assam. Assam a big state at one time, got fragmented due to the encouragement by the centre to the forces of disintegration. North-East is vulnerable due to the Christian missionaries working there to convert the tribal people to Christianity and make them hostile to a predominantly Hindu country that is India and Assam problem is due to the infiltrators from Bangladesh.

And you know the Gorkhaland agitation in the Darjeeling area of West Bengal had the full support of the central government of Rajiv Gandhi because there is an opposition leftist government in Kolkata. Then we can see also how badly the Punjab problem was handled and manipulated by the centre. Remember the problem in Punjab is not new, there were the days of people like Master Tara Singh and Sant Fateh Singh who used to go on indefinite fasts to create a *Punjabi Suba*, when they got it the Akalis, a Sikh fundamentalist party, started to speak for the Sikhs, only to gain power in Punjab, when they got into power on the basis of religious politics, some power hungry politicians started to become more fanatic. The central regime of Indira Gandhi started to approach religiously oriented politicians to be on their side. In the process they had people like Zail Singh and Buta Singh in their ranks over people like Darbara Singh, and encouraged people like Bhindranwale, the propounders of Khalistan against the moderate Akalis to play the politics of religion. In the end Bhindranwale slipped out of everybody's control and was killed in Operation Blue Star in the Golden Temple and Indira Gandhi was assassinated soon after. There was no sincere effort to solve the problem. Rule of the bandits had taken over Punjab and the country was paying a heavy price in terms of men and money to control the situation and in fact, it was a bloody dance of death and destruction that had been let loose by the anti-social elements and the state terrorists. The game was named 'killings'. The Punjab problem could have been solved in no time, had there been a sincere approach and men of integrity in power in Delhi. Likewise many of the violent problems in the country are due to the negligence by the regime in Delhi. The Naxalites problem is due to our indifference towards poverty. All these slogans of socialistic pattern of society and *Garibi Hatao* have caused insult and injury to the thinking people among the poor. The violence by the bandits is due to the collaboration of police and the politicians with the dacoits for material and political reasons, and mishandling by the police. The violence against women is because of the thinking among some stupid men that they can hit a woman because she is weak.

It is true that the power hungry people have now no regard for the philosophy of non-violence that was the hope of disillusioned people after the world wars. The influence of Mahatma Gandhi had put India so high in the eyes of the civilised people of the world. It is a pity that the India, i.e., Bharat of Mahatma Gandhi and many other sages and enlightened people, is being known and seen for its poverty, ignorance, disease and violence all over the world. I am really upset by the state of affairs in this country, in the neighbourhood and all over the world, that there is still violence and it is mostly in third world countries where there are a lot of uneducated and uncivilised people that have control over the rules in these countries. Still there is some hope to defeat violence?

Most of the time we are non-violent, we are living without fights and wars, we do not need police. We wake up every day and after some activity we go to sleep, because our body needs rest and that is a state of non-violence as well so we see how important it is to be non-violent. A person when he gets angry even for a minute, it can spoil the whole day for him. Similarly a man can get killed in just a minute by a fire shot or can be hanged for a crime in the same time. You make a house for two to three years and then it is complete and you can destroy it again in one minute. Now with the nuclear bombs you can destroy the whole world in matters of minutes. All I mean to say is that the negative power is so strong and fast that you have to watch it continuously. Non-violence is a creative energy and it takes time to grow and create things but then the negative power can hit you any time like death. It is only some time that violence spreads out. If we can live without violence for most of the time, we can live without violence for all the time as well.

Whereas most of the people have food all the time to eat, some people do not even have enough to feed themselves two meals a day. And we know that we can provide food and basic human rights to everybody, same way we can achieve a state of society without violence. It is a question of basic human rights being provided for everybody and the feeling of responsibility among the managers of the country towards everybody that a social harmony could be achieved and that is the beginning for a state of non-violence. Only then we can educate people about the importance of non-violence. Non-violence is a spiritual state of mind and body. It can come only when you are satisfied with yourself and you start to know yourself. You have to educate the children in schools not with the stories of hero worship of the heroes of the past and the great leaders and dear leaders of today but towards our social behaviour and attitude towards other people and our responsibility as members of this human society. Only then we can achieve peace and contentment in the society. As we have discussed earlier that people in this country still do not care that spitting is a bad habit and that it causes disease and spreads it, and releasing of human excreta everywhere is an insult to civilised life, because it stinks and it is unhygenic for health and thereby anti-social.

Unless we understand these basic things of life and social behaviour, we cannot improve on the non-violence issue, because non-violence is not a principle of weakness but a state of higher developed mind. New Zealand and USA are almost on the same economic level, but the rate of homicide in the USA is 50 times more than New Zealand, simply because the USA believes in policing of the whole world, resulting in military involvement and selling arms and making the life of the people miserable. Power has made the USA a country of snobs, arrogant and reckless people, that is why its citizens have such a high rate of crimes because of the *Karma* of the managers there. Back home in Bharat we had no murder case in Ladakh till 1973, but now you see violent agitations there. If the judge and the police can kill the enemies of law, then one individual can also think of killing his enemy. Therefore, the death penalty has to go and people be given education in *yoga* and meditation so that we can improve on the quality of life in this world.

People had made so much noise about one case of *sati* some years ago in Rajasthan, but nobody does any serious thinking on these cases of sure *sati* now being affected by contagious diseases like AIDS. It is also no consolation to say that four billion people out of six billion people in the world have no sanitation that the same ratio exists in India, because of poverty and ignorance. Cleanliness is next to Godliness, with this slogan the western developed countries have made great progress, we can do the same.

The colonial legacy of the British and feudal cultural heritage of the Indians have created an elite in India that is alienated from the main stream. This is due to the over use of English in our daily lives. Probably our country have a history of the elite being alienated from the masses. In the old times it was through Sanskrit and now its English. We have created a new class of snobs in all sectors. There are still others who indulge in sarcastic commentaries. With the advent of confused western tastes into our culture, the pressure is taking its toll on our family system.

Now with this consumer culture developing, our senior citizens are becoming helpless spectators of this decadent nuclear family system. Their life is coming more and more miserable and insecure. Many of them are living a sad life, even getting killed by servants or committing suicides. Similar is the case with many children who escape being aborted, they survive death being in poverty and disease. Growing in hostile environment is another problem. Cultural changes are inevitable but we should do it gracefully. The campaign to rewrite the history needs to be proved. However, we cannot live on the leftist projection of history. We criticise British for their colonial occupation of India forgetting completely that they made the present India. Similarly we hear criticism of the upper castes who are supposed to have exploited the *dalits* forgetting again the sacrifice of the whole lot of *kshtriyas* for the defence of the country. Culture based on lies cannot be promoted by saying that Kalidas was the Shakespeare of India. It is like putting Karl Marx before Hegel. We need this cultural transformation like Kalidas had after the marriage.

4

Economic Reforms and Quality Products

"India is a rich country inhabited by poor people". We have heard this before and I have mentioned it earlier. When we talk about the economy of this country, and the new coined words like globalisation and liberalisation, it is important that we start from the same proverb and try to understand and sort out the economy. The liberalisation is another name for naked faceless monstrous capitalism. People have always in the common sense misunderstood the meanings of so many words like nation, liberalism and anarchy, etc. If I say India is not a nation but a state. Most of the people will surely think I am wrong. So is the case with liberalism. Liberalism means more and more capitalism free from controls, less state interference and influence including less questions about tax evasion. In reality it is with the collapse of Soviet Union that the threat of socialism to capitalism seems to have diminished and socialism is no more in fashion, that the people led by USA are talking about economic reforms and their counterpart in India have coined a new meaning for liberalisation for the new form of naked capitalism.

India started its economic development, after it attained freedom from the colonial rule on a socialistic pattern. The world situation *vis-a-vis* Indian situation was such' that India and its leaders at that moment had to care about so many things. They had recently gone through the second world war, because there have been the communist revolutions in Russia and later on in China. At the same time, when the country was planning its future and because we had just attained freedom from a colonial capitalist country, India was bound to think on the lines of a socialistic pattern of society. During the freedom struggle which was very long, there were different groups of people who were for different kinds of economic policies. There were some people who wanted socialism, there were others who wanted communism while the majority of the leaders were for mixed economy. The forces of *status quo* wanted capitalism; they opposed even the mixed economy. There were, however, few personalities who could have influenced the course of our progress. The great communist man M.N. Roy had turned into a radical humanist. Jawahar Lal Nehru was influenced by the Favian socialism and Mahatma Gandhi had purported the theory of trusteeship. Subhash Chandra Bose probably was for a nationalist socialism but not like that of Hitler. And as he had already disappeared, Nehru took the middle path that of mixed economy that did not hurt any side. Not only because of the international situation, but because of the backwardness, illiteracy, poverty and feudal conditions in the country and moreover freedom and democracy had to reach the people. The government led by Nehru had to take a progressive path.

Hence the five year plans and the public sector undertakings were necessary to build the infrastructure. The country did make progress under Nehru but the bureaucratic syphillis and corruption and the trade unions and finally the attitude of the people and the politics of some vested interests turned the country into a very chaotic society and sick economy.

India have already spent 55 years of Independence from the colonial rule only being replaced by the indigenious brown *sahibs*. These brown *sahibs* are worse than the colonial *sahibs*. At every step they ask for *bakhshish* in every office that includes the bureaucrats and the ministers and the politicians. Once this is done, the business *sahibs* become a privileged class. They can evade taxes, they can ignore all the rules for industry and they can be involved in all the scandals in collaboration with the politicians and the bureaucrats. And the poor people who are more than 70 per cent of the one billion Indians, get almost no share in the economy of the country.

In the western countries the capitalist States had to and have to provide people the basic human rights and the social security. This has not been done because the capitalists have realised their social commitment. It has been done for two reasons: first, the threat from communism and second if the majority of people once achieve a well-off level, it is more profitable to make more money and make all the people work in such a way that they have to work for the capitalist system. So it is not a favour from the capitalists that the economically developed world have achieved a higher standard of material gains for the common man. On the other hand, the collective education level in those countries is also very high that the common man demands their basic human rights and the state has to concede because it will look very uncivilised in such countries if somebody dies of starvation. To give their citizens a better standard of life, socialism has influenced all these countries. Therefore, in the Scandinavian countries, the people have achieved a really fair deal for the poorest of the poor and for this, in a country like Sweden people pay over 60 per cent tax on their earnings and in Germany it was nearly 40 per cent on every earning hand. Perhaps this will open the eyes of the liberalisation freaks in India to open their eyes to their social obligations, otherwise the country is doomed and the capitalists soon will pay the price.

To provide basic human rights to every citizen in the country, the economy has to pay to the state and the state to its citizens. Taxes are to be collected to serve the needy people and not for freighing them to Swiss banks or abroad. Better standard of life is better for everybody, for the common man, for the capitalist and for the politicians as well. Otherwise chaos and not anarchy will soon overtake everything if we are not already there. But it seems we are in the hell hole of organised chaos.

To make the economy more responsible and vibrant. We have to take simple measures. Reform the tax structure and implement the social security programme. A very simple but effective tax system can be developed. To start with, the state can say that all the business is to be taxed, that all the money shall stay in the banks. That all income will be taxed, that there will be no income tax on the money saved in the banks, because the inflation has to be considered. That everybody will invest only that money in anything which have been cleared as tax paid money. That everybody in the country will have an identity card, health book and his total financial book that shall have the entries made of all the property of the individual. Everybody has to prove from where they have got the money. The liberalisation freaks will definitely oppose this idea but the needy people in the country can force this issue on them. However, we have to scale down the income tax rates and at no point they should be higher then 50 per cent. It is very ridiculous that you can ask an individual to pay 95 per cent of his income as tax. This was during Indira days. Now it is 30 per cent. Who will pay and who will be honest. These rates have been fixed by the extortionists from the politicians and bureaucrats down to the Mafia to make everybody unsafe in this country and live in the hell hole of stinky corrupt system. This kind of people have a saying, "it is better to be a King in the hell than to be a member of heaven." Honestly speaking, we do not have a system where an honest tax payer can be born. We do not compensate anybody if the person looses money in business or profession, but we can think of charging people 95 per cent tax on their income.

And on top of this tax structure, the country has most urgently to concentrate on the quality of its products. The quality in this country is very low in every field even on the grain fields. To start with, we are using chemicals in the production of food-grains, fruits and vegetables which is bad and have no future but a poisonous future that will kill us all. Second, every industrial product in the country is of poor quality and lot of wastage is being produced. It is this section of quality which puts us down and to rise, the only way is to produce quality.

Whether it is children or grains, things of everyday use or the missiles. It is good to know that in 1947 we were importing sewing needles and today we can make missiles or the satellites. It is also good to know that till the Dandi Yatra by Mahatma Gandhi we were not even allowed to make salt but it is equally painful to see that we are producing a lot of garbage as industrial products and it will be a great problem to dispose off this garbage.

Today we cannot sit and blame the colonialism and our past slavery on the others, we have to act and act properly. Our slavery as is known to everybody was due to our outdated war machinery and our tribal wars. But it is still a great honour to realise that out of that 1000 years of slavery, we are still the oldest living civilisation in the world. There is definitely no region in the world that have an older and more developed civilisation history and we still cling to that great past. It was great only because of quality Vedas, Upanishads and the stories of

Ramayana and Mahabharata, they are great only because the quality was great, the technology was great. But today we are sitting like mentally retarded fellows, it is because we have not cared about our education and the quality awareness that comes with education. Quality have the wisdom, if there is wisdom it is in the quality of life, it comes from the quality of consumer goods. The mind habitual to poor quality, performs poorly and is no match for quality, hence can be defeated easily. When you are surrounded by poor quality garbage you even cannot breath fully and freely and you even destroy the beautiful nature. You are better off in the pure nature than being surrounded by stinky garbage. Isn't it true? A wise man will not spend his time in making poor quality products, he will not even work his time in fruitless thinking and talking.

You can save a lot by using quality products, and different products for different uses. For example, today we lay down an electricity supply line on the wooden poles. First you destroy the forest, second the poles get rotten quickly, this way you waste that money and energy and then you have to spend the money again and repeat the mistakes again. So is the case with water supply pipes. You use low quality metal pipes. They rust quickly, the water is no good and then you have to replace them again and waste money and spend again. You can use top quality plastic pipes now that will be good for hundreds of years and every year you can lay down more proper water channels without waste. Plastic has to be put to proper use and with quality. The electricity poles could be built with proper material and design. You see very often roads and streets in the towns being dug by the diggers, because you have to replace a pipeline of water or sewage or telephone. These two examples are enough to prove that once we decide on quality we can save a lot which we need to provide to the people of this country for a letter quality of life.

The industrial products are very expensive in India. An industrial worker is paid ten times more money in the west than in India. But we pay the same price for our industrial products as in the. west and far worse we have poor quality. The country and the government never think of the very expensive spare parts industry, as why they should be so expensive. Most of the parts are made in the factories and very old factories like the Enfield Motor Cycle, for example, nothing has changed for the past 60 years, yet we have to pay 20 times for the spare parts than its metal value. The industrial products should be cheaper than the handicrafts. Few plastic products have become cheaper, but the pricing of things like cars, television and so many consumer goods is too high. At the level they pay the workers, we have to find that balance of cost and price. Unless we bring it to the same level as in the west we cannot achieve the standard of material life as in the west, also it will remain difficult to remove poverty. For long, people in this country have thought that the consumer goods like cars, television and washing machine, etc., are for the rich who live in high cost houses.

Sometime it can become ridiculous, for example, one fishing law in Himachal had the rich man to pay Rs. 100 as fishing fees if he was using the fishing rod. And the fisherman paying Rs. 10 who was using the net. Now with the net the fisherman could be catching 10 times more fish than the rich man with his fishing rod, but because it is luxury to have a fishing rod therefore you must pay more, never mind the loss by the net to the river life. Unless we change this attitude, poverty shall remain and unless we manage to produce the industrial products for public consumption cheaper and of better quality, the low level of living shall remain though no wonder so many industrial Charlies have become new sultans in India and made the country more stinky.

We have to make it a national morality to improve the quality of whatever we make. It is the best quality that will bring the demand for it. If people like the foreign makes of consumer goods, it is because they are of better quality. There is a need for a quality control department in the country. The ISI is not enough. It does not control quality, it only approves quality if somebody applies for quality approval but then it is again a matter of *bakhshish* as well. You must have noticed that there are people that produce good things in the beginning and when the product starts selling well they do not care for quality. They even sell their name while the things are produced by the others. Whereas in the international market the people are always making innovations, new systems and better quality. Whatever we export it is nothing when we take into account the size and population of the country. There is a great potential for export in this country because we have very cheap labour but we have not managed it well. The factory cost of the products is so high that there is not much chance for export. And also we do not take interest in exploring the markets. On the other hand, we import many things lawfully and unlawfully. This craze for foreign things, these defence deals of arms, guns and bombers take so much money out of this country which we really do not need to buy. India can become self-reliant in defence and we really do not need to import. We should be able to make what we need. Unless we improve our balance of trade in our favour, the rupee shall remain low and will further go down, should we remain as unwise as we are today.

Some people think that the exporters can make money if the rupee stays cheaper, that way they have a margin of profit only, otherwise they would not be able to export if the rupee goes up. This is a small man's thinking in this country and is very dangerous. India could be the third largest industrial country in the world even second, but the value of Indian rupee is so low that we are considered the seventh largest industrial power though the country is not the seventh largest economy because of the GNP which is measured in terms of dollars. The total value of our economy stands far behind many small countries of Europe that is because the Indian rupee is allowed to go down, this is why from the developed world even the students can afford to undertake holidays in India and from India even the rich people find it difficult to go for a holiday in the west and the common man and working class and students can only dream about it. Everybody knows that the value of Indian rupee which is non-convertible currency has gone down 100 per cent in the last 10 years in relation to other currencies like dollar, sterling and other European currencies. It had become stable in last two years. But it is strange that while dollar is went down with the New York terrorist's attacks in relation to other currencies, the Indian rupee has gone down in relation to dollar. It is increase of our import policy I guess.

Why has the Indian rupee gone down so much in relation to other currencies of the advanced countries after independence? Before independence the foreign trade was in the British hands who had worldwide trade. And when India became free, the Indians developed their own concept of development, policies and priorities. We started with the five year plans and not only we asked for economic aid but we started to import things disproportionately to our export and we started lot of borrowing and on top of that we started the deficit budget that caused inflation and inflation compelled the Indian rupee to go down and our balance of trade went against us and since then we have done nothing to change it. In desperation we are trying to sell the country to the tourists. What do we do to change that situation? We have to make things of international quality and produce everything. Unfortunately the producers of consumer goods in India are always looking to make duplicate things and call them desi. Desi Ghee may be better than the vegetable ghee but we belong to the vegetable ghee Dalda production. Desi Ghee generation used to win the gold medal in hockey and now we fight for the last spot. When the vegetable ghee came in the market, people used to buy it discretely, because it was considered like insult that you do not use desi ghee, but look, the time came when it had to be given on ration cards and people were fighting to get it, and the same vegetable oil they were selling in the black market. People even started to adulterate it with beef tallow.

In 1967 Indira Gandhi devalued the Indian rupee by 40 to 60 per cent and then Rajiv Gandhi is believed to have agreed to let the Indian rupee go down while the negotiations for an IMF loan were going on. Manmohan Singh further allowed the rupee to slump. Why do they do this to this country? Do you remember the story of a clever man who bought a village in Madhya Pradesh for a brass pot? because the villagers had never seen the brass pot before. And now the descendents of that clever man are a big industrial house in India. The developed world is exactly doing the same. The leaders in the third world who are no economists either accept these strings for their selfish interests or they are unable to do anything.

Indian rupee is cheaper because Indian industrial goods are expensive and that is due to the enormous greed of the producers and the government. Items of everyday use are considered items of luxury and they are heavily taxed and the tax do not reach the treasury. Our demand for imports is higher than the exports that puts pressure on the rupee. Our total foreign debt stands at 92 billion dollars today, i.e., about 92 dollars per head. Our per capita income is about 30 dollars per year. So you can understand why Indian rupee is weak against other currencies and to make it strong we have to control inflation. Luckily the new government has managed to do that the inflation rate went below 2 per cent recently and then we have to increase export. So what we can export? people? poverty?

We can export a lot of things. But because we do not have quality, therefore, we do not get further orders. Our fields of exports are, minerals, stones, iron ore, clothes, leather goods, tea, coffee, sugar and sometime fruit and vegetables and recently we are exporting software. But all together our exports have not crossed even the five billion mark. China is our great neighbour and developing country, its exports are nearly 60 billion dollars annually. Out of this total they export toys alone for ten billion dollars annually. We have the largest reserves of minerals, iron ore and the uranium and plutonium reserves, but we have not developed the instinct to export. The people here want to import the consumer goods, the talk of having imported things is an old disease here like the caste system.

The sugar that we use, eat and drink is one of the lowest quality. In the west this kind of sugar is used as preservative, we have to produce the table sugar and for cheap price. India has a great chance to make good handicrafts and there is a market for that. Also natural products are in great demand. If we can control the population growth in this country, we can even export foodstuffs. People of today and tomorrow will like to eat from the pollution free or less polluted areas and they even want organic stuff. The use of chemicals have to be discouraged and pollution has to be minimised. But our farmer leaders have to realise this.

The only field that India has made gains on the international scene is the stone cutting and export. This fine work is being done by few families of the Jains at Surat. Therefore, you can realise that you can do something that you know, that we export clothes made of cotton and wool and some crazy people import polyester rayon which is very unhealthy and causes many skin diseases and also we have to spend lot of foreign exchange. Yet the biggest polyester and nylon makers are those who are very close to the high List in the country. They can even bring in the polyester plants lock stock and barrel without paying any duty. These kind of imports not only harm the health in the country but the economy as well. You see now that the whole textile industry is sick. It was and still is the biggest textile industry in the world but we are so stupid to go for polyester. Now because the polyester is made by the plants, thousands of textile workers are loosing their jobs and millions of their dependents will suffer. Recently some cotton growers have committed suicide in Andhra Pradesh. Because of the failure of the crops and because it is difficult to grow cotton and because there is no improvement in technology to grow more and better cotton. So to increase the yield we need to do research and develop technology for future programme. The textile mills at Mumbai are forcibly closed by the Mafia and many people have lost their lives.

We import defence items like heavy guns, tanks, helicopters and bombers. Most of them we do not use, they we stored in our arsenals till they get rusted and outdated. First, India can become self-reliant in this sector. We can improve on the quality of these too. You know in 1962 the Chinese attacked us and we were outclassed and out gunned. In 1965, we could match the Pakistanis and in 1971, we not only out classed them but defeated them very badly because we had improved. We make MIGs in India and now we can make the Sukhoi as well and Russia is always willing to help us and assist us in making new models. The Russians do not need to import Miraj, Jaguars and Sea Harrier. Therefore, we need not spend our little foreign exchange on goodies like that. Same way helicopters, ships, passenger planes, submarines and heavy guns all can be produced in the country. If we can produce satellites, Pokhran tests and Agni Missiles, we can produce anything. But then how our defence dealers, leaders and the commission agents can make money as have been revealed. The politicians are so corrupt that they do not think of the country, no morality and they even say that the corruption is a worldwide phenomena. All they think and do is the foreign bank accounts balance and holidays in the west

India could produce passenger planes in collaboration with some countries like they are doing in Europe with the production of Air Bus industries India is on waiting lists for the deliveries of Boeing and Air Bus planes and then we have to part with the foreign exchange. If we can produce passenger planes we can sell them as well. Same way we can produce many things in India but we do not even try. For long many people in India have been asking, for going nuclear in the field of defence. People like Homi Bhabha could have produced the bomb in late 1960s and even America was toying with the idea in those years to help India do the same but we did not exploit that opportunity that had come in the event of China making the bomb in 1964 with the help from Russia. Then Indira Gandhi became dependent on the communists in India for her survival and she got portrayed as anti-American and USA under Nixon went to red China and for long even after the first Pokhran in 1974 India remained low and did not assert itself. Because there was lack of will and the bureaucrats made the leadership realise that India will loose foreign aid once we decided to be a nuclear power.

As we were going around the world with our legendary begging bowl and had made people paranoid to invest in the country because of socialist drama, Indian economy suffered. It was quiet late before Rajiv Gandhi realised to open up the country and stopped talking about socialism. V.P. Singh and many others after him could not take a decision to declare India a nuclear power because of the fear of world reaction and the possible economic sanctions. Vajpayee government took the bold decision as it was always the programme with his party and moreover there was the pressure for signing CTBT and NPT.

India needed to do the tests to sign the CTBT as a nuclear power and if we had not declared ourselves a nuclear power and had signed then we could have never become a nuclear power. Also the unstable government wanted to assert itself and go on record for making India a nuclear power. Mr Vajpayee and his government deserves medals not only for going nuclear but for managing the post-Pokhran period in the face of economic sanctions and actually raising more foreign money in hard currencies by selling bonds to the NRIs and the people of Indian origin abroad. India should not depend on foreign aid and it need not.

AIDS is a recent disease most likely a manufactured one, for which there is no cure yet and India has an estimated four million infected people that will double very soon. So we have to fight both kinds of Aids and both are bad for our economy. The foreign aid is not free, it comes as loans which we have to pay back and as said earlier it is 96 billion US $, at no stage our debts have gone down. And the second AIDS is going to be a national tragedy more than anything. It is going to be second Mahabharat and it will cost a lot of money and social problem Our economy will soon be burdened because the government agencies will have to work and that will cost money. It is a national shame that we have borrowed so much from the foreign sources and now we look for more aid and loans just to pay back the interest on the loans called aid. The situation is so bad and grave but not what we can not overcome. I think and can say that we have enough technology and infrastructure and money to invest that we do not need foreign aid to develop a strong self-reliant economy. The only way is increased exports and less imports and some burden of taxes on the people, but if the standard of living of the people goes up it would not be a tax burden on the people because when the consumption of consumer goods goes up the tax collection will go up as well.

We can save foreign exchange and money by producing more oil in the country, i.e., one of the very vital aspect of any economy, the energy source, after food. Though we are producing a lot of oil in the country and the offshores, but it is not enough, we still import more than half even if we have found vast reserves of petrol and gas. There is importation of more petrol because people are buying more and more cars everyday and every year. This import takes lot of money and foreign exchange and puts pressure on the rupee and the rupee goes down and when the rupee goes down prices go up and we have foreign debt going up. Therefore, we have to find new sources of energy like gas, alcohol, solar and wind systems along with the hydel and nuclear power. Though we have lot of coal in the ground but coal causes lot of pollution and until we find a technology to treat coal we should avoid coal. The day will come soon when we have to stop petrol and diesel, first because it is a great pollution producer and last, its stocks will soon dry.

We have to make energy costs very low, at present they are very high and with high cost energy we produce high cost economy and then we cannot compete with other economies. It is no solution to put up petrol prices because the government thinks, it is the rich people who use petrol, that makes the prices of everything go up and it is also not good that the government pays subsidy to keep down the petrol prices because then we have no money to spend on the developmental work. As this source of energy will dry soon we should not be found wanting in technology in time to come to use the other sources of energy and power. There are research works going on in the developed countries for a replacement of petrol. It is very likely that the technology already exists but is being kept under the carpet because of the petrol and petrol car lobby. India could revolutionise itself by developing a sound solar system, because we have about three hundred of fully sunny days in the year. Once we develop the solar energy, we can run our cars, buses and trains on the solar energy. This will be pollution free and save foreign exchange and the value of Indian rupee will rise and rise considerably. Already some people have demonstrated how they can run cars on alcohol and water. So the sooner we start on alternative energy, the better it is going to be.

Because of the poor shape of our economy we are thinking that the foreign tourists may help us. No doubt tourism is a big industry in many countries of the world, developed as well as underdeveloped countries. But India is not attracting many tourists. Tourists are a good source of foreign exchange and money that provides employment as well. They do bring some money but we have not many tourists coming to this country. About two million tourists came in 1999 and half of them were of Indian origin. So it is not much of a tourism industry if you take the size and population of this country into consideration. Think about the countries like Thailand, Indonesia, Jamaica and Spain. About five million tourists visit Thailand every year. Same number of people can be encouraged to come to India also. But we fail to sell tourism if not the country to tourists. If we can manage to bring in five million of foreign tourists every year, our tourism industry can earn as much as 100 billion dollars every year.

Foreign tourists started to come to India in the 1960s with the hippie movement. Hippies were a product of the Vietnam war in USA and came from the industrial and developed countries of the west. They found wars and industrial pollution and fast life suffocating. They were victims of materialism. They called themselves children of flowers. They had heard about India as a spiritual and free country. They traveled from the west to India and to Nepal. So during the 1960s and 1970s we had these kind of people coming to India. The hippie movement is no longer in fashion and we have also made it difficult for such people to come to India through the NDPS Act. So you see more and more straight people coming to India. No doubt there are some of the old timers around and some of them have become tourist guides. Most of the foreign tourists are travellers, mountaineers, trekkers and holiday-makers that make larger portion of the tourist traffic. India has six seasons in the north, beautiful mountains, lakes. rivers and many hill stations and ski resorts and in the south, beautiful seaside and sunny beaches and desert in Rajasthan and so many other things that people may think of coming here from far-off countries. The kind of tourists that India attracts are those middle-class and working class people and even students for whom making holiday elsewhere in the world other than third world countries would be expensive and they can not afford that. Moreover, India is not only cheap because Indian rupee is cheaper for the currencies of the developed world, it offers variety of things from religious, tribal, cultural colours, climate and geographic variations that the tourist just gets lost in the sea of variety. It is just a vast land with more than 4,000 kilometres of distance from one side to the end of the other side of the country and we have so many kinds of people and things that the tourists have lot of choice. On top of that, we have whole year sunny. You know all kinds of people come as tourists because there are so many kinds of people in this world. Some come for religious and spiritual reasons, some for *yoga* and meditation, some for looking around how it is like in India, some for mountaineering and trekking and some for beach life because our beaches are warm when it is cold winter in the west. Some of them also come for drugs and may be prostitutes.

There is no serious social implications of the tourists traffic because it is not much. It may be much in some areas but still bearable. People come into social contacts by individual visitors to this land. This way people can know better about other people whereas group tourists have different mentality. Their meeting with the people here is more of formality and business. People as tourists from the gulf and Arabic countries mostly go to one city called Mumbai for particular reason of seeking women as child brides or prostitutes and they are not many. The people to visit historical places are very few if you exclude the Agra visit.

There is not much influence of the foreign tourists because there are lot of domestic tourists. If we want to have lot of foreign and western tourists we have to provide them lot of facilities and less hassles and visas should be made available easily and it should be purely on grounds of money. We spend lot of money on our foreign missions abroad to promote tourism in India. But when they come we do not care that they get a good opinion about India. Our officers from customs to the police and then hotel and taxi operators and so many other hassle merchants, not to forget the beggars who hassle them a lot and nobody likes that. Though these kind of hassle makers are not many but no tourist escapes them.

It is strange but true that those people who bring money to India and like this country and are like friends of India but they are hassled continuously and rude behavior is meted out to them at places like visa offices and even a section of people in business try to cheat them. Whereas the people that sell arms and impose economic sanctions and dry out the money out of this land of the poor people, compelling this country to spend its money of the poor people on guns; are given a red carpet welcome at the airports on their arrival and are considered to be great, we have to change this attitude. And one more thing that the new government can do is to improve facilities at our travel agencies alongwith improved transport and hotels for the tourists and there is hardly any recreation facilities and if the tourists try to find that in *Charas* and *Ganjja,* we put them in bad jails for ten years. The parents of those people come and they fail to take them out and they go back and tell others not to visit this land of disease and poverty.

Recently the only good thing that has happened to India is that we have caught up with the developed world in the field of software, we can soon have a good network of computers and internet. We can also export the software and we have seen big names going for India. Our lead in this field may be shortlived if China can come up, but our knowledge of English is still helping in this field. Coming back to reality our economy is still in a mess and in a miserable position. No doubt, Rajiv Gandhi and his finance Minister V.P Singh did some ground work in liberalisation and Manmohan Singh started the actual change but in a silly manner. He started off with devaluation of the rupee and made it more worthless. He seemed to have learned nothing from the previous experiment of Indira Gandhi when she went for devaluation way back in 1967. No body can blame him for the poor state of economy but he did not do any thing to retrieve the situation. He did open up the economy for investment by foreign companies, that was done because that way some foreign money could come and we could pay back the interests on debts. In the process it was presented to the media which does not understand the western capitalism anyway, as something revolutionary to change the stagnant Indian economy.

These media people have no idea how the western capitalism works and what social problems and social security system they have over there in those countries. This new class of yuppies in India just want a cake for themselves. They simply know one thing because many Indians by habit of their desire to show that they know everything and they can talk endlessly without knowing anything just complain of the controls of the economic system. That it has to be free of the controls and they never bother to know how the tax system works in developed economies of the western countries like Sweden and Germany and how they have achieved basic standard of living for the common man. The Indian capitalists will never be bothered about their social responsibilities on the status of Indian rupee which is not worth the toilet paper outside India, because they can get the hard currencies by unlawful means which the system supports. The panic-stricken decision to devalue the rupee was simply the continuation of the Congress party's adhocism.

The foreign debt cannot be reduced by devaluation. Perhaps they know that it can only be reduced by bringing Indian rupee at its real value in the international market which is at least 5 to 7 times more than it has been brought at today by devaluation. This was done under the pressure of the imperialist IMF which believes in destroying the economies of the third world and make them good for nothing and colonise them again overtly and covertly and treat them as third class people, that is how they talk about the third world. Most of the people in the third world do not realise this and India is no exception. One German even told me once that India is not even a third world, it is the fourth world. This is because the third world countries have been victims of long time slavery. The amount of foreign debt that

India owes to the west is nothing for those people. India has accumulated this over the fifty years, this much amount they can spend on a stupid war in the gulf in ten days. The pressure from the IMF is nothing but to keep countries like India down so that they do not come up to be competitors like Japan for the US led western economic system. Because India can provide cheap satellite services and compete with USA, therefore, we have economic sanctions.

Indian economy is still looking for direction. It has no plans and the Indians are not aware of the national wealth in our natural stores. You cannot make Indian economy competitive by either devaluation of the rupee or by allowing foreign investments. Indian economy is still working on the demand and supply principle of economics. We have not produced surpluses. Indian economy can only be made competitive by producing quality. There is no restriction on providing quality. The quality control in developed economies are for producing quality. You cannot market anything below the quality level and also you cannot import cheap and low quality stuff in the country and sell it there. Many Indian manufacturers believe in reducing the quality once their products start selling, that is how the quality goes down and that is why Indian economy suffers. That is why Indian rupee has reached this low. Multinationals may have some technology but do we need technology to wash our bottoms, do we not know this already? The multinationals are not social workers who are coming here to serve us. They are coming here to make money. Some silly people may ask, if the Indian rupee is so bad why the multinationals want to make business here? Some time ago Coca Cola was banned by the Janata regime in India because they refused to show the contents. The Rajiv Gandhi government allowed the Pepsi Cola with the agreement that they will sell or export 25 per cent of their product and deposit the export earned money in hard currencies with the Indian Reserve Bank and change it into rupees so as to make foreign money. But the company exports Basmati Rice and takes its profits out by exporting Basmati that is the information, same will be the route of other multinational companies. India will sell the Basmati for formula drinks. Multinationals also create unemployment. The free market economy will also not help the country. Some imported consumer goods may reach the upper middle class in the country, but the poor not only won't be able to buy these goodies but will loose their jobs and become more poor. The time is not far when the unemployment created by the machines will result in the collapse of the whole system. If the communist economies have collapsed or suffered today, the capitalist economies will do that tomorrow. They are talking about the market economy in India as if it does not exist already.

India can develop its economy and pay back its debts only if it produces quality goods, that the consumers will buy at home and abroad. The Indian rupee can go up only if we can export more, and when the Indian rupee can buy more dollars, the foreign debt will come down, because the debt has to be counted for India in terms of rupees and not in terms of dollars. Because the Indians will pay their taxes in terms of rupees and not in dollars. So if we have to pay 90 billion dollars at the price of 50 rupees to one dollar the country has to collect and pay 4500 billion rupees. If we can exchange dollar at the rate of 20 rupees to one dollar, Indians will have to pay 1800 billion rupees only. So to improve quality, the ISI stamp of quality should not be a stamp for sale or a stamp to be bought but a system that leaves no field producing trash

Do the IMF and others know that you can rent a house in India for Rs. 3000 or 4000 for a month (excluding metros) for which you have to pay 10 times more in hard currencies in those countries for the same accommodation in the west. A newspaper is 10 to 20 times more expensive, if you can eat a meal in a decent restaurant in Delhi for 100 rupees, you will be happy if you can do that for 10 times more money in the western cities like London and Paris. So we should know the real value of Indian rupee from the price index and not from the exchange rates manipulated by the IMF and its hoodlums who sell goods like cameras, cars and watches that India does not produce in quality. We cannot blame the IMF and others alone, Indian industrialists, importers and the government are as much responsible for the poor and bad shape of Indian rupee. Unfortunately and sadly enough, we have complied with the west willingly because we cannot manage it better. Some bold and brave stands that we can take in the international forums like at the Seattle meet recently have to be real and not that we have to eat our words later on. There is, however, a problem with our mentality, we suffer from the inferiority complex that stings us because of our position, the mentality to show off and being a loud mouth and the attitude that there are still some people poorer and lower than us, that is how the Indians have not attained any position in the world in the field of any competition as a country. You can try your mind to revamp the economy and its balance of payments trap, but you have these corrupt politicians that have their election manifestos such as— one man, one family, or a temple or secularism. You cannot improve the situation for India unless we go for an intelligent programme and planning.

No doubt, many Indians have excelled in many professional fields and business all over the world. The Indian community in USA is the highest earning ethnic group as professionals and per family annual income. It is because there is chance and opportunities and also it is only the well-to-do people who have gone there from India. But back home we are at No. 142 in the community of countries for our per capita income. There is this parallel black economy in the country, tax evasion and corruption. That is why we cannot progress. Therefore, we have to find a solution and proper steps are needed to be taken to reach our goal of a healthy economy. We have to make a system where people have to put all the cash money in the banks. There should be no income tax on the interest. People with black money or unsettled cases be given a grace period of six months to declare their total assets and a general rate of tax be levied to pay by a dead line and close their cases. Nobody should be allowed to keep more than Rs. 50,000 in cash on his person or in his possession any way. That will stop a lot of black deeds. Everybody should have property card and all *benami* should be punished. All kinds of gifts, transfers and deals have to be checked. Gold policy has to be changed. No body should keep mint gold without license. Everybody should be allowed to bring in gold and a 5 per cent tax should be charged. But nobody should be allowed to make a stock without license. It is very strange that the Vajpayee government is asking people to put their gold in banks and get interest on that. This is not a healthy step. First these people are allowed to raise the prices of gold by hoarding and second, you are rewarding them by offering them interest. The concession that has been given to the people in export business should be reconsidered and they should pay the same amount of income tax as much as the others. There is, however, one very important thing for the banks and the people to learn that they must respect the rupee and not destroy by making holes after holes, paste paper and colour and write on it.

According to one estimate by one American University Indians have deposits worth $400 billions in the Swiss banks and more than that money is owned by them in various business investments around the world. This is definitely a proof of money flight from India and now our NDA government has a priority programme of disinvestments and the *Bania Karan* of the whole country. In this just presented budget there is no money for the social causes like health and education and sports. There is no money for social security, they even do not talk about it. The government says that it will retire 3 per cent people and take only 2 per cent every year to replace the 3 per cent. That it is not the job of the present government to provide jobs for the unemployed. The market forces and the private sector will create the jobs like the services and the IT sector. That the country is going to be an IT Super power. All this talk of raising the GNP by 10 per cent which has never gone up by more than 6 per cent. They think this is the remedy for social evils and poverty. There is no talk of quality. There is no concern about population control which is 2 per cent increase every year and there is no concern about global warming and pollution. The only thing on board is how to grab all the money and wealth for less than 1 per cent of the population of so-called yuppies like Margaret Thatcher did in England. She destroyed the British Car Industry and the social security of the poor people. There even grew up a new generation of unemployed and nowhere-to-go people who did not know that the government has social obligations. Similarly the *Bania Masters* of NDA are controlling and calling all the shots as this class has welcomed and approved the new budgetary policies and anti-people policies of the government. They all have agreed that the present government is friendly, so it should stay in power and the Congress must be led by Sonia another capitalist to make it easy for the NDA to stay in power, because of the foreigner issue. So you see the Hindujas and the Ambani's all Congress financers and holders of black money having direct access to walk into the PMO. The government is going in for privatisation in the name of Sick PSUs but it is also making disinvestments of the companies that are not sick. On one hand, they say that this will save the country some money and on the other front they are giving counter-guarantees for private 'good for nothing' companies like Enron, Hindujas and Ambanis. Meaning thereby that in power sector alone the country will have to cough up billions of rupees to satiate the greed of these people. In the public sector, electricity is free for the farmers in Punjab, but in Maharashtra the people pay may be Rs 2 per unit for which the government must pay Rs. 6 to 8 per unit. Now with this counter-guarantee what is good for the country? The naked truth about this all is that the NDA government will make it sure that the monstrous capitalism owns everybody in the country. A school drop out son of a rich man involved in all kinds of anti-social and criminal activities shall enjoy life and get away with every thing while others holding master degrees and diplomas have to starve and remain useless. A graduate or a matriculate if employed can get Rs. 10,000 to 20,000 in a government job while many others can be exploited for Rs. 600 a month by the private sector and with physical abuse. Is it the economy of the Ram Rajya that Mahatma Gandhi visualised for the country or is it the *Ram Rajya* by making Ram temple at Ayodhya. The prime minister the famous son of the school teacher like Mr Ambani and at 76 probably has forgotten the common man. He enjoys sitting and eating with rich and powerful people. The great poems and songs and speeches that he made to win the elections to save the country and its people are proving master allusions and have unfolded into natural calamities and misery for the country. In 1962 we could really blame Nehru for the insult heaped on us by the Chinese while our defence budget was probably Rs. 70 crores but today with Rs. 70 thousand crore annual budget for defence only, we cannot even control the terrorists and Mr Vajpayee often declares ceasefire for the holy month of Ramzan.

Coming back to this talk of globalisation, free market economies and the patents and the liberalisation *tantriks,* it is very clear that some people want to make money and make it fast. This is also the old bullshit in the new baskets. The globalisation talk is only about trade and investments. There is no globalisation of the labour. There is no globalisation about the global warming and greenhouse effect. If there has to be globalisation about trade and capital investments, there has to be globalisation about the labour and manpower as well, but it is not. The capital globalisation is that of the currencies of the developed countries. It is because the paper of some of these countries is managed to look better than the currency paper of the third world countries. Otherwise there is no real value for the currencies of the developed countries. Because the cost of living in those countries is as much high. Moreover, the workforce of third world countries including India has even problems to get visas to go to the developed countries and find jobs. If at all this country wants to be on a par with the developed countries of Europe, we have to adopt the tax structure and social security system plus the education system of those countries and moreover we have to eradicate corruption which has become our religion in this country. At the same time, we have to fight the American hooliganism of ridiculous patent laws.

For example, they have brought out the patents of Basmati and Neem, etc. These natural products of Indian origin cannot be the patent properties of some country or individuals just as the mountains, rivers and oceans cannot be the patent property of anybody. Monalisa painting can be somebody's patent or intellectual property but to say homeopathy or Ayurvedic medicines can be somebody's patent property is ridiculous. Tomorrow somebody can say that they have the patent for mango or apple or wheat. Can this kind of stupid ideas be allowed to rule the world.

Now there is a big plan to sell off the public undertakings for songs. There are so many songs and poets in this country. Some would like to sell the railways for a Kathakali while somebody will like to sell the Indian Airlines for a Banarasi pan. These public sector undertakings have been built with the public money and sacrifice. They cannot be disposed off to the musicians of the present rulers for a morning Raga and evening Baja. A national debate has to take place and a consensus has to be reached and then the experts have to lay down proper norms for disinvestment or sell the PSUs according to the law and not according to tenders or auction. Also you have to find out why any public sector undertaking is sick or running into losses. Now the government is talking about tough steps and hard decisions to be taken. Somebody has said why they did not speak about these hard decisions during the elections. It seems that the BJP leadership is trying to appeal to the hardliners in the party that they will act more favourably to destroy the socialist thinking in this country and the economy of subsidies and bring into the country the monstrous naked capitalism. It is tragic that the people in power are misled by the vested interests in this country who want to loot. Both the BJP and the Congress are agreed on this agenda of the capitalists.

However, intelligent people in this country should be given a chance by the public to sort out the future course and it cannot be the IMF or the American President who should give commandments. India, i.e., Bharat is a resurgent country and its economy can be the biggest economy of any single country. India's rate of industrial and national economy growth is 7 per cent per year and that is twice and more than double than the rate of growth of developed countries and many other developing countries. The size of Indian economy should not be counted in terms of dollars. It should be counted in terms of people and their property. It should be counted in terms of natural resources and in term of possible progress. It should be counted in terms of total consumption of consumer goods and petrol and cars need not be the criteria because it is really not necessary to have as many cars to as many people but we do have to remove poverty. Once poverty is removed and a better standard of life is attained for the masses, India's economy will be the biggest economy of the world. Because it is the real estates of the people that will count and for that we have to make our currency fully convertible and to do that we have to improve quality in every corner and in every field. We have to export more than we import. We have to improve technology and we must develop alternative energy sources like solar energy. India has lot of sun everyday. Once we start to run cars, buses and trains, cold stores and air conditioners on solar energy and remove poverty, there is no reason why this beloved country of ours should not be the leading light of the world. India cannot be allowed to become Aamrapali. If some people do not know the story of Aamrapali then I may repeat it here. Aamrapali was the most beautiful princess and daughter of a king called

Bindusaar. Bindusaar had a difficulty to find a proper groom for his daughter. He asked his courtiers for advice and his advisors were the aristocrats around him. As they were unable to find a proper groom for the princess Aamrapali and all of them in their dreams wanted to marry the princess, they all decided that the princess be married to that bunch of advisers as their common wife. The poor king had no choice and the beautiful princess was married to those vested interests of that day. India is in a similar position today. All the multinationals want to come here and they advise our Bindusaars to turn Bharat into Aamrapali. Our poet prime minister should be careful in having poetic planning for this country and save Bharat from the evil designs of vested interests of turning it into Aamrapali.

5

Presidential Form of Government and Direct Elections of the Executive

India opted for parliamentary form of government due to the education of our freedom movement leaders in England. Nobody can say what kind of a state and government we could have if the 1857 war for independence had succeeded. After that war whole of the British India was subjected to British rule and the people got to know the British laws. Wealthy people sent their children for education to England. Some of them came back and joined the freedom movement. Their way of struggle was to ask the British to give the same kind of democracy and rule of law for the Indians as the British had in England. Swaraj became the ultimate mantra for freedom. Over sixty years, the movement for freedom was not only for the freedom of India from the British, it was for democracy as well. Our leaders were elected for their party offices in the Indian National Congress party and other small parties as well. Through the various Acts of the British parliament, they tried to accommodate the Indian aspiration for Swaraj and give to Indians few rights to the privileged classes and some rights to elect assemblies in the provinces, that were not under any Indian rulers or princes. Therefore, the seeds for the parliamentary form of government were sown already.

During the freedom movement, the number of leaders continued to grow. Their personal interests and egos started to clash. People like Jinnah even demanded Pakistan. The land-owners and traders or lawyers occupied the elected assemblies that were based on voting by a few privileged people that nearly constituted 1 per cent of the total population, for example about 1 per cent of the Muslims. could vote when they were asked to vote whether they wanted Pakistan. During the 1930s, the number of top leaders in the Congress party grew considerably. By the time India got independence after partition, the need for a parliamentary form of government became a sort of a compulsion. Jinnah had got his Pakistan to rule and the Congress party had to accommodate all the power hungry politicians in the new set up. So they had to be in the council of the ministers. Since Mahatma Gandhi had opted out of power, the presidential form of government could not be adopted as Nehru had not emerged as a leader to replace Mahatma Gandhi. Since all these leaders have been educated in England, they opted for the Westminster model and wrote down the largest written constitution for India.

There have been great debates in the constituent assembly on each section and clause of the constitution. It will be appropriate to say here that after the constituent assembly had written down the constitution, there never was even any debate in Parliament to make any law and changes in the constitution. It was great luck that only highly educated people were members of the constituent assembly. Had it been an elected body like parliament or State assemblies where rowdies rule today, there would have been no constitution. Needless to say that the constituent assembly had debated all forms of governments and had concluded that the parliamentary form of government was the best. No doubt, it did work for about two decades after independence but shortcomings started to appear after the 1967 elections when Congress party was returned to Lok Sabha with a slender majority and in many provinces it lost power to other parties. And when the Congress party split in 1969, the parliamentary system started to become fragile. However, Indira Gandhi managed to get on to the centre stage and an absolute majority for her party was secured in 1971. But as the saying goes "that power corrupts and absolute power corrupts absolutely", the political system has become very corrupt and together with the corrupt bureaucrats, Indian system has become one of the most corrupt systems in the world. It is because of the corruption that political instability of *Aaya Ram* and *Gaya Ram* is becoming the norm of the day and there is a threat for democracy, because people are loosing respect and faith in democracy and that is because some vested interests led by the ignorant and uneducated people without integrity have managed to become leaders of some political parties. The number of political parties have crossed 50. there is a jungle of so many political parties, instead of well meaning politicians we have a breed of totally selfish and corrupt people leading the political system from Panchayat to Parliament and there is no progress. Therefore we need to find out why the corruption has become our norm of life, why the present parliamentary system has become redundant and how we can change and improve this shameful and disgusting political system into a vibrant, respectable social system where we can tell our children that we have a system that they could respect and be proud of it.

It has appeared that the parliamentary system has become corrupt. The members of provincial assemblies and the parliament have lost touch with morality and their aim has become to grab power for personal gratification. In such a scenario, the chief ministers and the prime ministers are all sailing in the same boat. There is a need to change the political and administrative set-up in the country. Frequent elections in the country have brought us to a sad situation. We stand as a hopeless lot. We have seen that the parliamentary form of government at the centre and in the provinces causes a lot of horse trading, instability, and gives place for undesirable activities, corruption and disruption. So what is needed is the direct elections of the executive heads of government at the centre and in the provinces. India should have gone for a presidential form of government. It is good that we have seen and tested the parliamentary form of government and come to this conclusion that this system has proved counter-productive. Our experience shows us how one family and one party has misused and abused this parliamentary system with one person holding the offices for 17 or 18 years and passing the power to the next generations of the same family. A sort of dynastic rule. The parliamentary form of government is inherently a weak system of administration though, it could be seen as more democratic. The widespread corruption encouraged by the parliamentary system is getting more organised with every passing election. When we have a prime minister not elected by the people directly but to be elected by the majority party or an alliance. There are chances of somebody pulling down the verdict of the people.

Let us discuss the prime minister first. Soon after the Independence or on the day of independence Nehru became the first prime minister of India. He remained PM for five years without elections and became prime minister again on the first general election in 1952. With Sardar Patel having died and Rajendra Prasad already the president there was nobody within the Congress party who could challenge Nehru for the prime ministership. So he remained prime minister for life that is 17 years till he died. A sort of hero worship had taken over the country and nobody even got a chance to change the government even after its China debacle. Nehru made it sure that Indira will succeed him one day. Not only she succeeded in becoming prime minister but imposed her son Sanjay first as the future ruler of the country during the emergency days and when he died, she thought of Rajiv; her first son, who succeeded her when she was assassinated. Had there been a presidential system, where a president is elected for four years and not more than for two terms, India would have overcome many of its socio-political evils like corruption, casteism, secularism and even poverty. A two party system could have emerged and the whole country could have been more united to elect a president and those regional outbursts of people and thoughts of secession could have been easily avoided.

Let us discuss how a president could be less corrupt than the prime minster or the parliamentary system. When a president gets elected, he does not have to worry for his chair for four years. Therefore, he is stable and an energetic president. He has enough time to look after the administration and implement the programme of his party. If he is good he could be re-nominated by the party and elected by the people for the office for a second term. And when he retires there will be another president and there is no instability. Whereas a prime minister has to win a majority in his party and then win a majority in parliament to remain in power. To elect a prime minister there are different lobbies and groups that the prime minister has always to win and keep in good humour, otherwise he can loose his power. So many vested interests emerge and they blackmail the honest man who could have won the party election. Therefore, a lot of corruption develops and the corrupt people get away with it. The prime minister is a humble man who is to be blamed for every lapse and the omissions and commissions of his partymen as well. Our experience has shown how the Desai government was pulled down by defectors, how Charan Singh became the prime minister without facing the parliament, and how the people had to vote back the discredited Indira Gandhi back to power. It should be appropriate to comment on this particular development for the sake of history.

That Morarji Desai could not lead his colleagues to a successful completion of a five year term while the Janata Party enjoyed a clear majority in Lok Sabha. First of all, he was not a good captain. Secondly, the issue of Raj Narain breaking law by addressing a public meeting in Shimla in a prohibited place started it all. The then chief Minister Shanta Kumar should not have made such a fuss over a trivial matter. Raj Narain was made to resign and Charan Singh took it as a matter of personal prestige. That is where people like Sanjay Gandhi found an opportunity to fish in troubled waters and they succeeded. Even then Desai could have managed it, but the former Jan Sanghis insisted on taking back Charan Singh and Raj Narain. By that time Raj Narain had already made a deal with Indira camp. As is known, the Congress had split after the 1977 election, and there were about 80 MPs led by Y.B. Chavan who were recognised as the official opposition party in Lok Sabha. Like normal activity of the opposition party Y.B. Chavan had moved a no confidence motion. Soon Indira camp joined it and Charan Singh faction came out of Janata Party. Even Y.B. Chavan was not willing to pursue the no confidence motion in the new situation, but he had no choice. Desai was voted out. He refused to resign as the leader of the party. So the party could not elect a new leader. Some people thought that in that situation on that day, Indira, Desai and Charan Singh all made it sure that Mr Jagjivan Ram did not become the prime minister. There was a possibility that given a chance he might have succeeded to align enough members on his side. But as Desai did not resign, Jagjivan Ram could not be elected the new leader. At the same time Charan Singh became the prime minister with support from both factions of the Congress party led by Y.B. Chavan and Indira Gandhi. Soon Indira Gandhi withdrew the support and Charan Singh kissed the ground. At that moment I think the Jan Sanghis made a big blunder by siding with Jagjivan Ram. They should have supported Charan Singh and joined his government, they could have saved the Janata movement and the government at the centre and in several states where Jan Sanghis and the Lok dalis were running the provincial governments, but political immaturity was probably the reason why the Jan Sanghis did not take a proper decision. In the mid term poll people voted Indira Gandhi back to power. Again Indira Gandhi could not improve on the administration and the poverty of the people remained like before. But one thing is clear that the parliamentary form of government proved fragile and the peaceful revolution that took part in India in 1977 was soon compromised by the vulnerable parliamentary system. Had there been a presidential form of government, the people's verdict could never have been overturned so easily. Again in 1989 when V.P. Singh formed the government, the Congress party played the same game. It was Devi Lal who played-up Raj Narain to support Chandra Shekhar, who was promised support by the Congress. Devi Lal was furious with V.P. Singh for removing Devi Lal's son Choutala as the chief Minister of Haryana. Mr Choutala was blamed by the Congress party for the murder of a candidate who was contesting against Choutala as an independent candidate for the state assembly. This charge was never proved but was good enough to throw out V.P. Singh, who had brought in the Mandal Commission report and accepted it for implementation. This was not good for both the BJP and the Congress, they were together in the streets to oppose V.P. Singh. V.P. Singh, however, had a major awkward situation. His government was supported by two opposite poles in the Indian politics namely BJP and the communists. It was doing well but Chandra Shekhar managed to get Congress support to get rid of V.P. Singh, firstly, as many people who were and are corrupt found, V.P. Singh as a major hurdle. Second, BJP had sensed the downfall of V.P. Singh government and they did not want to be on the sinking ship. Hence Mr Advani started his Rath Yatra for the construction of Ram Temple at Ayodhya and managed to get out clearly. People realised that BJP was not part of pulling down V.P. Singh. It was Rajiv Gandhi who supported Chandra

Shekhar. Soon the Congress party of Rajiv Gandhi withdrew the support to Chandra Shekhar under the pretext that two policemen of Haryana were seen spying or shadowing Rajiv Gandhi's residence. This was nothing but an excuse to withdraw support. This has been repeated in the case of Congress supported governments of Mr Deve Gowda and I.K. Gujral. All that the Congress wanted to convey to the people is that the non-congress governments are not fit to rule and they always end up in mid term polls.

BJP was leading for a major success in that poll of 1991 but the assassination of Rajiv Gandhi in the middle of the elections and the arbitrary postponement of elections in south India helped the Congress party to gain sympathy votes. The main opposition party BJP did not make any trouble for Narasimha Rao. The party even did not agree with rest of the opposition parties to have an opposition candidate elected as the speaker of the Lok Sabha. Mr Advani even went to the extent of saying that Narasimha Rao was the second Lal Bahadur Shastri. Later Mr Rao acted very strangely. He is reported to have used brakes on the nuclear defence programme of the country, he generated the Hawala scam in which most of the assumed people were his cabinet colleagues and few members of opposition parties. To please the BJP, Narasimha Rao established full diplomatic relation with Israel and allowed the demolition of the Babri Masjid. Soon the urea scam broke out and he fell as well and the Congress party lost the elections of 1996. BJP emerged as the single largest party and was invited to form a government, but Mr Vajpayee could not muster majority in Lok Sabha, so he resigned. Deve Gowda of Janata Dal was installed as the next prime minister supported by the Congress party from outside, when he started to function he was pulled down by the Congress party led by Mr Kesari. Mr Kesari demanded his replacement to which the Janata Dal agreed and I.K. Gujral was elevated to the post of PM. The Congress party again withdrew support to I.K. Gujral as well without any reason. The only reason was the old game of congress patty to prove to the electorate that only they could rule this country and that the other parties bring in unstable governments. Fresh elections of 1998 brought in the Vajpayee government whose pre-poll alliance parties did not get a majority yet again the BJP emerged as the largest party and the alliance roped in few other parties that were not willing to support a Congress party led government. As there were corruption charges and cases of corruption against a few people in the courts, the BJP led government refused to compromise, specially when everything was in public eye. Therefore, the opponents of Vajpayee government came together to vote it out. Jayalalita the communists and the Congress party could do that with the support of other small parties just by one vote. They were claiming all the time that once the Vajpayee government falls they would make a new government within five minutes, but they could not, Mayavati the leader of the BSP said on the floor of the house that her party will not vote on the confidence motion, but the next day her party voted against the motion. But when it came to form the next government, every faction started to sing a different song, and the net result of the whole exercise turned out to be a most disgusting situation where a fresh election had to be ordered.

So now we have seen in these last 47 years since the first election in 1952 that apart from the elections of 1952, 57, 62, there have been elections with hung Lok Sabha, soon after the split in the Congress party in 1969. Indira Gandhi could manage to survive only due to the support of other political parties. Though she won a comfortable majority in 1971, she had to impose emergency after she lost her case in the Allahabad High Court in 1975. When the Desai government lost the vote of confidence, there and then the Congress party had started a new political culture in the country. All the non-congress governments have been destabilised by this party. They have mastered the trick of destablising of non-Congress governments from Desai to Vajpayee. They have used the same trick. Help the renegade to become the prime minister for few weeks and then ditch him. This had been done at least five times and still they found such persons of straw to fall in their line. It is amasing how some people like to be the PM even for a day.

All these 20 years we have seen that the parliamentary form of government has become a liability for the country. It has become very corrupt, very expensive and very unstable, resulting in the uncertainties causing the country a great loss of money and time and no time to solve any problem of the people and the country. The coalitions do not work and do not last as different people have different interests and personality clashes among the ambitious people are the causes of sorrow for the people at large. Therefore, it is high time that the state of India and its people decide for a different system other than the present one and the sooner it decides the better it will be.

There are few options before a state like India. As we know we are a big country with very big population and diversity of culture, creeds and regions and religions. Therefore, we have to find a system that will unite the country and promote unity in diversity. Since we have a federal structure in the country, we have to develop a political and executive system that will be truely federal and yet united. There are few well working systems in the world of federal states. The systems of USA and Germany could be models for India as the British parliamentary system is proving fatal for this country. It was good in the beginning because Britain is also multi-cultural and multi-lingual state. But it is not a multi-religion country. USA is a very large country. It is federal but again it has no resemblance of India. First of all it is predominantly a white Christian country, the minorities are of very small number of 12 to 14 per cent. They are just small ethnic groups. But they all speak one language. The case of Germany, a federal state was another example for India to imitate. They have over a dozen provinces like India. They have the parliamentary form of government, but the parliament is constituted on the proportional representation of the popular polled votes and parties who get less than 5 per cent votes do not get any representation.

India's constitution has been framed after great deliberations by the great learned people of those days. Yet it proved not very good for the country. There are reasons for that as well. But since we have accepted universal franchise for the country, we have to find out how best we can use this opportunity to develop an efficient system of administration to make the country a great place to live in. The American system of a Presidential form of government is probably the best for India to accept. Though the President there is elected by an electoral college which is elected by the people. But practically it has become a formality and the President is voted to power on his own merits. Now in India where people have experienced slavery and emergency for a short period of 18 months, people are bound to think that a President once elected could become a dictator. It has not happened in USA, so far. There is a system of checks and balances and democracy in India has got institutionalised. People should exercise their option carefully. There are three major organs of a state namely, the administration, legislature and the judiciary. Since Indian constitution is a written document, everybody has to play by the rules. Therefore the executive which shall be elected by the people directly shall have the provisions of rules, a limited term of office and there will be no dynastic rule, which seems to be the choice of the Congress party.

Frequent elections since 1989 and specially three elections in the last three years and three prime ministers have not only resulted in political instability but have been done at the cost of the country by some vested interests. It has cost India billions of rupees and more dangerously the people have lost interest in the elections as is reflected by the low turnout of voters in the last election of September 1999. This is very dangerous for democracy. Elections are great occasion for the country and democracy but frequent elections put everything in jeopardy. The fixed term of five years for the assemblies and Lok Sabha have been tampered frequently by good for nothing people. The proposal by some people that in the event of fall of a government on the floor of the house there should be a new government or the old one should continue if nobody succeeds to form a new government, does not sound proper. First, there is already a fixed term of five years. Second, it will become a game of manipulation for the vested interests which are always anti-social and corrupt elements to play their evil games of buying and selling and the true representative of the people will get thrown out. Therefore, to avoid wheeling and dealing by unscrupulous people it is not worth even trying.

India is a federal democratic state. The diversity of culture and languages and political opinions make it necessary that we continue to be democratic. To keep this faith of democracy intact, we have to care for the regional aspirations of the people and their concern about the frequent elections. Since the political hotch potch in the country which is the outcome of some disgruntled elements and vested interests joining hands in politics, the country and its people are loosing sight of real issues and there is no discipline or direction to guide the destiny of the people. Therefore, the need to have direct election of the chief executive of the country and suitable provisions is the call of the day. To make it work, we have to separate the legislature from the executive. The president of India could even work better than the president of USA. The chief ministers of the provinces should all get elected for a fixed term of four years. The removal of the president or the chief ministers could only be done by impeachment which shall be the right of the legislature by two-third majority.

Presidential system does not mean the absence of legislature or parliament. It means that the three chief organs of the government have got separate functions and they are not controlled by one person. Whereas we have seen in India that the executive and the legislature have come under one umbrella of the ruling party. Laws are made and unmade by the parties to suit their own interests. Schemes are launched with political gimmickry. The politician in power even interferes in the judicial process. Whereas in presidential form of executive where the chief is directly voted to power by the people, he is not involved in legislature. The legislative institution is separate like the judiciary. The president can only request the legislature to form new laws and provisions if need arises. The president does not depend on the legislature for a confidence motion, his term of office is fixed, his succession is fixed and the time of election is fixed. He cannot become dictator because he cannot make laws. He is there only to implement the law and administration according to the law which is made by the legislature and the legislature is elected by the people. In case he dies during his term, the vice president takes over. In case he breaks any law of the land he is liable to be impeached and voted out of office by the legislature with the two-third majority. A president has to be elected by majority vote of 50 per cent plus one vote of the total votes polled. In case there are more than two candidates and nobody passing the 50 per cent mark, there have to be second round of polling between the two top candidates. The system in USA is different here. They have federal system, where they elect an electoral college. According to the system, in each state the majority party gets all the votes of electoral college. Thus, it can happen that a president could get elected without winning the election by majority votes of the people but the margin in that case has been very low. That system of the electoral college was conceived as a federal device and moreover to avoid a second round of polls. But the second round of polls has been accepted in Russia. It can also be done now in India where the polling is getting stretched over one month. It does not have to be done all over the country. We can have second round in only those states where a candidate has not received 50 per cent plus one vote. The election should be based on the federal concept and not on the unitary system. There can be a situation where a candidate has received very low percentage of votes in one particular province and a loosing candidate at the national level has received more than 50 per cent of votes in that particular province. But here we should make it clear that we are electing a federal president and not a provincial governor or a chief minister. Therefore, second round of polling in any province will mean the contest between the first two candidates, that the country has thrown up. Then a clear winner for the job gets identified and selected and that is for a fixed term and nobody can overturn that verdict by wheeling and dealing, whereas in a proportional representational system there is a chance of wheeling and dealing. People can get elected because some people control some political parties. The lists of the names of the persons are prepared by the political parties and the parties who do not get more than 5 per cent of votes are kept out. Then the other parties get their votes on proportional grounds. The political parties can nominate any candidate that the people may not like at all. Again they must secure a majority in parliament and if there are groups of different political parties they will create political instability. The scope for wheeling and dealing is there. Therefore, when we opt for presidential system, the legislature will be the house of representatives and the members should be elected by 50 per cent plus one system, only then we can keep away the sectarian representatives. In the present system, a person can get elected even by polling 10 per cent of votes polled. Does such a person represent his constituency? Therefore, we need to have this 50 per cent plus one system and separate the executive from the legislature and develop system where it works and people do not loose interest because of frequent elections.

India urgently need the presidential form of government because there is no need to keep two offices that of the prime minister and the president as the two offices of the top executives. The parliamentary form of government is proving unstable and expensive. Moreover, a lot of scandals have taken place and the prime ministers have either been unable to take action against the guilty or have been themselves involved in such scandals. Therefore, to make a man perform his duty it is our duty to make a proper system. Like the chief minister whose future depends on the MLA's, the prime minister has been suffering in the same way. With no political party getting a majority the election of a prime minister has become a scandalous business. All the corrupt people have become powerful in retaining or disposing of a prime minister. Therefore, it is very dishonest to expect a man as prime minister to perform honestly. He is not even given time to do his job. In a situation where every month or every year you have a new prime minister or fresh elections, the parliament has become a *Subzi Mandi* or a fish market. The country of India's size and problems need a strong system, only a presidential form of government a bit better than the USA is needed. We should be able to elect a man whom people know, who will have a reputation to be considered worthy of this high office. Otherwise in the present form of wheeling and dealing we have seen a lot of Charlies.

The people who are saying that the era of coalitions have dawned are directionless people, they also do not know as what is needed to take this country out of the hell hole that we are in. Once president is elected directly for four years, he or she will move in right direction without worrying for the beggars and the robbers and will not waste time in cheap tactics. The parliament can stay there for its legislative business and approval of ministers by the president. In the event of a president resigning or dying, the vice-president should be the new president. Therefore, to avoid uncertainty, the line of succession should be laid down clearly. Once we manage to provide a stable government and a system where people have direct say and where the president is elected with 50 per cent + votes, the political and economic health of the country will definitely improve. The Charlies and the vagabonds will disappear from the top brass and then you can expect a cleaner staff down under as well. Otherwise the stink will further engulf everybody and a big chaotic volcano will sweep us all. In the present system of parliamentary form of government we have seen how people have tried to get power by putting on a dynastic rule, by manipulating the insane and old people and changing the prime minister to suit the needs of the vested interests. The country has a mafia system already there and we do not need more. The political parties with their limited pockets of influence have managed cakes of power for themselves and they no more think of this mess that the country is in, they only think of being in a position to grind their axes.

In presidential form of government the two groups who have to come together to elect the president shall eventually turn into two political parties. Therefore, the communal, casteist and regional forces will disappear automatically which is in the interest of the country. Once a man is elected president, he will nominate people of standing and reputation as ministers and secretaries. The president shall be bound by the constitution and there is no likelyhood of him becoming a dictator because Indian democracy and its institutions have taken deep roots. Indira Gandhi imposed emergency because of the threat to her government but had to lift it 18 months later. On the whole, Indian democracy has reached the people politically and they will never tolerate any dictator. But if the problems of poverty and population of the country are not solved soon, then no form of government can save this country. The blunders of good for nothing politicians will see this country through unseen chaos and people who think that they are sitting pretty well in their glass and marble houses will not live to see the ruins of their dreams. The hungry and the unemployed and neglected people sooner or later will move on the streets and nobody rich or powerful will escape.

The president of India thus elected directly shall be a powerful man and not worried about loosing power all the time like all the prime ministers of these days who are thrown out because they cannot please and appease everybody. If a great leader gets elected as president by the people, he will have great power and should be able to enforce the programme and discipline in the country. With all the checks and balances already in place that of judiciary and legislature, such a president shall remain within his limits. All the prime ministers from Indira Gandhi onwards have faced threats of dismissal either from the presidents or from the parliament. We have thus seen lot of them ousted and the stability of the government and the country has suffered a great deal due to this. We can also see how political instability can be dangerous for democracy in the country as we have seen sixteen prime ministers in 25 years of civil rule in Pakistan and three army dictators in 27 years of Pakistan's 52 years. Therefore, not only India but the whole Indian sub-continent needs a proper political system.

The Post of Governors or Pradesh Pramukh

The post of governors should go or the chief minister should replace him. The chief minister should be directly elected by the people with a 50 per cent + votes and should be elected for a fixed term of four years and not more than twice. He should be elected along with his deputy who should succeed him in case the chief minister is removed by God or by impeachment in the legislative assembly or by parliament or he resigns of his own. We have noticed and seen that the chief minister's job is very difficult and the political parties decide who will be the chief minister, the MLA's decide who will be their leader and not the general public. Many times it so happens that somebody gets elected because he has been controlling the party or is imposed on the state legislature party by the central high command of such a party. Many chief ministers has a problem to act, they can act freely or they can act in an arbitrary manner. If it's a regional party, the chief ministers can be the final power for that party, but such a chief Minister have to care about the central power at Delhi as well. And if there is a strong provincial leader who has good relations with the central government either belonging to the same party or in supporting the ruling party at centre, he or she could be in a good position to serve the people. There is also a problem of the person getting arrogant because of power, who can ignore the feelings of his rivals and opponents in the party or outside the party for too long. Many chief ministers have been paralysed by the corrupt legislators called MLAs. There is always a lot of horse trading and wheeling and dealing to emerge as a candidate to be a chief minister. He has to keep his MLAs happy and to keep them happy means lot of corruption. The people have to pay for that. All these problems can be curtailed if the chief minister is elected directly by the people for a fixed period of four years. The people are better judge than the MLAs to elect a chief minister: It will go a long way to elect a chief minister directly and to make a stable and able active administration than a chief Minister who is always worried about his chair because of the MLAs and the midterm poles. The chief minister has to be a man of the people to serve them and not a man of some vested interest and corruption and this can happen only when a person is elected directly by the people with 50 per cent + votes polled. There will be no governor to dismiss him because the prime minister does not want him or the MLAs are not happy with him because they want to grind their own axe. This way an honest able man and a man of integrity could get elected as the head of the government as the choice of the people. The chief minister could appoint his ministers from among the members of the legislature subject to confirmation by the assembly or could drop any minister who is not found good enough or because he is corrupt and involved in illegal activities. The chief minister could only be removed by impeachment by the assembly or by the parliament with permission of the High Court or of the Supreme Court. The impeachment resolution could be passed by two-third majority. A chief minister thus removed shall be replaced by his deputy for the remaining period of that term. Thus, there will be no mid-term poll and uncertainty and instability and there will be no extra expenses. The total strength of his ministers should not exceed 10 per cent of the total number of the members of the assembly and should not be less than 10 in any case. This way there is going to be a limit on public money spending on the jungle of ministers. That will also enable a chief minister not to worry about the self-seekers.

Now a problem or a question could arise about a thug chief minister or a secessionist one who could not be dismissed by the president of India because the removal of the chief minister is through impeachment. This question can be sorted out with the permission of the Supreme Court and the Lok Sabha could do the impeachment job quickly if such a need should arise. But it is very much unlikely that such a situation could arise. Since there will be a checks and balances systems at work it is likely that the partisan attitude of politics in the country will take a back seat. However, the important question is that the people shall fix minimum qualifications to be elected as a chief minister and MLA. At least a post graduate or equivalent degree should be the academic qualification for a chief minister and a graduation degree for being an MLA. All MLAs should also be elected by 50 per cent + votes system. That will help in containing the sectarian politics and a party of the chief minister could get elected only if they could carry majority of the people with them. For example, a party or a person could get elected even with a twenty or thirty per cent of the votes polled in the present system in a multi-cornered contest. That is no representation of the people. Therefore, if a person is not elected in the first round, there should be a second round between top two candidates and the winner will get elected with 50 per cent + votes. Such a system will bring peace and progress in the country. A chief minister will not attend any proceedings in the assembly. The chief minister will be the top executive and the legislature will do its own job of legislation and budgetary allocations.

This type of election shall improve the quality of the election and political system in the country. The family dynasties will not have much say and only the experienced and qualified people shall occupy the offices. The election rigging cannot take place and hardly anybody could be tempted to capture booths all over a province. Because capturing few booths cannot make much difference. The caste and religion based politics will take a back seat and the social causes and concerns shall be the major issues. However, personality cult could be a drawback. People may be negligent to elect a proper person, because they seem to be tempted to vote for some silly film star or a dynastic folk. But the qualification restriction will put most of them out of contention and there will be a law that a person could get nominated if he has the support of at least 1/10 of the legislators whether in the parliament or the state assemblies. The second house of provinces should be abolished. So there is no harm in having a new system for the country.

We have seen how the system has been misused and abused over the years. Indira Gandhi, as president of the Congress party in 1957 tried to dismiss the leftist, communist government in Kerala and later on when she was the prime minister she did get naughty about that and many provincial governments were changed, dismissed and president rule was imposed very often. Chief Minister Rama Rao of Andhra Pradesh was dismissed while he was away in USA going through a heart operation. The Janata Party in 1977 got the Congress governments in nine provinces dismissed as the Congress party has been routed in those states in their Lok Sabha elections that year. The Supreme Court has finally ruled that the state government cannot be dismissed arbitrarily and the floor of the House is the only place to test the majority of any government. Even then, Narasimha

Rao had dismissed BJP governments in four states after the demolition of Babri Masjid which was in U.P. But the Congress party without any regard for the constitution and the democracy had the four state governments dismissed by the president.

At present there is big demand for the abrogation of Article 356 from the constitution. But if we go for the direct election of the state executive as is proposed above the article will be of no use as the CMs will get elected directly by the people for a fixed term and their removal will not change much because he will be replaced only by his deputy and there will be no president rule or a mid-term poll.

A new political system will develop in the country and it will help in improving the political and social environment in the country. The leader will have to emerge from among the legislators and when there will be only two terms for anybody, there will be no hurry for many people to get the top job. There will be less corruption in the country and people will get more united in sorting out the social problems. There is no danger of personality cult developing because of the time limit. A very important thing will be to fix a qualification standard for the president and the chief ministers. For example, there should be at least l/10 of the legislators to propose the name for either the president or a chief minister that will eliminate many possible candidates from the very beginning. So the serious candidates would not be many and then if at all a second round has to take place it would not be much of a problem.

There are power hungry members of the state assemblies and parliaments who individually or by associating themselves into groups make pressure groups to influence the chief minister or the prime minister and for their support to keep the man in place they always expect rewards and unless they are satisfied, they try to topple the man. So in such a system it is too much to expect a man to be honest whose tenure is dependent on such greedy dishonest people. So if a chief minister or president is elected directly by the people there is little scope that an unwanted person could capture power by hook or crook or by proxy. In the last thirty years we have seen how difficult it has been for the chief ministers in different states specially in Haryana, UP and Bihar to stay in place. Many have been toppled and many have managed to survive by unfair means. Therefore it is not fair enough to blame only a chief minister that he is corrupt and charge him only. Our whole system of government is corrupt. Therefore, we have to elect a person directly to the post of the chief minister or pradesh pramukh. This will enable the public to make their choice clear and save many unpleasant situations. Once a strong honest person with a programme is elected at the top, the bureaucracy under will have to take order and mend its ways. The top man shall be stable and careful about his reputation. The people will also learn that if they elect a person who is not fit to rule and serve, they will suffer and that they will have nobody to blame, but themselves.

In India we have noticed in the past that there was always a situation where the unfriendly government at the centre tried to topple the state governments under one pretext or the other. The politicians change their parties and bring down the chief minister or a chief minister is dismissed because he is not liked by the central government. When a chief minister is elected directly for a fixed term it will be very difficult to dismiss unless there is really a constitutional crisis. Therefore such an election will definitely improve the health of the politics in the country and there will be very less corruption and nepotism. Only a person with more than 50 per cent valid votes shall be able to become a chief minister. Hence there will be no sectarian chief minister and he will have to take into consideration the larger interests of vast majority of the people. He simply will not be able to become chief minister without taking all section of the society with him. Therefore it is very good to have the chief minister or a pradesh pramukh directly elected by the people for a fixed term and this post of the governor must go because it is not needed. Now the central government can not use Section 356 frequently if they do not have majority in the Rajya Sabha to approve the central rule.

The same way the Panchayat system has to be improved. The direct election of the Panchayat pradhan should take place and the term should be fixed for four years and not more than two terms and again a pradhan should get elected with 50 per cent plus one votes. The members of the Panchayat should be elected on the same pattern and the members should be given different duties like proposal and programme and the judicial section should look after the disputes and law section as empowered by the Panchayat Act. A lot is needed to be done on the Panchayat level. The members of the Panchayat should also be elected on their 50 per cent plus valid votes system because we have noticed that in a multi-corner contest many times a member gets elected even by polling 10 per cent of the votes polled. The Panchayat should be turned into a village secretariat and many public servants should be assembled under the pradhan of the Panchayat. However, the three tier system of Panchayats should be abolished and there should be only three tier election system in India, that is, the Panchayat, legislative assemblies and the parliament. The elections of the executive whether it is the Panchayat pradhan, pradesh pramukh or rashtrapati, all the elections should be direct elections.

This will minimize corruption and wastage of public money. It is very likely that the system of electing the executive directly is going to be effective because it will be very clear who is the commander for that period. A question can arise about any one of the above executives indulging in illegal and anti-constitutional and extra-constitutional activities but we have seen from the American system that there are certain safe-guards and the institutionalised democracy in the country will take care of such situations. Moreover, the Lok Pal Acts will take care of the corrupt practices on the part of such individuals like the Election Commission in the country. Hence we as a country are likely to be benefited by the above system and we can save lot of money to invest on the social welfare of the people.

6

Reforms of Laws and the Judicial System

Twenty millions of civil and criminal cases are pending for disposal in the various courts in the country. That is, more than 10 per cent of the population is involved in such cases and that is a sad commentary on our judicial system. There are major drawbacks in our legal and justice system. In 95 per cent of reported cases there is no justice or it is not proper. The criminal cases are on the increase and the life of the people is becoming more and more insecure and vulnerable everyday. The criminals are becoming more and more brave and habitual. Because there is so much delay in trials and justice that the criminals have found a safe place in India to do crimes. The nature of their crimes is becoming more heinous and sickening everyday. Just think of the most revolting cases of rape, murder and terrorism. A girl below 5 years of age gets raped by more than 3 men and thrown dead into a gutter. A housewife gets burned to death by the in-laws and there is no case registered, a child gets aborted and is thrown out in the dustbin and is eaten by the crows. Some poor villagers get killed by a gang of criminals and there is no arrest. Somebody gets murdered and the police says that its suicide. Somebody gets arrested for daylight robbery in front of eye witnesses and the judge says there is not enough proof. A minister or a chief minister is charged for corruption & the charge never gets proved, even if the whole country knows that the person is really corrupt. The whole world knows that prostitution is one of the oldest professions in the world but is never legalised. Now with the spread of AIDS, it is becoming really dangerous and the issue is never addressed. There is news that the Home Minister is talking about imposing a death penalty for the rapists but is our system doing anything under the present laws which are adequate enough. Talking and framing of laws is something but implementation is another thing. There is talk about the Lok Pal Bill which the prime minister says shall cover the prime minster as well and the Congress party says that the prime minster should not come under such an Act because they think either the office is too great to come under such a law or they do not have any candidate who cannot be corrupt. All this said and discussed, can the prime minster explain what the prime minster is doing about other corrupt people under the existing laws or we shall know that corruption has already disappeared? It is about time that BJP leaders should demonstrate to the people that they are doing something about the law and order situation in the country. I doubt that they can do anything about it under the present system of parliamentary democracy and the Indian mentality that has developed in the last 30 years and our leaders are part of this mentality.

Actually, the Indian Judicial system is very rotten and disgusting. There are so many laws in the country that it is very difficult for the people to know them all. Hence it is very likely that the laws are not obeyed by the people. Many people take pride in ignoring laws of the land. There are so many outdated laws in the country that of the British time and nobody has bothered to replace them as the country is still being ruled by the laws of the British time. The justice system is so complicated that people only know that whoever has the money he will have the law machinery in his hands. It takes such a long time to have a judgement made in all kinds of cases. Therefore, first of all it is necessary to know which kind of judiciary we have in the country. The lawyers, the police and the judges are hand in gloves in this judicial system. It is like a regular Mafia. In criminal cases the police is first to take bribe, if the person cannot dole out the money he will be booked, then you will have to pay the lawyer and if you can not then you will stay in the jail without bail or trial. The police refuses to register cases unless you pay them. If you have not paid, they take time to act and by the time they act you are already suffering from the second assault. If you have been attacked by other people the police is open to be bribed by the other party and shall leave enough loopholes in their report so as to enable the accused party get acquitted of the charges, it is a business as usual. Similarly in rape cases the suffering party goes through such procedure that it is another assault. The lawyers in criminal cases will ask for lot of money, they even bribe the single judge and get judgements in their favour. The longer the case goes on the better for the lawyers to make money.

In lower courts the magistrates and judges are the real monkeys. They do not do their jobs properly. They come at 10 am then there is lunch break at 1.00 pm. Then if they go to sleep it is assumed that the magistrate or the judge is gone on spot inspection and the people that he had called for that day to be present in court are called for next week or the next month. This goes on forever and people have to pay because these careless and good-for-nothing people are immune for the negligence and wrong judgements. Under this judicial immunity they can even send you to jail for contempt of court if you try to plead yourself that you are suffering as a result in delay of justice. You have to address them as My Lord and many of these judges and magistrates behave in such a manner that they even put to shame all the dictators and on top of that many of them take bribes in criminal as well as civil suits. They are open to political pressures and for this the politicians are responsible. And single judge cannot sit on judgements of serious nature, so they make mistakes and it takes also long time to make these mistakes and then for the aggrieved parties to get those mistakes rectified by the upper courts. Where there are further single judge judgements, by the time the cases get disposed of by the supreme Court the whole system seems to be a complete farce.

For example, the lower courts find a person guilty of murder, the High Court says he was not guilty and then the Supreme Court says the man was guilty. Again in both civil and criminal cases the judgements of courts at different levels are so different that it seems they are based on different laws. And if a court declares a cow as donkey, and if you are little bit late to go to the upper court to rectify that mistake they tell you that it is time barred. So a cow shall remain a donkey because the court has said that and if you refuse to accept that cow as donkey it is contempt of the court.

The higher courts have got another system where they can even refuse to entertain your appeals. They can simply shut the doors on you because they think they are overloaded with work. They have ears for high profile cases like the Hawala Scam even if they find no substance. But they are not ready to look into cases where people are suffering due to wrong judgements. In our rust and dust kind of files system, laws have to be updated and the system upgraded otherwise people will not care any more and the system will be rejected by the people. In a corrupt society where corruption is on in every field, the judges do not bother to see whether the judgement has been made according to the law or whether the advocate hired by the party has done his job for what he was paid. When the lawyer is bought over by the other party, the judges just shut their eyes as well.

There is no justice in this world. Sometime it is even difficult to do justice, for example what justice we can provide to a man who has been murdered, we cannot bring him back to life. So if his murderer is sent to jail or to the gallows it is only the control system where the fear of punishment keeps the crimes in check. What is justice? Giving a man his due is called justice. But can you give to a mad man his gun? Still we can make the judicial system more functional and the credibility of the system can be restored in a way that it helps people to get their grievances redressed within reasonable time and in acceptable manner. For this we have to change the laws and bring in reforms in the judicial system.

To start with, there should be only a four layers system. The local body stage, the district level, the state level and the union level. In all the levels, there should be two types of courts, the civil courts and criminal courts. In all the cases, there should be bench of three judges at all levels and they should pass a judgement unanimously or by majority. There should be time limit on the disposal of cases. Every case should be entitled for appeal till the highest level. No case should stay normally in any court for more than two years and nobody should be called to a court only to be told to come the next time. The business should be done on that day. When we shall have the three judge bench in a case it is unlikely that you can say to the people to come next time, because the judge is gone to sleep. Moreover, the judges should be asked to explain their judgements and make them according to law and that they should not be immune against wrong judgement. The laws need a review and the jungle of laws should be made simple and effective practically. The judicial system in the country should become also a national service like the IAS. There should be a judicial service where we can have a national academy of judicial system and the judges should be trained for at least five years and then they should start their career from the bottom line. The whole judicial system should work under the Supreme Court's direction and the ministry of law and justice should provide and cater to all the needs of an overloaded judiciary. The legal system in India needs a total overhauling. We have to make the laws simple and few, the system efficient and honest. To start with, we shall have common civil court and there shall be only one law for everybody. The lawyers qualifying system should be upgraded and the judicial service should be reorganised on the basis of top professional training and tests from the lower courts onwards, there should be bench of three judges at each stage of the courts and decisions should be written by all the judges with the majority upholding the decision. Every decision should be confirmed by the next court. The lower court judges should at least have a degree of master of law and experience as assistant judges for three years. There should be at least five years of distinguished service for promotion to the next court and the Supreme Court judges should have a degree of doctor of law.

To get all the cases in various courts of the country settled and justice done in time without delay and clear the backlog we have to fix time limit on all the cases, civil or criminal, to be heard and decided in reasonable time because Justice delayed is justice denied. Therefore, we have to appoint more judges.

Talking about the Laws and the Crimes

Crimes are as old as the mankind itself. Society calls them crimes. When the man was living in the stone age, the crimes were of the stones, by the stones and now they are of the diamonds and dacoits. Crime should mean a conscious act on the part of an individual against the society he lives in. An act may be a crime in one society and not so in another society. So is the punishment for crimes. It all depends how much civilised a society is and what a certain amount of people in power think the rules of the society should be. There are many kinds of crimes: physical and material crimes, individual and mass crimes, but both of them or all of them are supposed to be against the society. All societies have framed their rules and laws or regulations by individuals, assembly orders, traditions, conventions and regulations. Whatever become an irritant or threat to society is called illegal and to break those laws called crime. Many people commit crimes because they are not so much committed to the society they live in, or their need of the hour calls them to make an offence which is called crime. Crime is only a crime if you can punish the offender. A powerful person or a clever person can get away with all sorts of crimes if the society cannot get hold of him, but you know the limit and hollowness of the system called society.

Modern living styles and many kinds of people and so many kinds of their activities have brought in so many kinds of laws, making together so many kinds of laws makes it a jungle of laws. The jungle of laws makes people's life confused and miserable and controls the freedom of the people. Many power hungry people in power always think to control the freedom of the people and in a way they are jealous of the freedom of the people that they frame laws to rule them. Even in a democracy, people talk of ruling people. These kinds of feudal people are always trouble makers.

So what does a law mean literally. It means the generally accepted code of conduct. A law is that social behaviour of an individual which is expected by the society of such an individual as members or visitors of the society. While some of the social behaviour can be voluntary and most of it obligatory. To break the code of obligatory behaviour is called crime. Because there are different societies based on different religions, tribal traditions in India, but there is no need to make different laws for different people. India is a country of multi-religions with the freedom of religion. What laws we have are for general obligations, and the voluntary behaviour could be covered under those religious and traditional things.

Laws can be changed, dropped or framed whenever the legislature thinks there is a need with these amendments of the constitution so many times, people may think that the people that made the constitution were fools or they did not see the things what the Parliament sees today?

Well the constitution of the country is not a sacred book.

Even it is up to the people whether they like one sacred book or not. But it is the most important law book in the country. The makers of the constitution were distinguished and intelligent people. They were inspired by the freedom and the thoughts of freedom of the people, whereas many laws and amendments have been made to restrict the freedom of the people or to suit the whims and wishes of the rulers. Because one or two PMs haven't been the champions of the freedom, they want to rule this country by hook or crook. In their desperation they have brought changes in laws and indulged in amending and downgrading the Constitution. Indira Gandhi has damaged the constitution and the law authority in the country and social norms of democracy to a shameful extent. She was not a person motivated by freedom of the people or service of the people. She desired for personal power and her desire of family dynasty led her to so many black laws and amendments of the Constitution. Even today you see that when they fail to solve the problems they talk about the need to change the Constitution as if it is the Constitution that is the responsible person for the problems and is supposed to solve the problems of the people and not the government.

Some people may think that these kind of reckless changes and making more and more laws confuse the people and they no more care about what the laws in the country are, and even the Constitution. When India attained freedom, the purpose of making the Constitution was to ensure to the people their basic human rights even though they were not aware of them. Today the Parliament takes away their rights even if they have got awareness of their fundamental rights. The difference is in the thinking of the leaders. The post-independence leaders were those, who were freedom fighters and they wanted to serve the people and the country and make it a great country. But today's leaders are leaders of corruption, they serve and fight for corruption, they love corruption. If anything like freedom of the people comes their way, they have to fight not for freedom but to fight the freedom out itself so that they could rule and keep their regime and the lustful administration in power.

There is a need to bring this awareness among people about their rights and the anti-people laws. We should all fight them out and keep only those laws that are good for the people and the country. The people must fight for their basic human rights. It is a shame that the freedom of the people has remained a concept just on paper. The dream of a free country that is free from want, hunger and disease is still far away. It is disgusting that the Parliament under Indira Gandhi and Rajiv Gandhi had turned itself into anti-people and anti-freedom organisation rather than the institution for protection of the freedom of the people. Instead of representing the freedom of the people and their cause, they work against them and work as the loyal servants of the royal rulers of corruption which stinks.

Despite all these amendments to the Constitution more than 85 times, they have not framed one law to guarantee the people the basic human rights of life. They have not even thought of providing the starving people (to death) two meals a day, not to speak of clothes and shelter, public health and education.

It is possible that we can provide all the people the basic human rights with guarantee who do not have them and until these basic human rights are not guaranteed to all without regard to race, religion, caste and class, our fight for such a goal should continue. This can be achieved with the co-operation and support of the people. Otherwise we cannot claim to be civilised people. It is a crime against humanity that people in this world die of want, hunger and neglect. The crime against humanity is bigger than the crimes against society. All these governments and societies are criminal that do not provide the people the basic human amenities of life, that is food, clothes, shelter, house, health and education. All these amenities have to be provided by the state to such people who cannot afford. Only then we can claim to be civilised and to be a true democracy, otherwise there is no freedom.

Laws are made to serve the people, the society and the individual. The state makes laws for the welfare of the people. But can a jungle of laws really serve the people who even are not aware of the fact how many laws actually exist. Can we not reduce their numbers and make them practical and simple, so that a common man understands what the law of the land really is. We can make the laws of the land simple and less in number. For example, there are many sales tax laws and sub-laws and many different kinds of sales tax rates, creating a big amount of confusion and leaving a vast scope for corruption. We can just say that everything that is sold at shops be subject to a uniform sales tax. That every shopkeeper shall have a sales tax number and there should be just one rate of sales tax for all the consumer goods, so that it will leave less scope for corruption. It is very impractical to sell twenty kinds of goods to the consumers, with as many kinds of sales tax rates. It is a time killing system, and the consumer will not bother to wait for the sales bill and that is how the government looses revenue. It should be obligatory for both the buyer and the seller to use bill book. The consumer should always insist on the receipt. He is paying the tax anyway.

So I suggest that there should be just one limit on the consumer goods as a percentage of sales tax, say five to ten per cent whatever it is, on the whole bill. All the consumers and the sellers should be obliged to keep an account. Yes, this way seems simple and wise. But think about the items that some people think are for the rich people and they be made to pay more on the luxury items. The poor should not be taxed so much.

It is these type of discriminatory laws that generate corruption. The rich are supposed to pay income tax and wealth tax. On consumer goods we have to see that we encourage more consumption among the people, thereby encourage more production and more employment and our aim should be to lift the living standard of the people. There are these customs and excise duties that could be taking care of the luxury items because in that case the items can be separated easily, whereas in a shop where you have hundreds of items for sale, you only complicate the things.

Think about the demand of abolishing the sales tax. It is like asking for abolishing the whole tax system, you know tax system is like a contribution towards a common pool and because we want to make the state a welfare state. We will need money to make that and the money has to come from taxes. There have been no governments without taxes in all the history. We have noticed that the people in power and around them are so corrupt that they stink worse than anything. Take, for example, FERA, a law made by the parliament to control the foreign exchange, and you know how much money we have seen and found going out of the country and all is done by the people in power or in connection with them, and they are the ones who make laws like FERA, for whom? It is no secret that in all those defence deals a lot of money has been made and stashed outside and also in so many other deals of importation. The black money generated and channelled out of the country, even when the value of the Indian rupee has almost no international value because it is not fully convertible. The people in power, political or economic have never bothered to clear themselves of all the charges, No prime minister has ever bothered to tell the country, how much money he or she has, before the election and after the election. Then who is accountable. It is a power game to grab power and never bother about the responsibilities, or accountability What a state of affairs? An economy of black money.

Black money is the money that has been generated by avoiding taxes or by illegal means, I cannot say that we can eliminate the black money. But we can control and recover it. There could be a law that above certain amount you cannot keep money in cash in your possession. All the money above that has to be in the bank. Moreover, all the money recovered from anybody above that limit should be confiscated and all the transactions made above the limit be made through the banks. There will be no need for trial and the money thus recovered should be deposited with the treasury of the state. One thing that I would like to suggest is that if we accept such a limit, we will have to bring down the income tax rates to a reasonable limit. I mean it cannot be 95 per cent, it is really too high and even immoral, like its immoral to have made black money.

Agreed, but what do you think about a man in power whose money the law enforcement agencies would fear to touch or people who are protected by such men in power. You know these corrupt officials in all the departments. On the other hand, the men in power can really harass the people in opposition by such laws or blackmail people that have got the black money. We have to think about these kind of situations that are so obvious in India.

As I have mentioned before, you have to vote such people of integrity to power who could be trusted. Second, the wealth and black money department could function as an autonomous body like the supreme court and as there will be elections in the country, the governments would change. The new people and party in power can look into what the others have been doing.

One more question, about this department that is to be made concerned with black money, could it be a part of the income tax department? It could be, but there is a need to make a complete department. You know that all the workers or employees are paid their wages by the governments or by their employers for the work they do. Same way the employees of the income tax department, customs, police and the revenue departments are paid for their jobs. Isn't it strange and corrupt to pay commission money for the employees of these departments that I have mentioned, particularly on their unearthing cases of revenue, customs, smuggled goods and things like narcotics. What else they are supposed to do? Is not it a discrimination against other people in other professions?

Yes it is indeed a bad practice, that the people in those departments are rewarded commissions. It is a very corrupt practice. The foolish idea is that the public servants who catch huge amounts of money or gold, could be easily corrupted. But it is all corruption. The people in those departments should be able to perform their duties for what they have been employed like others. What else are they supposed to do. It is the same corrupt way of taking commissions on defence deals.

People in the army die fighting for the country. Teachers in the schools teach all the way till they are retired. Nurses in the hospitals serve the patients even in the middle of the nights. Drivers of buses, trains and trucks work in odd hours and so many farmers work in the scorching heat of the sun and toil their fields. Many people sweep the streets and even carry the shit on their heads, we do not reward them with millions, why these tax people should be treated like a class by themselves. The fact is that such lubricant jobs are given to the near and dear ones of the ruling party. Postings are made with premium money. Like such and such person can get posted in profitable position and place if he have paid such and such person in high up position or is related to or recommended by the high ups. These departments that are supposed to raid people some of them even steal things and money from the houses of the people on their raids and searches. Is it possible to clean these departments of corruption? I am sure you will say yes. Corruption is very bad and the people who are corrupt are really sick. The choice is with the people what kind of society they want, if they want to change they can do it without being misled or if they choose to be misled then it is their choice. There are many corrupt practices indulged in by the party in power during the election times that people do vote for the corrupt people because that way they think that the party in power will look after their interests. Now this mentality has to be changed.

Alcohol, Tobacco, Drugs Abuse and Awareness

The addiction to alcohol and tobacco is a very old disease. Many people die because of these habits. Sometime you see one province like Gujarat imposes prohibition and it does not work towards it. We have so many alcoholics all over the country. Alcohol has destroyed many people and has driven many families to poverty. It is because of the man who turns alcoholic and then his family suffers because he spends the money on alcohol. The wife and the children suffer because of this man and it is because of alcohol. There is no provision by the state where a family or a wife can complain about this alcoholic person and state can refrain such a man or put him in a rehabilitation centre. It is the state that makes money along with the brewery man but they take no responsibility and instead the state allows the alcohol products to be advertised. Many people commit crimes under the influence of alcohol, many accidents take place because of alcohol. We have so many patients with liver problems because of alcohol. People are corrupt because of alcohol. Most of the crimes including rape, murder, scandals, prostitution and corruption in all the departments are instigated by alcohol. Yet alcohol is the king that rules the world.

Tobacco is the biggest killer of people around the world. twenty-five per cent of people die prematurely because of tobacco. Yet its not a prohibited item. On top of that the Tobacco companies are sponsors of many sports events. Not because they want to help people get good health but because the popular sports events can be used to advertise the use of tobacco. No doubt, tobacco and alcohol are heavily taxed but that does not solve the social problem. Instead in many criminal cases where the persons are involved under the influence of alcohol, the judges become lenient and the criminals are let off. The people who suffer because of these smokers and alcoholics are never compensated. Alcohol is very old stuff, but the entry of tobacco is very recent. Hence, it can be controlled and all its advertisement should be banned.

The world today is alarmed of the rampant drugs abuse and there is allround campaign against it. There are many laws against the users of these psychedelic drugs all over the world, and many people are punished for it and in some uncivilised countries the punishments are inhuman and harsh. Still many people think that the laws against the use of these psychedelic drugs by the people is against the human rights. While some others who have had bad experience among their relations, ask for severe laws. It has become a social problem in the cities and there is a very heavy law against it now. Drug abuse is as old as the history of mankind, the plants that produce the drugs are as old as the other plants around. The plants with their narcotic and psychedelic substances are growing in the nature. They are there from *dhatura, bhang,* opium, poppy plants to coca plants. They are spread all over the world. The historical vedic stuff called *Soma Ras* is also derived from the concoctions of various herbal plants that have a hallucinating effect. The folklore in India traces *bhang* or *vijya* to be the cultivation of Lord Shiva. Many sadhus and babas of the chilum type believe that to be near Shiva Bhole Nath bhang or charas helps and it is not only an addiction but a ritual to have chilum and safi, etc. For them bhang is a satvic stuff and not a tamasic stuff like alcohol. It is really not addiction because you can live without it. Opium is derived from the poppy plants. The drug has more medicinal uses than bhang. But the opium products like heroin are killers, for its users. There are a lot of other drugs as well, like cocaine LSD, Mandrix, speed, and crack, etc., and other chemical drugs that have psychedelic substances that need to be discussed in detail.

First of all Ganja or Bhang alias Marijuana and *charas* or Hashish with its various forms have almost the same effect as a drug when used in its different forms and ways. Until 1937, it was not illegal in USA. It was legal in Nepal till 1973. It has been legal before that for thousand of years. It was made illegal recently, i.e., in the last fifty years. All the countries have banned it by law because of international convention against the narcotics. There is American pressure on the third world countries to make strict laws against drug abuse and narcotics.

But cannabis alias marijuana does not have narcotic content. As the folklore goes among the babas that Lord Shiva cultivated or invented Bhang, cannabis and all the Shiva devotees think that Shiva likes and has been consuming Bhang for many reasons as he was the one that took poison for the Gods because the other Gods could not. Therefore many Shiva devotees among the Babas do smoke or some smokers feel closer to Shiva. It is not necessary for every Shiva devotee to smoke it, that everybody knows. The plant is growing also in places where people do not believe in Shiva. The age-old cultivation of Bhang and its wild growth like any other plant or herb is natural. Things that are natural cannot be illegal. People cultivate the plant to make shoes and rope out of the peal of this plant. How you can deny them the cultivation of Bhang when you do not provide them jobs or money to buy shoes and ropes. If you deny people their livelihood without compensation, you are a criminal. People are poor and the new laws have made their life worse.

There is no serious medical effect of smoking Ganja or cannabis. Nobody has ever died or gone insane by consuming it. Though it can damage health but people can commit suicide while they are intoxicated. The religious right of Babas have been seriously affected, which is a shame because so many worse things are not only legal but bad. Here is, however, a question, why it has been banned, specially in recent times, all over the world. Though in Muslim countries and tribes who arc prohibitionists, *Hashish* is cultivated and smoked like anything, they do not care for international law. What is international law anyway; if you look at the opium wars with China during the British rule in India then you will see that there is politics in banning cannabis. It was during second world war that cannabis was made illegal, why? Because people who smoke or use cannabis do not like violence. They enjoy life with lots of laugh and fun on one side and on the other the drug helps those people to concentrate on themselves and they get a sense of Karma. The outcome is that the man who is smoking Charas does not like to join the army, to fight some bloody wars for stupid reasons of the king, a dictator or imperialist. He likes to live freely and even does not like to work when he or she does have to. This is bad for the capitalist or the state. Therefore, they who are rulers now must ban such a drug. It is a simple truth. Once they did it in the west, they asked the other countries of the third world to follow them. Most of the third world countries that have been former colonies just accepted the advice of their former masters. Nepal did it in 1973 and that was from much pressure from the US.

It is rumoured that Hitler gave alcohol and yava for the soldiers, cocaine for officers and consumed morphine himself to keep on the war. But no cannabis that shows that cannabis is for people who don't involve themselves with wars.

But narcotics are bad, there is no doubt about that but alcohol and tobacco should also be as bad as any of these prohibited drugs. Only then we can have full prohibitions. But we have seen that it has been very difficult for any government to continue with prohibition. Therefore, a new law is necessary to modernise the whole concept of alcohol and drug use. For example, all the dangerous drugs should be separated from mild drugs and the penalties should be on the quantity bases. We have in the country Adulteration in Food Substances Act as well. Many people had died of poisoning adulteration in mustard oil few years back. It is playing havoc with economy of the country and the life and the security of the people, but as always, nobody will get punished, but if you find somebody with 20 grams of ganja in his pocket, our great system will send them to jail for ten years and a fine of Rs. 1,00,000. This wonderful life in India needs to be investigated.

There is a need to classify the prohibited drugs. The Indian government has passed very stupid law, called the Narcotics Drugs and Psychedelic Substances Act, which makes no difference between these drugs and their quantity. Everybody knows that Bhang or Ganja is not Charas and Hashish. That Bhang is not Cocaine, LSD, or opium and that the opium is not heroin and morphine. But the senseless government in India has not bothered to know anything, all they have done is to make a law to show to the Americans or their stooges that they are hard on drug abuse and narcotics. In the process they have made a very stupid law that does not make a difference between a tola of grass to that of a ton of heroin. The result: there are more heroin addicts in the country than ever before. As long as the people and the government in the country keep going with the new laws, it will be making the country safe for heroin monopoly. How? Some idiots will ask. Simply because heroin and Brown sugar whatever they call it, makes people addicts and this addiction drives the users do anything mad. There are people at times who try to know these narcotics to see the change even for fun. When they do not find easy and soft stuff like grass, they take to heroin which is easily available in the metropolitan cities. Now people will ask why you see heroin is easily available. The answer is simple that the drug traffickers as they are called do the business to make money. Heroin people are those without conscience. When you see one person with one *tola* or 100 grams *charas* or *ganja,* it is very easy to find out. This almost harmless stuff is the option for the small man in the street to handle. This small man cannot corrupt the narcotic officials with his small money, so he is more likely to go to jail. On the other hand, a gram of cocaine or ten grams of heroin is easy to hide and much money and enough to corrupt a narcotic official out for *bakhshish.* Because the addicts of these hard drugs are desperate to get anything, because they need it, it is easy for the pusher of hard drugs to sell his stuff than the small dealer of *ganja* who even would not make two times meals for himself. There is this difference in smuggling. Smuggling a kilo of grass of few hundreds of rupees is difficult than smuggling of few grams of heroin worth lots of money. The small man who is less of a risk to society disappears from the scene and is actually thrown out by the mafia of heroin, which is a killer.

It is, therefore, time for people to wake up against the new law to make a difference between a tola of grass to that of a ton of heroin. People should make distinction between alcohol, charas, opium, heroin, cocaine, crack and LSD, etc., and classify them and provide different forms of penalties. There is a genuine voice for legalising cannabis, but it remains to be seen when some democratic people will manage it. President Carter thought of legalising it but could not prevail over the alcohol and arms lobby. There is another lobby against legalising cannabis also yet hidden, that is the cocaine and heroin mafia. In case marijuana is legalised they will loose lot of their addicts to cannabis and the big trade in hashish will also get out of their hands to the common man. Therefore, they have a vested interest in treating all the drugs on a par with each other or at least keeping them illegal. On one hand USA is trying to fight the drug menace with its public speeches and postures and actions and funds, with its other hidden hand, the well known CIA, it is trying to grab the heroin business. It is no secret that organisations like CIA and their agents among the mafia of the world over make the biggest deals, narcotics and the arms. This wheeling and dealing is going on while people, their own are hunted by the law agencies. Remember the case of red brigade in Italy. It was wiped out by the police eventually, but when the same chief of police expressed his determination to finish the mafia in Italy, he was found dead the next day. President Reagan spoke against drugs but never appeared for drug test though he appeared for AIDS test, his vice president Bush went to Pakistan and addressed a meeting of people against the drugs and those people appreciated his concern. Later, it turned out that the meeting of high officials and people that he talked to was none other than the international syndicate of heroin pushers.

The reason why they are putting pressure on the third world countries is because the money from the industrialised countries is going out to the third world, and thc value of their currencies will go down in terms of the currencies of the third world which they never cease to exploit. Therefore, they do not see the cannabi cultivation in the USA. Where it is called the Hot-Pot. Some countries of Europe like Holland and Spain which are moderate towards drugs of this kind, still they do not legalise cannabis but at least they make difference between heroin and cannabis. The Indian government did not take any advice from the medical or social scientists and the result is this stupid law that they have now. They say it had to be enacted under the international conventions and law. What is international law any way. A handful of countries led by USA, what they think is international law. Will they make a law to ban arms trading and gun running. Will they stop to make nuclear bombs and international pushing, dealing and blackmailing of arms? That is the trouble of the whole world. No that is how they make money and the rest-of-the-world has to follow them. The US president is the biggest arms seller for his country, so are the Russian, English and the French heads of governments. They make money and the western European countries make money by selling arms to the third world where the men in the governments make money as commissions and stash that money in Swiss banks. The black money from all over the world is good but a man cannot do with his life what he wants to do.

President Reagan told the prime minister of India that he will take care of the Sikh terrorists in the USA if Rajiv takes care of the narcotics going out of India. Therefore, the prime minister went to welcome the Catholic Pope on the airport on his arrival who drinks wine on the public stage, but made a law against *ganja* to put the Hindu *babas* in jail should they be found smoking. Now what is left of India. The hippie movement started in the USA, as the children of flowers. The young people did not want to fight the stupid American war in Vietnam. So many young people fed up with the American system started on their way to the east and they landed in the countries like India and Nepal for seeking spiritual solace. They met some smoking *babas* as well and some of them joined them, while others went to meditation and *yoga*. So stories of disease and starvation started to appear in the western media about India. And now they talk about the drugs. Drugs are as old as this world, but the present problem is emanating from the social degeneration of indifference and spoils. Western world with its industrialisation has brought the present generation to the shelter of drugs. They have to find out why they have failed.

The reason to make a heavy law about narcotics in India is due to the concern about it in the high middle class of the cities. The children of the high ups in Delhi and Mumbai are getting hooked. So they are worried because their children are affected. Therefore, wrong law. Where there are millions of the poor who are dying of want, hunger and starvation, there is no law. The government has nothing to do, because the people and the children that die because of starvation are not the children of the ruling class. Even those unfortunate people have a desire to live a life. Those addicts whose addiction is a matter of choice will not have this choice. They can drink alcohol though alcohol against which the father of the nation stood so high, alcohol that makes people so aggressive, that is the cause of so many crimes and lawlessness in the country, alcohol that is destroying many people and families, the people under the influence of alcohol are the worst kind of people, ask any woman, they will tell you how these people misbehave, molest and rape the women under the influence of alcohol. Yet it is legal and the army and police are free to drink it. It is amazing how a man under the influence of alcohol can be justified to arrest another harmless happy man smoking *ganja*. Islamic people are against the alcohol, Sikhs are against smoking tobacco and the Hindus are against beef but will the international law respect these values of other people. Alcohol is legal because the pope drinks it, so his followers, who have a history of war mongers and colonisation of the world. Mahatma Gandhi's *samadhi* have to be buried deeper down than it is today.

There is a strong case for legalising cannabis in India. No drug laws have succeeded in controlling the drug abuse in the west. All it has done is that more than half of their prisoners are drug laws offenders. The money of the common man is being spent on the police, on the jails and on those drug law offenders. Same is going on in India, the poor man's money is either squandered away by the politician or the police. Can we not spend this money on developmental work? In Morocco there is hardly any law against cultivation of cannabis. The country so close to western Europe, the country has become rich because of the cultivation of cannabis. Otherwise it would have been one of the poorest in the world. Where is the western concern for drugs buried in Morocco. If they did not allow the cannabis in that country that country would have gone communist. So is Lebanon where the army is supported by the money from cannabis. There are ten million smokers in Germany alone on a conservative estimate. Out of these, one million must be smoking cannabis. Even if they smoke one gram a day they will need one ton of cannabis per day. This is going there every day. So at least in the western European and Scandinavian countries they are having a supply of ten tons per day. India is being blamed by the west either for supplying these drugs partially or being used as the transit point. The government of India confirms their charge that India is being used as transit point. Whereas the truth is that India does not even produce or transit one per cent of what the world is consuming. Pakistan supplies 90 per cent of the heroin to the west. At least this have been confirmed by the studies and records of heroin catches in England, and yet that country under Zia who was himself involved in the heroin trade, got a favoured deal in economic and military aid by the USA block. The Mujahidin in Afghanistan sold *hashish* and heroin to the agents of CIA that gave guns to them to fight the Kabul regime. It is also possible that a part of Pakistan's nuclear programme is being financed by the heroin trade.

There is a heroin mafia emerging under the new law, so that they could control the heroin trade by politician, police and the courts. Otherwise how they can make such a law that makes no difference between *ganja* and heroin. There are many psychedalic drugs that have not been covered under the new law. What shall be the position of law about drugs like crack that have not touched the market in India yet. Therefore, it is time that the people and the law-makers in India have a fresh look at what they are doing to the people and the mankind, by making such laws. The right of the individual to do with his life what he wants to do, has to be respected. Second, a difference has to be made between psychedelic drugs and their quantity. Third, the addicts could be educated about the drug menace. To give the advertisement for occasional catches in the paper is not in the national interest, especially when the papers mention the high prices of such narcotics in the international market, that makes people curious and adventurous.

There are people that can also plant any drugs into the other people whom they want to put into trouble and bad name. Just a little bit of dope and they can send their enemy to ten years in jail. If the country can make money on alcohol cigarettes and sugar, etc., it can also make money by legalising cannabis, etc., and the money can be spent on the development and social work in the country. There are people that like one thing or the other, why people should be dependent on alcohol. Millions have died around the world by consuming alcohol, tobacco and sugar. Millions are dying of acid rains and pollution. Millions of abortions take place every year legally or illegally, billions of animals are being slaughtered by the people around the world, all these evil things are legal around the world but you cannot do with your life what you want to do. Good or bad, putting people in jails for using drugs on them is a clear violation of human rights. Nobody has ever died of smoking cannabis for thousands of years. Therefore, this law against cannabis, only the evil people or the ignorant can make such a law. In India where Shiva devotees among the Babas have been using cannabis for thousands of years, it is clear violation of the fundamental right of religious freedom and practice, is it not? Or the government will compel people like these vegetarian Babas to eat beef and drink alcohol to take them into the 21st century.

Penalties and Punishments

The nature of punishment depends on the nature and seriousness of crimes. It could be different in different societies and states in the world. The democratic countries have different ways of the trials of the offenders while there are different ways and punishments in dictatorships and they all differ in their character. Here we have to discuss our way of laws and punishments for breaking of laws, the mode of thinking of the people, and the outcome of those punishments. Whether they have succeeded in their mission to make this society free from crimes because the punishments are supposed to be exemplary, so that the other possible criminals are deterred from attempting those crimes.

Now we all know that there are different laws for different crimes all over the world for various offences and crimes. But here we have to discuss whether such laws and punishments have succeeded in making this world crime free? The answer is simply no, the rate of the crimes is on the increase everywhere. The punishment for crimes have not succeeded in either preventing crimes or providing justice. In most cases where people have been sent to jails they have come out as hardened criminals. This has not improved the lot of the society. Jails in India are money making wells. Where even the most dreaded criminals if they have money or connections in the higher centres of power, can take over the management of the jails from the superintendent of jails. In the jails there are these thugs that have to be obeyed by the newcomer. All kinds of crimes are planned and organised in and from the jails by the *dada* inside the jail. Even innocent people that could be jailed by the blind law agencies, because of the stupidity and wickedness of some policemen, or are framedup in false cases, could turn into rebels who indulge in crimes when they go out of jails. While some people come out of the jails totally recks. This is just a little bit of introduction of the jails in India. There are more harrowing aspects of the jail life in the country, like sodomy, rape, violence, and abuses of all kinds. The inmates of the jails do not get things to what they are even entitled to. The jail staff is corrupt like any other departments. The system of jails and punishment in India is totally outdated. The living conditions in jails are inhuman. In police lockups and judicial custody the conditions are worse. People are tortured to death even if they have not committed any crime, just on suspicion. If you could pay somebody money, you may be spared of all that trouble, even if you have committed some petty crime. Such things are well-known about the system in the country, they need no introduction. What we have and need to know is whether we want to change the state of affairs or let it go on like it is. What we need to know is the fact that aim of punishment and jails is to make the society safe from crimes and we have not succeeded. Therefore, we have to know why? This is not a small why.

We have to trace the causes of the crimes. If you make a survey of the people and win their confidence, you will come to know that most of them could have been punished for the crimes that they have made or the laws which have been broken and offences that they have committed—consciously or without. But they have not been caught or punished by the law. Then why we should punish just few of us. Then as we have not guaranteed the basic human rights to all, there are people that have no choice but to indulge in petty crimes. Because they need to fill their stomach, and they need clothes. You see there are so many beggars, there are people that have no jobs, now all of them cannot be expected to wash the dishes in somebody's house for nothing. Then there are these temptations to make crimes, coming from the media, movies, folklore and teenage sensations. More serious crimes come from ignorance.

Now the new awareness among people, the educated and civilised ones is that you do not keep people in jails as a matter of punishment or revenge, you keep them in jail because they are a threat to the individual and the society. Moreover, in some countries the jails are used as reform centres. Then we have to see how we can eliminate this threat to society and the crimes. Is it possible to eliminate crimes? Yes, it is possible to reduce the crimes and nearly eliminate them. Most of the crimes are taking place in the urban areas with the chaotic life of the cities. Material lust, wrong ideas coming from the wrong information motivate some people to attempt crimes. So many kinds of crimes from theft, stealing, cheating, corruption, violence against women, murder and wars all arise from ignorance, ignorance of the Karma, and the ignorance of the human rights. All kind of aggression being thought of emanates from the stupid ego of the people. Every need has an ego to feed and ego is the breath of crimes, the negative attitude of the offenders towards life drives them to commit crimes. Though there are people that might do so just to get it easily. There have been no crimes in the mountains until they were exposed to the people outside. People used to leave their homes unlocked and murders were not known till 1973 there was not a single murder case in Ladakh and now there are violent agitations going on there. The problem of crimes is mostly a state of mind. Though we are known as a country of great holy people and saints and sages. and on top of that producing Mahatma Gandhi and then our professed belief in non-violence, the country still hangs on to its barbaric methods. The spurt in violent activities and movements in the country and their suppression by violent ways and means have proved to us that we are still uncivilised as a country together. Strange are the ways of this world. When you kill a person in the society it is known as murder and when you kill people in war or fighting of small groups it is not murder.

I think it is all a question of human evolution, the human awareness has not touched yet a higher form of mind, these sages and saints we talk about had attained that higher state of mind that they were known as preachers. There are people like that among us today also, but our problem is that we suffer from wrong notions about people. Therefore we fail to understand the message of those great people, we have this stupid idea in the head of the people that those great persons of the past were just the reincarnation of gods. We called M.K. Gandhi, Mahatma Gandhi, because of his thoughts and ideas. Instead of following him or making good use of his thoughts we simply declared him Mahatma. Our political leaders every now and then pretend to follow him, and all they do is that they go to the *samadhi* at Rajghat to offer flowers and get photographed. Mahatma Gandhi does not live at Rajghat, most probably he lives in his thought in the books and with practising Gandhians. There are so many barbarians in this world that will not agree to give Gandhi a chance. I think Gandhi, our Mahatma, has answers to our social problems though not perfect, yet very valuable.

The way out is not difficult. First, we have to guarantee the basic human rights to everybody, which we are capable of.

More awareness of human rights of every individual and respect for them, social security of life and care. More harmony in the society, the child limit will work wonders. Again it is the question of education. We have to introduce Yoga and meditation practice in jails everyday. The inmates of jails could be asked for their options, if they like to stay in jails as usual or they want to learn Yoga and meditation to change their lives for the better. The people who will opt for Yoga and meditation should be separated into different jails, where there should be classification for those who have made more than six months and who are the beginners in Yoga and meditation. The people will change in their personality and outlook towards life. There will be no crimes inside these kinds of jails, and when the people will go out of such jails which should be called reform *aashrams,* they will be an asset to society rather than dangers. Those people will not suffer from any kind of complexes because of being in jails. In return they will not hit at the society again for revenge, Instead, because they will know better about themselves and the life, they will guide others. More people in gang stories or any other crime thrillers will not find any guru in the field of crimes. Instead, there will be these reformed people coming out of the reform Aashrams that will be better sensed than the ordinary people in the society. Even the police, the lawyers and the judges will learn from those people. Yoga and meditation should be developed as a new culture in the whole country and the world. Because this is going to be the common culture of all the people irrespective of their backgrounds and will bind all the human beings together with a new sense of society. People will respect each other for their opinions, professions, cultures, races and nationalities. Because they will find the new awareness in them that the civilised people have nothing to fight against each other, but to co-operate as human beings. The individual should also be free from the social clutches, and the individual should participate in social exchange out of choice and not of compulsion, this way we can make this world a better place for living.

We therefore need reforms and reviews of the laws and the judicial system in the country and the conditions of jails and its inmates have to be improved. There have been no improvement so far and there are many innocent people suffering from the rotten system while the rich and the organised criminals have become the politicians and they rule and continue to do their job in league with the law and order set up in the country. So it is about time that we do something about it as well.

Few clauses in the law on homicide and criminal assault have to be added for the sake of criminal justice. That the murderers be made responsible to pay not only the fine, which has to be raised, but a reasonable amount of blood money as compensation to the next of the kith and kins so that the loss of such a person could be compensated. In case the murderer is not able to pay, his/her sentence should be doubled and the state must pay compensation to the victim's party. Because state have failed to provide security to its people. The other clause that may be added is about the group assault where in situations like communal riots and gangwars, the courts fail to fix responsibilities because there is this law that a group of more than 8 people becomes an unruly mob and not a criminal gang. So this criminal gang or group, that could be responsible for mass murders and looting escapes the grip of law because the witnesses could not be relied upon or the unlawful activity could not be punished because it could have been done by any one of that group. Therefore to control such criminal acts, and save the sufferers from such attacks, it is necessary to blame all those people for such offences collectively so that such groups are restrained to be formed and activated in such manners. Therefore carnages like we witnessed recently in Gujarat cannot be repeated again.

7

Orientation in Foreign and Defence Policy

"If you want peace, be prepared for war", is a saying that really matters in our case of defending India. More than two thousand years of attacks through the Hindukush, since the days of Alexander, India has suffered loot and plunder by the foreigners and was enslaved for a long time till 1947. As there were weak rulers in the frontier provinces and there were no federal arrangements of defence between so many rulers throughout India to identify the enemy threats and develop a common defence system, against the alien races, India continued to suffer. Inspite of the Chanakya *nitis* and the glamour of Mahabharat we allowed the continent to suffer aggression by foreign and alien races. And since Independence we have got a different borderline to defend.

When we think of the defence of India we have to go back to its history as well. Though we had those wars in the Mahabharat and Ramayana periods, it will be more relevant to trace the need of our defence line from the days of Alexander, the great. Before that India had only wars within the continent. It was only in India that Alexander not only met resistance, but he decided to go back as well. Later on, we have had two thousand years of aggression from the foreigners and most of them came over Afghanistan and finally most of India was occupied and enslaved by the Mughals after the war of Panipat and later on by the British.

After India became free, it got not only a different border-line to defend but a different neighbourhood than the British India had, so our defence needs started in that perspective. Right from the day one India under the leadership of Nehru, the first prime minister, neglected the defence of the country. As a result of such neglect we were attacked by Pakistan and later on by China. Now we have managed to make India strong militarily, so that we are able to throw back any aggression. Still we have to look more into our defence needs and plan the defence system accordingly.

India is surrounded by seven countries. Out of these seven countries five were part of the British India, and now we have borders with all of them. Two of our neighbours are nuclear powers and hostile to India, i.e., Pakistan and China. These countries have a very long border with India. With Pakistan we have a border from Gujarat to Ladakh and with China from Ladakh to Assam. Burma is also not a friendly country with a long border, as well. That is several thousand kilometres of border with hostile neighbours to defend. Though we can manage our border problems with Bangladesh, Nepal, Bhutan and Sri Lanka, there is long coastal line to defend as well. From Kolkata to Kanyakumari and to Daman and Porbunder in Gujarat, this is another 3000 kms. Any body can attempt to attack us by sea. Therefore, the picture should get clear that we have to defend a very long defence line. India has a distinct and totally different security threat than most of the countries in the world. It is because we are a predominantly Hindu democratic state. There is only one country that is a declared Hindu state and that is Nepal which is our friendly neighbour. Bhutan is another friendly country and Sri Lanka and Bangladesh are not hostile towards India. Ever since Pakistan has been created, that country has remained hostile and inimical towards India. China is a communist country and looks upon India, since the takeover of China by the communists led by Mao Zedong, as a feudal capitalist country that needed to be turned communist. They started doing the same in Korea, where they were stopped by the Americans. So till now we have those two Koreas—the north communist Korea and the south democratic Korea supported by the USA. Recently we have noticed that this north communist Korea has helped Pakistan in the nuclear field and has supplied to Pakistan long range nuclear ballistic missiles. There was a time when the communist China was not allowed to be a member of the UNO. In those years India used to advocate China's entry into the UNO to make the world body more representative and yet China attacked India in 1962. China shall remain a threat to India as long as there is no democracy in China or a new strategic understanding is not developed by the two countries. China after the clash in 1962 has remained distant and has been maintaining close links with Pakistan. These two countries have created and remain a threat to India all these years. They have attacked us, taken our territory and have not developed friendly relations. Recently China created some confidence building measures on the borders and has stopped acting in a threatening manner. It is still not enough that they could think of friendly gestures. The Pakistanis have got nukes and they keep threatening India and supporting the terrorists against India regularly for the past two decades. They have their supporters outside India who need not be named that keep on helping Pakistan financially. USA and Saudi Arabia are two of them. Pakistan had joined SEATO in the 1950s and USA has helped Pakistan militarily and financially. Also during the war of 1971 President Nixon of USA had thought of dropping nuclear bombs on India.

Therefore, when we have problem with Pakistan we have to talk to so many countries whereas with China you can finalise anything without a third party. Since India has become a major power in the world with our nukes, the security concern of the country is greater than ever before. A country like Pakistan can drop a bomb on India like they sent in infiltrators in Kargil. Pakistan is not only a danger for India, it is for the whole world, because of their poverty and small size they cannot match India, therefore they are vulnerable to inducements from other parties. That is the most dangerous aspect of Pakistani nuclear power, because they can pass on the nuclear weapons to other countries for considerations other than Islamic fundamentalism, in that case many countries can suffer other than India. During the war of 1971 we have noticed how vulnerable India could get in times of crises. Therefore, we need a strong naval presence on both sides of coastal area, east and west. Though India has the largest volunteer army in the world, it is still the fourth largest army in the world. There are several countries combines that have as much soldiers as India. Since India has become a nuclear power, the combined armies of many countries against India would not be much of a threat. All that India needs now is a well equipped fighting machinery and sophistication in training of our soldiers. Indian people are second to none when it comes to patriotism and sacrifice. But we are not the best in training and equipment. It is these two fields that India has to improve. No doubts, a lot is being planned and done, we also need a proper political leadership in the country, we cannot afford to be lax. Until now we have found ourselves always unprepared.

The three wings of the defence department have to be enlarged, specially, the Air Force and the Navy. A lot remains to be done about the Navy. We need ships, submarines and highly trained men with bases far away from India on both sides of the country. We have to develop star wars technology and should be in a position to hit anybody anywhere in the world who could threaten us. At the same time we have to develop strategic understanding with many countries round the globe and form friendships, so that we could eliminate our enemies before they could think of adventure. At the same time India should pursue a worldwide campaign to limit the defence spending by all countries. India is one of the lowest defence spenders. We spend less than 3 per cent of the GNP on defence while Pakistan spends 13 per cent. India's total defence spending is one-fifth that of Britain and we have 15 times more people and area to defend than the British. So the per capita spending of Britain is 75 times more than that of India. The defence budgets of China and Britain are almost equal. So we can see even if our defence budget looks huge we are not spending too much. But we have to watch also that the money allotted to defence is not being misused or pocketed by some corrupt people. The working conditions of the soldiers have to be improved. The National Security Council should work and draw out a comprehensive future plan. When we talk of defence system it is meant to defend the country from external dangers. The external dangers could be economic as well, therefore, we have to really work a plan of military and economic defence.

As a result of cross world movement of the people, India has become vulnerable to not only military and economic aggression but cultural invasion as well. Therefore, when we talked about the education and cultural reforms we must find out the cultural threats and neutralise them, whether it is coming through people or any media. Defence of the country means that we save this country from all sorts of danger from the enemy, from the epidemics, from weather and from pollution and from the evil. The negative energy is so quick and destructive that we have to really care about it, in our lives. The positive energy is good but slow. It takes long time to build and grow, but the negative energy can destroy anything and anytime. Therefore, we have to be always alert and active about our defence line. In future we can be threatened by not only star wars but manipulated weather wars, bacteria wars, biological weapons and chemical weapons, that could be the handiwork of even the terrorists. The policies of the world trade organisation and the concept of globalisation only serves the interests of the capitalist advanced countries. Hence the economics of the underdeveloped and poor countries are vulnerable. Therefore, defence of economy is as much and even more important. India has to ask for global labour liberalisation and also pursue a policy for saving the planet from greenhouse effect. In sum, we have to identify our defence needs and develop an effective defence policy supported by a good foreign policy.

Detonating the nuclear devices and achieving self-sufficiency in the field of defence for the country is very much necessary. A poor and militarily weak, racially and religiously isolated country like India could have serious defence problems and it has been proved time and again that India has been attacked militarily by China and Pakistan because we did not have the matching military might to face these hostile countries.

Foreign Policy of India

The foreign policy of any country means thc policy of a country towards other countries of the world, the relations of one country with another country, and if there is a group of countries, that believe in the same philosophy and outlook, their relations with other country or a group of nations. It is meant to serve the national interests of a country in the best ways that are available to it. It is shaped to serve the interests of defence and the economy. The basis of foreign policy should be self-interests. So far as international relations are concerned there is no place for charity, morality or justice and principles, as it stands today. There should nevertheless be an international consciousness and awareness of the problems of the countries of the world and exploitations by one of another.

The foreign policy of a country is mainly decided by geopolitical situations, defence needs and economic realities. Ideology, if any, comes next. History of a country can be also a big factor if the country is a theocratic state or a conservative isolated regime, a racist or a fascist, or a crusader of liberty. These factors are the choices of the governments that represent or are in the control of the country. It all depends who wants what, but we are concerned with the foreign policy of India, what it should be like and how it can achieve the goals set by the values that India stands for.

India arrived on the world scene as a free and democratic country in 1947, after getting the independence and the partition of the country from the British. This was the time when the second world war had ended and the cold war had started and the two opposing blocks of the countries led by USA and USSR were trying to involve as many countries as possible and align them on their sides. Since then the balance of power and balance of terror systems have come up. But at the same time there were some people and statesmen in the world that did not want to go with those blocks and they were intelligent enough to stay away from this cold war strategy of the two blocks. Also they were not ideologically close to any of these blocks. Because one side represented the capitalist world while the other communist world, so most of the third world countries that had just got freedom and wanted to develop themselves opted not to be slaves to any group. They wanted to be free, yet not capitalist, progressive but not communist, so in the broad sense they opted for non-alignment with India as one of the founders.

When free India arrived on the world scene, she had the unique and tremendous opportunities open to her in the international relations. (1) The socio-political environment which India inherited at the time of independence and the big size of the country both in population and area and a champion of freedom everywhere; (2) the advantage of Mahatma Gandhi's influence on the minds of the people and governments all over the world; (3) the end of the Hitler's Germany; (4) weakening of Britain; (5) the crudeness and ruthlessness, authoritarianism and lack of sophistication of Russia; (6) America's hysterical crusade against communism, and the emergence of free countries in the world, that have been under the colonial rulers, like India. These and many other factors gave India a place on the world stage with many eyes on, looking for guidance and co-operation.

Partition of the country and the creation of Pakistan bought with it problems for India in the diplomatic world, and put India's diplomacy on a big' test from the very start. Pakistan which was created by the imperialist axis of Jinnah and Churchill to check India's growth as a giant of Asia, kept its anti-India propaganda alive since its creation. It turned out and slaughtered all the Hindus and Sikhs and other communities in Pakistan. The non-Muslims had to leave that country of fanatics. Only a small number of non-Muslims could remain behind in east Pakistan (now Bangladesh). The Islamic base of Pakistan's creation, has been used by Pakistan to gather support in the Islamic world in its opposition to India. Not only that, Pakistan invaded India in Kashmir, it entered into SEATO and made India more vulnerable. As a result of the creation of Pakistan, our western and eastern borders became vulnerable. India wanted peace and progress, her future plans were based on the Gandhian outlook of life and the world. There was no place, for force, capitalism, dictatorships, or fascism in India's national and international policies. Hence India's policy of non-alignment, secularism and panchsheel came up.

We should have an enlightened foreign policy in the self-interest of Bharat and the world at large. We should look upon all problems of war and peace viewing the interest of the nation and the mankind. Permanent peace is not possible without a strong country. So long as there exists political slavery, economic exploitation, social discrimination and selfish lust for power, India cannot progress as a strong country. History has shown time and again that weakness is a curse, and that if one wants to live freely and with honour it is essential to have military and economic power. The foreign policy of a country is a necessary adjunct to its defence policy. India's foreign policy needs to be reoriented to make it a fit instrument of winning friends and isolating enemies. International policy of a country is a matter of relationship between two countries irrespective of the type of governments it has for the time being. It is to be determined by the national interests and not by the interests of the people that may be in power. To tie the foreign policy down to the ideological likes and dislikes or personal whims of any individual or group of people who may happen to be in power in any particular time in disregard of wider national interests is indefensible. Therefore, a non-partisan national policy instead of partisan and coloured policy should be the normal practice.

Hence India should not look at the world in terms of blocks, rather it should look at the world of individual countries. Therefore, the need and will to enter into bilateral relationships with each one of the countries on the basis of mutuality of interests and reciprocity arises. To contain our hostile neighbours, China and Pakistan we should develop friendship with the countries of the region through bilateral alliances and pacts of trade and technology and contacts of people. It should not matter which blocks they may belong. Therefore, we should normalise relations with Taiwan and the ASEAN group of countries and help Vietnam economically and in defence. Other SAARC nations should be helped in their growth by India. Israel, the west Asian country should not be ignored. It was foolish that India did not develop cordial relationship with that country for long.

Every country has a right to choose its friends and allies according to its own assessment of its interests. Therefore, in the present international situation and more particularly keeping in view our relationship with China, the talk of non-alignment is wrong and irrational and uncalled for. The aim of foreign policy is to win friends and when we say we are non-aligned, it leaves little space for other countries to think before having friendship with India. This talk of non-alignment should not stand in our way because no country can afford to be non-aligned and you see it is these super powers that have got these blocks. China-Pak connection and there is hardly any country that docs not have any alliance. For India, who is neither a factor for peace and nor a terror of war, talk of non-alignment is just wishful thinking.

The decision to be non-aligned was bit legitimate in 1947 and the continuance of such a policy simply led to tragedy. Non alignment could have been used as a policy of peace making strategy in the 1950s. When the bipolar system transferred into the multi-polar system, we should have adjusted our foreign policy accordingly but till now we find ourselves so unprepared, till recently because this was never done the Dogma of non-alignment became the cause of our failure.

If Pakistan and China had not been inimical and hostile towards us, our foreign policy might have taken a different shape altogether, but since they have not improved, we have to keep in mind our relationship with them while formulating our foreign policy. Therefore, necessary steps should be taken to recover the territory aggressively taken and occupied by China and Pakistan. Both China and Pakistan have created for us conditions of hostility not only on our borders but in the world family as well. We have no friends in the world. The so-called friends show their backs when approached to support us. A complete failure of our foreign policy in south-east Asia, in Europe, Africa and America is a living proof. Indian interests and the interests of the people of Indian origin are not safeguarded. We are always isolated. It is no solace to feel that Russia supports us sometimes. The not so past history of the relations between us reveals that USSR was never a good friend of India till 1969. It has become friendly due to the recent developments in the balance of power system that has shaked Russia considerably.

It was in India's interest and in the interest of world peace for India to keep out of the cold war that was raging and going on between USA and USSR, and concentrate on its own development. India wanted peace and did not want to spend the money on armaments and raise a big army. They wanted to spend the money on the progress of the country. In that context, the policy of non-alignment that India developed and adopted in respect of the two super powers being USA and USSR, had something to commend. But success of such a policy depended on two things: first, India should not have given the impression that it was leaning on or favouring one side or the other in various disputes between them. It demanded some kind of self-restrain and self-abnegation, in the sense of deliberate silence on issues involving USA and USSR in which India's interests were not directly involved. Second, India should have built up its economic and defence strength at the fastest pace. It should have reduced its dependence on other countries particularly USA and USSR. But while the makers of Indian foreign policy talked of non-alignment, they failed to fulfil this idea, these two so important for its success. They leaned on one side or the other by turns and not necessarily by merit, thus making India a suspect in the eyes of both the blocks.

The policy of keeping aloof from the Russian and the American blocks was in the best interest of the country. But the way it has been pursued has given the impression that India is a friendless country. The way in which the promoters of this policy speak, gives an impression that this policy is something sacred and for the maintenance of which even the interest of the country should be sacrificed.

When the world was divided into two blocks, there was some sense in this idea of non-alignment. The world situation has changed now. In the 1960s why does it seem that our investment in international relations had proved and turned disastrous for the country. Why and how China, Japan and Germany that were lying prostrate in the 1940s had overtaken India so rapidly. With the emergence of communist China as a major power and its attack on India in 1962 gave rise to a new situation with China entering into the nuclear club. It became a real threat for Russia. The Sino-Russian relations which were getting cool became further strained. This resulted in a thaw in the east west cold war, the USA and USSR developed a common interest in peace in the face of a new threat from China.

The cause for China's attack on India in 1962 is attributed to China's ambition to weaken India, which could be a rallying point for the weaker Afro-Asian countries. India was emerging as a giant of world peace on the world scene because of its role between Russia and USA and was becoming popular. China felt jealous and gave India a humiliating reverse by attacking and grabbing thousands of kilometers of its land. This situation made the world multi-polar in which India and China became two new poles and the policy of non-alignment became irrelevant and out of date. To call China's attack against India, a betrayal is ridiculous and an insult to intelligent and thinking people. On the contrary, Nehru thought that he could take care of China's aggressive action through his self elusive foreign policy. Nobody in the world came to India's help. People like President Prasad had warned Nehru when China overtook Tibet, but Nehru did not protest against China. Instead he tried to appease them by accepting Tibet as part of China. He then allowed Dalai Lama with thousands of Tibetans to take refuge in India. This infuriated the Chinese and made India a suspect in the eyes of China. The power game in China between Chou and Mao is believed to have been one of the reasons for Mao to attack India, because Chou was getting in international stature through Nehru. China had watched the Bandung Conference of non-aligned countries and had seen how popular India was.

Then followed the 1965 war with Pakistan, again nobody came to support India. Pakistan was clearly the aggressor, but India found itself lonely. Loneliness may be good for a lunatic but not for a country. In 1971 Bangladesh action when India relieved millions of Bangladeshis from the genocide by the Pakistani Army, the American President threatened India of dire consequences. It is reported now that he thought of a nuclear attack on India, should India go into West Pakistan.

Foreign policy is a policy and not a principle. Therefore, this talk of non-alignment is unnecessary, uncalled for and not in the best interest of the country. Instead, India should have a firm, solid and independent foreign policy which may help India to gain friends and allies against the combined menace of China and Pakistan. The four fold objectives of foreign policy are to make friends, to strengthen relations with the old ones and to minimise the number of the enemies and to neutralise those who cannot be befriended.

The Indian foreign policy makers never thought of the country whose foreign policy they were making. They just looked at it vaguely. They never thought that India with its predominant Hindu population which no other country in the world had. Though the kingdom of Nepal is an exception, but how much Nepal matters in the international politics. Great principles were incorporated in the foreign policy and India allowed itself to be used without any long term gains. Our hostile neighbours made a joke of our foreign policy. Nobody supported the cause of the largest democracy, yet the poorest democracy of the world. We have to take into consideration that India has been a land invaded by everybody, over the last 2000 years for loot and plunder, and finally has been enslaved and colonised. And that the idol worshippers will never be praised and liked by the Christian and the Muslim countries of the world. That is why we are a friendless country. Apart from economics, there are four major factors in the world politics that is race, religion, region and ism, and the Indians have no support on these counts.

First, India itself is racially mixed up and we do not look like any other people of the world. Second, religiously we are a predominant Hindu country simply because of the Hindu population. Hinduism in itself is non-partisan in its outlook but how many non-partisan countries are there in the world. There is no country in the western democratic world that is secular, though they have the social liberty, but they have a dominant Christian traditions and outlook. They just do not understand Indian culture and, therefore, you cannot count on them for friendship or an Oscar award for any Hindi movie. Those very small number of people among these countries that are interested in the Indian culture are branded hippies and India is not kind to them either.

Then apart from the Christian block we are surrounded by the Muslim countries. It does not matter how many times these countries fight among themselves, but when we have a dispute or war with Pakistan, most of them will call for an Islamic solidarity. Though India has the largest Muslim population in any single country of the world after Indonesia, yet the Muslim countries do not take this into consideration. And Buddhism does not count in international relations like Hinduism. Though the Hindus and Buddhists together can be two billions. Therefore we should not forget that racially and religiously we have no support. Though these factors appear ugly to modern man, the fact remains that most of the countries are still under the rule of ugly and uncivilised men.

Regionally we have this Indian sub-continent label and in the sub-continent we have this SAARC association, which is an experiment. In the SAARC the participants do not feel equal, and they believe more in leg-pulling than in cooperation. All the countries in this region are different in their political set ups. We have Pakistan either under the army or democracy sometimes but Islamic always, and hostile to India. Nepal, a kingdom resisting Indian domination over that country. Bhutan, a non-entity in international politics and Sri Lanka with its domestic problems. Burma not a member yet, Bangladesh another dictatorship with Islamic colour and now democratic and under the leadership of Awami League is still experimenting democracy. Within India, the communal and regional parties weaken India's stand internationally. All the countries in this region have a friend or a judge in the international politics with opposing interests. Therefore, the SAARC can be wished well. We have found, therefore, that India has problems rather than solidarity in the region. Now the question of ism. The world is divided primarily into two blocks after the second world war into communist and the capitalist blocks. Free India though capitalist and feudal, preached socialism, annoying the western block and the communists never looked at India as a socialist country which we are not. So on both sides we do not have solid connections as far as the ism are concerned. Ism has been a strong factor in the international politics. Though both the blocks are not as united as before in their perceptions of the world, but the factor is strong as before.

So on all these counts we have seen that India stands alone and lonely. The last and most important factor in international relations is the economic strength, trade and communication between the countries. India can count on this according to its relationships with other countries. Success of such a policy depends on the trade between India and other countries. Investment by individuals and countries and not by the multinationals. We need collaborations and balance of trade in our favour. Balance of trade could establish India, but though we are the sixth largest industrial country in the world we do not count for much in international trade not even one per cent.

We are neither good buyers nor good exporters. We are not good buyers because we buy petrol, guns and bombers and we are not good exporters because we do not produce good quality and we do not keep ourselves up in technology. We buy outdated systems. We have to open ourselves to the international levels of investments, technology and trade. Even if we do not make much progress in international trade, we should be able to keep balance of trade in our favour. Bharat, i.e., India has an image of a country that is poverty-stricken, where millions are dying of starvation and disease and there is no sanitation, which is true. Unless we improve on this front we cannot get any medals at the Olympic.

Apart from the economic strength and self-reliance, India needs a good defence policy. Foreign policy goes together with defence policy. India's defence policy suffers from guilt consciousness and inferiority complex. Guilt consciousness is coming from preaching peace and disarmament, and inferiority complex is our heritage, complicated by our English medium schools, bureaucrats and policy-makers who do not know much about India. That is why Nehru neglected India's defence, Indira Gandhi had asked for foreign interference in our domestic affairs because of her visionless mind. Rajiv felt at home with his western style tastes and friends. India's bad luck has been its Prime Ministers who have been of mediocre, calibre and mind. They do not know how to build up this country and establish itself in the world community. If India counts internationally it is because of its size and population and big possible market for the international trade, and not because we have a foreign policy. Therefore, I will conclude that India has to make two things clear, to promote its foreign affairs. First get rid of its poverty among its citizens and second make India safe militarily. Only then we can have an independent foreign policy and dignity.

Self interest is inherent in every individual and country, the great saints and kings who served humanity, doctors or nurses, teachers and social workers, everybody did their bit because of their nature and to do things of their liking was and is their interest, that pleases their aspirations. Now India as a free democratic country aspiring for socialism, secularism and peace as a champion of freedom, not only contradicts itself domestically but finds the world outside conducive to its principles. As must be clear to everybody that the free democratic world need not look for a guide in India, the socialist countries do not need to learn socialism from India and the Islamic fundamentalist have no ears for secularism. The world is full of these three types of countries, so what use are these principles that we preach to outside world. At home we have not been able to get rid of regional and communal parties, and on the issue of freedom and liberty, we are suffocating it by making internal laws that make the freedom of the individuals a risk of life. Therefore, we cannot preach liberty to the outside world while many of the countries remain under dictatorship. With our economic and defence system so weak we cannot sustain such principles. India could have democracy and peace as its principles and we could work for such principles and ideals but we have not and could not do anything. For example, we agreed to have monarchy in Nepal and Bhutan could not sustain democracy in Bangladesh soon after its creation and have earned the Sri Lanka problem. We let the Chinese legalise the invasion of Tibet. Our whole neighbourhood could have been democratised, we deal with dictators everywhere. We have not succeeded in protecting the interests of the people of Indian origin outside India. The case of Fiji is most recent and biggest failure of Indian foreign policy, where an elected government of the majority of the people of Indian origin was thrown out by an armyman of the ethnic minority. In countries like Uganda, Tanzania we could do nothing for those unfortunate people of Indian origin who got kicked out and their properties confiscated. There is hardly any country in this world where we do not run into difficulties even to get a tourist visa. So you must see the contradictions of our principles. In most of the voting at the UN, India could not manage more than half a dozen countries on its side just because there is no place for preaching and principles. We criticise Israel for its occupation of Arab territory and refused to have diplomatic relations with that country till recently, but we want friendship with Pakistan and China who have not only attacked us but have been holding our territory. We are doing nothing for democracy in the sub-continent and the world over, do we have any principles?

Some people may ask how Indira Gandhi invited foreign intervention in our domestic affairs while she has been known for complaining about the foreign hands, so common a statement when things became unmanageable. Since the split in the Congress party in 1969 Indira Gandhi sought the support of the Communist party of India which is known to be pro-Russia. It was to the so-called syndicate in the Congress which to some extent was pro-west that wanted to throw out Indira, not because of her policies or for anything, but because they had this power game going on. Russia had interest in supporting her because she will support them in return. This arrangement worked till her end. In her appeal to Russians in 1982 she asked the Russians to discipline the communists and the left parties in India, which was an open invitation for the Russians to intervene in our affairs. During her visits to USA, Europe and Australia she went out of her way to blame the right wing parties for causing damage to the economy and for attempts to destabilise the country. Did she mean that the capitalist countries should bring pressure on these parties to fall in line with her. Still before the 1980 elections she had a dinner party with the ambassadors of Arab countries and exploited the occasion to make it appear as if the Arab Muslim countries supported her and that the Indian Muslims too should support her in the elections. That was an attempt to involve the Arab countries in the internal affairs of the country. All these and many other attempts were totally against the dignity and sovereignty of the country. She got away with it. She forgot conveniently how the Indian delegation headed by Fakhrudin Ali Ahmed to the Rawat Muslim conference had been humiliated. For a secular country participation in such a religious political conference is a clear violation of Indian constitution. Mrs Gandhi's remarks against the communists were not in good manner. The communists were and are trying to come of an age and had begun to take an independent line on domestic issues. This was a far out development from the behaviour of the communists during the second world war when they sided with the British, because the Russians have been at war with the Nazis during the Quit India Movement, when they abandoned the nationalist movement for freedom. The accusation of destabilisation shows only one thing that they do not know how to manage this country and the very often repeated stories of foreign hands are nothing but misleading and cheating the people. If they cannot stop the foreign hand from operating, they should resign, but they won't.

Think about the leakage by Mrs Gandhi of the secret visits of Israeli minister to India during the Janata rule. First, Morarji should not have kept it a secret as a true Gandhian, and the country should have been taken into confidence. I am sure the country would have appreciated the visit, and the majority of people in India wanted better relations with Israel. If the visit has been kept secret then Indira Gandhi was not serving any national interest by revealing the secrecy. It only made India a suspect. Her political interests to mislead the Muslims were more valuable than the national interests.

Israel is a democratic country in west Asia, India being a democratic country should have full diplomatic relations with that country. We shall gain more for the country. The Muslim countries did not make any protest to the western countries having diplomatic relations with Israel. If India did not take this step it was because the party in power did not want to loose the Muslim votes, which they believe that they could always mislead. In fact India with its diplomatic relations with Israel can help in bringing peace to west Asia and help the Palestine and the Israelis to reach a settlement and such a settlement will be good for Palestine. Otherwise I doubt they could even achieve anything by confrontation. Israel is the Karate champion of that region, the more you attack that country the more it will feel insecure and it will attack back more ruthlessly. They do not have any doubt about their interests like India. India can very much benefit from the friendship of Israel. The Israelis have the best solar energy technology. The Jews know that India is the country where the Jews have never been persecuted. Egypt has not suffered in its relationship with other countries in the region because of the Camp David agreements. It should be made clear to those countries that India believes in having diplomatic relations even with those who have attacked us recently and have occupied our territory. If a country chooses to strain their relationship because of our better understanding with Israel, it will be their choice and India should deal with them accordingly. We need to have an Indian foreign policy and not an Arab foreign policy.

As far as the Indian Muslims are concerned they have not made a serious protest on such a policy. It is only the Congress policy of abuse and misuse of the religious feelings of the Muslims in India for vote catching that they assume that the Muslims will resent it. Like the Khillafat movement in British times when even Turkey was not protesting but Gandhi had made it a point that the Indians should participate in the protest. How many people have cared for the Iran Iraq war. India as the Chairman of the non-aligned movement could not convince them of the futility of war, but in the end they accepted the western sponsored ceasefire after so much devastation. Peace in west Asia cannot be achieved by throwing the Israelis into the sea. The cause of peace will be better served if Israelis are made to talk across the table. The peace in that region is not only good for the people there but for the whole world. Hence there is no need to think that our relations with Muslim countries will deteriorate, as a result of better relations with Israel. I want to add that it was funny not to allow Indian Tennis team to go to Israel while we allowed the Israeli team to play in Delhi the previous time. Also in the Asian Games the Indian government took a very immature stand by not allowing the Israeli team. India only has made a laughing stock of its foreign policy.

The first prime minister Nehru had told the Israelis that the question of their recognition and full diplomatic relations depended on Israel to solve the problem to the satisfaction of Arabs, that of Palestine. The former foreign minister in the Janata Party A.B. Vajpayee had said that Israel was more close to India during 1962 and 65 rather than, when the Israeli foreign minister visited during Desai's tenure.

Enquiries confirm Mr Vajpayee's claim that Israel was more closer to Delhi in 1963, 1965 and 1971, than under the Janata Government. In January 1963 the then army chief General Mr J.N. Choudhry had invited Israel's chief of the army, and chief of the military intelligence to visit Delhi on their way back, then on an official visit to Rangoon, to exchange views with India's top military intelligence in the wake of India's military debacle against China. General Choudhry could not have done this without Mr Nehru's clearence. Again Mr Vigel Alon, a member of the Israeli cabinet, visited India in 1965, and not only met Mr Lal Bhadur Shastri but Indira Gandhi as well.

During Mr Nehru's time, three secretaries of the Congress parliamentary party visited Israel on special passports and they submitted reports on their return to Mr Nehru. With the change of government in Delhi in 1977 and Mr A.B. Vajpayee becoming foreign minister, the Israelis had developed optimism by Mr Vajpayee's two visits to Israel as a Jan Sangli M.P. and leader, who had publicly supported the Israeli case for diplomatic recognition. Therefore, Mr Dayan, the Israeli foreign minister expressed a desire to meet the new government. The visit was undertaken by Eisenburg who represented some top companies of the British, French and the Germans in India. Dayan arrived *incognito* in Mumbai by an international commercial flight and was received by Eisenburg along with the men of RAW and was brought to Delhi by CBI chief John Lobo in an IAF plane. Desai handled the entire operation personally and kept it a secret. Neither Vajpayee nor the foreign secretary Mr Jagat Mehta were taken into confidence. Mr Vajpayee was called in when the Israeli minister arrived at Desai's residence. The meeting lasted two hours. Dayan stayed overnight in a RAW guest house and expressed desire to see an Indian village. He was taken around Gurgaon.

Contrary to reports, Dayan did not come to Delhi only to secure establishment of full diplomatic relations with India. Tel Aviv was aware of Nehru's views and notings on the subject of having no diplomatic recognition and relationships unless the Palestine question was solved to the Arab satisfaction, indeed Desai's stand confirmed their fears. Originally the idea was to seek Indian permission to upgrade the Israeli consulate in Bombay and further shift it to Delhi. The Israeli consulate in Bombay had been barred from visiting Delhi without the permission of the external affairs ministry. Dayan was here also to persuade India to extend support to Camp David peace talks at a time when President Carter had run into difficulties with the Saudis and the Arabs.

The crucial question is : did Mr Desai and Mr Vajpayee compromise India's interests? There is no mistake if they met the Israeli minister, actually it should have been done openly. Do we not talk to the Pakistanis with whom we had wars and who have occupied our territory, and the Chinese who have attacked us and are still holding our land? Mr Desai did take care to protect, preserve and promote India's interests. He and Mr Vajpayee made it clear to Mr Dayan that India appreciated Israeli view that it cannot be thrown into the sea. However there could not be diplomatic recognition of Israel as long as the Palestine question remains unsolved. Mr Desai also told him what could be helpful in arriving a settlement. The important thing about the trip was that Desai shared his views and the Israeli reaction with Egyptian Vice- President Mobarak and the Syrian President Assad when they visited Delhi.

Now there will be another question as well. Why Mr. Vajpayee did not extend diplomatic relations with Israel, to which he was committed as Jan Sangh leader. The answer is simple, that he was not the foreign minister of the former Jan Sangh, he was the minister of the Janata Party which was dominated by the former Congressmen including the Prime Minister who took the traditional line of cowards. Mr. Vajpayee's mission as foreign minister was not just to extend diplomatic relations with Israel but to do many other things. But he could have managed the Israeli affair with efficiency if he was given the chance. Even now it is not too late, if India and Israel want good relations, there should be no obstacles, the friendship could be achieved in the cause of world peace. Finally, Narasimha Rao could be given the honours for making full diplomatic relations with Israel. Israel and India can develop a strategic relationship not only militarily but economically as well.

Vital national interests have been and are being recklessly sacrificed at the altar of power politics. Little has been gained and much lost from India's point of view, in the foolish and unfortunate controversy raised by Mrs Gandhi over the visit of the Israeli foreign minister to Delhi in early 1978 and the meeting of the former Prime Minister Desai with the South African foreign minister at Frankfurt. India's credibility has suffered and suspicions aroused all around especially in the Arab world and in Africa over Delhi's basic intentions as distinct from the declared policies. India's decision to recognise the PLO has no doubt helped out, the damage caused will take time to repair. India's policy of tilting cannot help it. The stories of the so-called visits and meetings of the two ministers during the Janata rule cannot be projected as crime on the part of the Janata government. Indeed Mrs Gandhi had damaged India's credibility abroad and committed a breach of trust by making those statements uncalled for. She seemed to have preferred personal interests over national interests, which is a preference she had taken many times. The utterances by her were meant to please the Muslim and the Russian lobby in India, it did not serve any national interest. Mrs Gandhi did use that as a political weapon against the opposition, which promoted Mr Desai to reveal another secret that the Russians had asked him to teach Pakistan a lesson, when Pakistan started to oppose the Russian involvement in Afghanistan. India could have used that opportunity to hit Pakistani nuclear refinery at Kahuta with the Israelis. Because of the Israelis, the Americans would not have made much fuss about that as they make stands against India very often.

Mr Desai saw nothing wrong in meeting the South African foreign minister at Frankfurt at the latter's request and what is more, it was done at the pressing behest of some prominent people of Indian origin settled in South Africa. The South African minister wanted to seek Mr Desai's guidance in regard to matters concerning persons of Indian origin to South Africa, such as certain adjustments in the government of the country. Mr Desai saw through the game which was meant to delay the rising tide of anti-apartheid movement. The South African regime wanted to win over the Indians by offering them more autonomy in predominantly Indian areas. Mr Desai wanted the Pretoria regime to accept the majority rule thereby serving the cause of the freedom of the people. In fact, he told the South African minister that he had advised the King of Nepal and Shah of Iran to be realistic and democratise their regimes before it was too late.

Secrecy is vital to diplomacy as it is to any other business, even in the present day of satellites and push button communications. All countries have used it to advance their national interests. India is no exception, Nehru kept the country in dark for four years about the Chinese border, hoping to sort it out secretly. It is believed that Mr Morarji Desai while serving in the Nehru cabinet disclosed the secret. The ill advised disclosures need to be investigated in depth, nobody should be allowed to say hell to the interests of the country. We in India were taking a sharper and stronger position against South Africa than many other members of the UNO and more especially the African countries themselves. In sharp contrast to the firm stand that India had taken over the years, almost all the African States did trade and other dealings with South Africa, in one way or the other.

There are more than 3 million people of Indian origin in South Africa and we have not been able to do anything for them either. We had the most hostile foreign policy towards Johannesburg than any other country in the world. Because of the racist regime there who believed in the total separation of people on the grounds of race and colour, and due to that policy of the ruling white minority, it was not only the coloured but the majority black people who had been denied their legitimate place and share in the set-up of that country. The Indian Passport was not to be used to go to South Africa. The Indians could not even go to see their relatives in that country and, therefore, in a way the Indian government had compelled its people not to have even the contact with their relatives in South Africa. On the other hand, the Pretoria regime had approached the Indians to help solve the race problem by offering more autonomy for Indian areas which the Indians have always rejected. India had even refused to play sports with the South African players even on a foreign land other than South Africa. Whereas the Pretoria regime feared a black backlash if they handed over the power to the black majority who may not be able to provide a government with rule of the law and democracy. The plan of the Botha regime was to share power with the coloured people and slowly adjust them in the ruling of the country. The Indian government thousands of miles away did not understand the reality and the compulsion of the situation. On the other hand the frontline states of South Africa did business with that country. India remains a champion of democracy in that country and even avoided playing Davis Cup with that country, the only time India could have won that event. Even in those days of apartheid South Africa wanted to play cricket and invite Indian and Pakistani cricket teams to South Africa. They also wanted cultural tours by Indian artists to South Africa. This showed that they were not ultra racists, all they feared was mismanagement and reprisal by the black majority.

Since South Africa has become a democratic country and rule by majority have taken place, India has established diplomatic relations with that country, the historical relations of our two countries should be developed further and friendship, and cooperation between us should be further consolidated and enhanced. There is a tremendous opportunity for India to expand trade in Africa and develop better understanding. South Africa could become our strategic partner without causing concern to the western block led by USA. Not only is there a big Indian community in South Africa but India has contributed a lot towards democracy in that country. India should not remain docile towards the people of Indian origin in other parts of the world as well.

The case of Fiji is a clear demonstration of India's pathetic condition, where the majority population of people of Indian origin was subjected to dictatorship by the minority ethnic group led by an army dictator. No democratic country including Australia and New Zealand protested against such a take over by a military dictator. Just having no diplomatic relation does not solve any problem. There has to be real action. India simply should avoid being a prisoner of unpractical ideas. India has diplomatic relations with so many authoritarian and dictatorial regimes of the world. All kinds of dictatorship whether they are of ism or of individuals, have been of a small minority against the majority. It is for the people in those countries to make and unmake their government, though we can help those people by all possible means to attain freedom and democracy. What we could have done for the human rights in the communist countries. Some years ago in China they had massacred thousands of students and people who were asking for democracy, and what we have done for the rights of non-Muslims in the Muslim countries and people of Indian origin that were thrown out of countries like Uganda and Tanzania. India can only talk and make a world opinion in favour of human rights, but as long as the rule of the gun dominates the world affairs, there have to be some practical and realistic behaviour on our part otherwise India will continue to be dismissed as a country, of talkers.

Because of our hostile foreign policy towards South Africa and Israel till we established diplomatic relations with them, we had earned their hostility for nothing and it was becoming a threat to our national security. Why India should have made enemies of the likely friends. Because of this, South Africa, so distant a country had started gathering intelligence information, and Israel had already penetrated in Sri Lanka. Therefore, we can see how our policy will serve us in future. Israel with its anti-Islamic compulsions and for its anti-Islamic nuclear bomb curiosity is trying to find a foot near Pakistan. Because India refused to participate with Israel to attack Pakistan's nuclear refineries, it has found a place in Sri Lanka's insecurity. From Sri Lanka Israel can even hit Indian nuclear installations in the South. Our country has become more vulnerable, because of our adventures in Sri Lanka. Indira Gandhi is known to have approved the Tamil Tigers policy of disruption in Sri Lanka, as if it was Bangladesh. It is known to the people that India allowed the Tamil Tigers to use its territory for anti-Sri Lanka activities. The result is that India lost more than two thousand soldiers in Sri Lanka and was spending 20 million rupees per day since it went down to discipline its own cronies. Such a reckless policy and adventure will cause only harm to India. During Rajiv Gandhi's tenure our relations with our neighbours became sour. The Indo-Nepal relations have been so good all these years and suddenly we had a policy of confrontation even with our small and weak neighbours, like Nepal, Sri Lanka, and Bangladesh, not to speak of Pakistan and China. Why India has such a hostile neighbourhood.

There are mainly two reasons for that : Firstly, India has the potential of a world power so it is being curtailed by USA and China. Second, our own leadership has failed to convince our neighbours that India is their friend and not a bully in the sub-continent. The visionless policy-makers in the South Block do not know how to use the newly gained power of the country, they are just arrogant and tactless. The Prime Minister Rajiv Gandhi probably thought that the heads of the neighbouring states were as small like some chief ministers in India and they should be shown their place. The childish pranks of the South Block are so visible. India needs a respectable mature leadership to deal with the countries not only in the sub-continent but all over the world. The image of the Prime Minister Rajiv Gandhi had sullied as heavy corruption charges were made against the government and the image of a very poverty-stricken country still hangs in the balance. Therefore, to change things for the better we need a new set up of leadership in the country who can mend old mistakes and hold the country as a champion of peace and progress and freedom. There is little bit of hostility by our neighbours because there is hardly anybody of them democratic. Sri Lanka imposes emergencies very often in the country and it is believed that India has had a hand or it allowed the Tamil militants of Tamil Elam to operate from India or get training in armed struggle against Sri Lanka. Though we did liberate Bangladesh in 1971, the country went back to the dictatorship of the army and its Islamic base became more rigid after the army dictator had declared the country an Islamic country. It was designed to be anti-India, so that democracy was kept out of the country. The lame democracy in Pakistan under Mr Nawaz Sharif could not take long to be befriended and stop the hostility of that country towards India. The American involvement in that country will never allow that country to be a friend of India, neither the stupid fundamentalists in that country will agree to stop hostilities against India. The overall belief of Pakistani rulers is that they exist or benefit because of being anti-India. India can only hope to neutralise Pakistan and China militarily. The ruthless suppression of the democratic aspirations in China brings that country back to old days. It is possible that relations with our neighbours will improve when they will become democratic. Pakistanis is the proof of it, whenever it had a democratic government we had no war with Pakistan, but the friendship with that country is a distant dream. Kargil was done to stop Sharif to normaise relations with India and eventually he was thrown out by the armed coup. But how can we change the lot of our neighbours to become democratic and be friendly.

India's freedom struggle after 1857 in the beginning of twentieth century AD under Tilak and Gandhi and other leaders was not only for freedom from the British but for democracy. The whole movement was directed democratically under the democratically chosen leaders. The country had a history of more than 60 years of peaceful and democratic struggle against the British. After the freedom India framed a democratic constitution for the country and the system could sustain democracy in the land and whenever there was an attempt to scuttle democracy, the moves have failed. Our neighbours got freedom on platters, because India attained freedom. These countries never had such big movements for freedom. They are still not ready for freedom. Whenever there is a movement for freedom, it is put down by the forces of anti-freedom, like the police and the army. Therefore, India can not be blamed for the hostilities of its neighbours. As far as our concern for democracy is concerned, we can say we can help democratic forces in those countries, but how we can do that while we keep voting one family to power in India. So many laws against the freedom of the people in the country and the system has already received comments from the Amnesty International. But India does have a system and capability to change the system at home and in the neighbourhood. Our aim should be to have democracy in the whole sub-continent and the world over. USA, USSR and China are those super powers that are anti-democratic and they dominate the world. Indian subcontinent is vulnerable to these powers. All that India could do is to develop a strong nuclear weapon system with a real democratic system at home with a really intelligent leadership. Only then we can help our neighbours to become democratic and friendly towards us. Only a strong India can help the world to become more free and democratic, and not a poverty-stricken India full of disease, pollution and corruption.

Is it because of the Monarchy in Nepal that the relations between India and Nepal had become sour, or was it due to the personal reasons of our Prime Minister Rajiv and the king of Nepal that the two countries were at pain with each other and the Nepali public was suffering so much, due to the trade embargo imposed by India. Soon after Independence when Pakistan attacked India in Kashmir, it was the Nepali army that came to help India. This was because of the common ties of religion between the two countries. Nepal is the only Hindu state in the world and Pakistanis are anti-Hindu. Therefore the Nepalese were emotionally ready to fight on India's side. During the British time the Nepali Gorkha have been a regular soldier of the British army and there are still Nepali Gorkha. recruited in the Indian army. There was a treaty between the British and the Nepali government after 1947 that the Gorkhas soldiers in the British army will never be made to fight against India in any future war. So because of our religious and military ties with Nepal we have an open border between the two countries, and the people of both the countries do not need any document to cross over to the other side. We have had friendship and trade agreements with Nepal. Because of India's secularism and democracy, Nepali monarchy feels uncomfortable, not because of any hostility between the two countries, but due to the freedom for democracy movement in Nepal. Though it was India that helped the royal family during any democratic change in the system. The family have tasted absolute power and it is not willing to accept even small suggestions from India and it is finding friendship with the authoritarian China. With the brutal massacre of the Nepali Royal Family in 2001 by their crown Prince, Nepal has been put to the test of time again. On the other hand, the Indian, Indira Gandhi, ruling family had developed an ego trip and the prime minister Rajiv expected the Nepali king to behave like a deputy of the Delhi regime. So all that trouble on the border and the people of Nepal suffered. Because Nepal is landlocked country and is completely dependent on India for its outside supplies.

Because Nepal does not produce any industrial goods that could be sold to India, the Nepalis have developed an economy that is dependent on smuggling of goods into Nepal and then into India. It is not only the Nepali people that are doing this, most of the smuggling that is going on the border is done by the Indians because they got the money to invest and the market to sell. The Indian and the Nepali custom officials are the same corrupt people of the sub-continent. India and Nepal cannot afford to be hostile to each other. Therefore, they should sort out the matters amicably. All that the two countries have to do is to arrive at a mature relationship which is not guided by the likes and dislikes of the rulers but by the traditional sense of friendship between the two countries. Nepal needs democracy and India needs to get out of the dynastic hangover. Only then the two countries can prosper and help each other. Two individuals, one in Kathmandu and the other in Delhi, cannot be allowed to bring the two countries and its people into hostility to each other.

Since the solution is democracy, we are not doing any thing in our neighbouring Burma, which was a part of the British Indian Empire. The movement for democracy is being ruthlessly suppressed and there are reports that Pakistan is supplying arms to the dictatorship in Burma. Many Burmese youths had taken shelter or crossed over to India, but they were either told to go back or make no political activities in India, whereas the Burmese border has been continuously used by the insurgents and forces of disintegration in the eastern provinces of India. There is need for democracy in Burma too.

There is a need for democracy all over the world. India is too much preoccupied with the problems at home, in Sri Lanka, Nepal, Maldives and on the border with China, Pakistan and Bangladesh and the Afghan problem that they are not brave enough to interfere in Burma. Interference in the internal affairs of another country is also against the international law and understanding. Because Burma has kept itself all aloof from rest-of-the-world, therefore it is not much of a news for the people around the world as to what is happening in Burma. May be the situation is not ripe for India to help the movement for democracy in Burma. The Indian politicians are a different breed who are not bothered for the human rights around the world, all they are concerned is what they can have in India. That is why neither the ruling party nor the opposition parties have said anything about Burma. It is a shame, is not it? Tibetan people have spent now over 40 years in India as refugees but no solution have been found yet. We treat them as refugees from Tibet. They have settled down now in India but we do not give them Indian citizenship nor we plead their case for free Tibet so that they could go back. Now what shall the Indian government decide about the citizenship status of the Tibetans that are born in India. As India has accepted Tibet as an autonomous region of China, we should talk privately with China for the solution of Tibetan problem and also make China agree to a solution acceptable to the Tibetan people and also secure permanent passage for the people of India to visit Mansarovar and Mount Kailash as this place is a place of pilgrimage for the people of India.

India's cause of sorrow in international relations is the Anglo-American baby that is Pakistan, that is flirting now with the Chinese. As is very clear and known that Pakistan has been created by the Anglo-American block to check India, so that a strong India does not have access to the oil rich Muslim countries like Iran, Iraq and other Gulf countries. Also that in collaboration with communist Russia, India does not venture into these countries. To this day Pakistan has done its job of blocking India's links to these countries by road and rail. So we do not have a direct oil and gas line with them nor do we have any other culture and business link of reasonable quantity. In India we can go from one corner to another crossing three thousand kilometres for anything, but with Pakistani block in the way, we can neither do business with Pakistan nor with other West Asian countries. Pakistan has been the most hostile country towards India and we have not overcome this problem as yet. The fault is that we have remained poverty-stricken country and people like Nehru mishandled Pakistani threat and nuisance from the very beginning. India accepted the creation of Pakistan and did not exchange the population as suggested by Jinnah. So Pakistan has remained always fearful of India because they think that India thinks of taking back Pakistan as the Indians do not support the two nations theory. Further down the nallah Nehru with his no war thinking allowed Pakistan the pleasure of occupying half of Kashmir and ever since then the Kashmir problem have remained main cause of war and peace between India and Pakistan. India had plenty of opportunities to kick the Pakistanis out of Kashmir but to this day we did not have the leader who could do that. Now with both countries getting nuclear, it becomes very difficult. But it is not impossible to neutralise Pakistan. India has to opt for a Presidential form of government first of all. Political instability is very bad to handle Pakistan. Secondly our poverty-stricken India has the inherent weakness and after that India has to develop very good relations with countries from Iran, Iraq and to the former USSR's Asian region. For this we need to have good relations with Putin. Now with the Taliban regime coming to an end in Afghanistan with the interim government needed by Karzai who has been educated in India, we can have good relations with Afghanistan again. To neutralise Pakistan we have made mistakes and neglected many things in the past 50 years. Our great mistakes were not to push back the Pakistanis out of Kashmir in 1947-

48. And again in 1971 we had a chance to settle that issue but Indira Gandhi failed and surrendered under the Shimla agreement, does not matter what threats the Americans were holding out to India. With better guts India could have managed Pakistan to sort out all problems with that country. After the Pokhran test in 1974 India could have handled Pakistan in a better way but we did not.

During President Carter's time during the 1970s when the Russians went into Afghanistan and Mr. Brezhnev had offered India help to teach Pakistan a lesson Morarji Desai could not see the wisdom. That is why he was awarded *Nishan-e-Pakistan* award and he was happy to receive it from a dictator. Again Indira Gandhi on her return to power did not neutralise Pakistan while Pakistan was supporting terrorism in India. She might have thought of doing so, but the opposition leaders were starting to accuse her of adventure and preparing a ground to win elections after 1984. Soon she was assassinated. Then we had this Kargil bloody encounter with the Pakistanis in 1999. It reminds me of Afzal Khan' s stabbing Shivaji Maratha in the back when he came to make friends with him and in the process lost his own life when Shivaji anticipated it and hit him instantly and killed him. But Nawaz Sharif did exactly the same after the Lahore declaration, may be it was Musharaf. However, Pakistan is still vulnerable to India because it can not match India and it has internal problems. Therefore, to neutralise Pakistan, India must keep on the pressure on Pakistan and wipe out the terrorists.

India is a nuclear power today but it has been a spiritual power for thousands of years. Gaining the power of Bhasmasur today is not a great achievement for this country but that is what the worshippers of evil around the globe understand and appreciate. We have found it important to protect our land of *Yagya,* truth and non-violence with the nukes because the evil respects only the evil. However, we can live in peace to enhance human development into human enlightenment.

Since the second world war the Americans have assumed the role of global policeman. They have been creating nuisance everywhere, in Korea, Vietnam, Pakistan, Afghanistan, Grenada, Latin America, South America, North Africa, West Asia, Iran and Iraq. They have problems with their own agents turned terrorists every now and then. In the name of containing Communism they have sold guns and drugs all over the world. They have cowboy mindset. The country was occupied by the Europeans since it was discovered 500 years ago by Columbus, whose mission was to land in India. So when he landed in the opposite direction, he called the natives Indians and later on it was changed to Red Indians or the Bush man in Canada. The present day Americans are the descendents of the colonisers. They started their lives as cowboys and they have inherited that culture from their past and rooted in that culture at their best. Today they are the same hooligans who think that they can colonise the whole world for themselves if they had the power to do so. Since the first world war and communist revolution in Russia and after the collapse of the European colonial powers in the second world war, the Americans with the nuclear bombing of Japan emerged as the second super power vis-à-vis Russia. Since then they have emerged as the leader of the former colonial powers who have taken a road to democracy. Since then, the USA has started to poke their nose in everybody's affairs and hence considered anybody who is not with them in their opposition to the communist block, as unfriendly and opposed to them. They supported dictatorships around the world if the dictators suppressed the democratic aspirations of the people. They thought that the communist could take over by democratic means because most of the people are poor and they will turn whole world into communist world. Since then, they have always looked at India as the potential communist country and developed anti-India policies by supporting the Anglo-American creation Pakistan. They armed Pakistan against India and even befriended China because they could make business with them. Today USA is more friendly and supportive of China than India. It is very clear now that the Americans are a country of hypocrites. They say they can bomb any country even if some individuals branded as anti-American terrorist indulge in some terrorist activities against the American from those countries. The recent terrorist strike at the World Trade Centre at New York and its repercussions are enough evidence of American retaliation. But the Indians cannot do the same even if the terrorism is sponsored by the government of a country like Pakistan. Of course, there is a danger of war in that case but the fact remains that if you ask for an international effort to condemn and eliminate terrorism, you cannot have double standards. They do not approve of Indian idea of hot pursuit. Here clearly Indian government have not done its home work. They should stop the talk of talking to Pakistan. They should make it very clear to Pakistan that Pakistan should stop sponsorship of terrorists against India or there will be no talks. Further the international community should force Pakistan to stop terrorism tactics against India. Otherwise, India should assert its position to handle terrorism and anybody who barks at India for human rights violations or anything else vis-à-vis the Kashmir problem. India should ask such countries to stop supporting terrorism as well and their evil hostility towards India should be exposed and treated adequately and if need be reciprocated.

We as Indians must reveal to the world as who has invented and introduced AIDS on this globe and who is most responsible to increase the global warming. How is it that the great democracy of USA flirts with the biggest dictatorship of the world and its henchmen against the largest democracy of the world. India do not need the advice from the land of cowboys and hooligans and from those criminals that have invaded the virgin lands and occupied them and who continue to spread naked capitalism. It is better for countries like Japan and Germany to ponder over the fact that they still have foreign troops on their land to boss them. They should free themselves and solve the problems before they should find themselves fit to give advice to India. It is a shame for Japan that it should have the army still on its land that dropped the Bomb on their motherland. Only those countries should be able to get to the permanent seats of Security Council that do not have foreign troops on their land because otherwise they will only speak for the forces of occupation and not for forces of truth and peace.

India's foreign policy till recently has been the continuance of Nehru's thoughtless and euphoric foreign policy based on the three most meaningless words that have been used and abused all these years. These words are socialism, secularism and non-alignment. It will be an eye opener for the people who still use these words in the Indian context to preach their political views how they have been harming the interests of India and its people.

Firstly, though India started as a democratic republic, the country was and still is an orthodox, feudal, and capitalist country. The use of socialism as our goal antagonised the American block and made them hostile to India. We could not befriend the communist block because we were not socialist. So it is very clear why we did not succeed in our relations with these two blocks. Secondly, the talk of secularism is most misunderstood word in India has no meaning for anybody outside India. Secularism according to the dictionary means no religion. Secularist means one who does not believe in traditional theology. This word was, also addressed to the outside world with different intentions. To the communist ears for their being anti-religious, to the Western and the Muslim world to cheer them for creating Pakistan and that a predominantly Hindu India was not a theocratic state. This talk also did not help India in any way but it did help the Congress Party to use the Muslims as vote banks. The non-alignment talk was bit better than the use of the two other words. But soon it appeared that this was a major disadvantage for India. Alignment means to put the soldiers in line and the non-alignment means the opposite. It can appear bit amusing for us today because India is better militarily today. But we should realise the tragedy that this word caused to India. The cold war blocks were there. No doubt, it was also good that India stayed away from these blocks. But that simply proved for India the non-alignment of soldiers on the Indian borders with Pakistan and China. The result was that Pakistan invaded India soon after the independence and took over one third of Kashmir and China attacked India and took twenty thousand square kilometres of our land. Again the Pakis attacked in 1965, another war in 1971 and then in 1999. Therefore, it is about time that we stop using these most disgusting words of socialism, secularism and non-alignment and be honest and realistic and say that we stand for basic Human Rights instead of socialism and a militarily and economically strong India instead of a non-aligned India. India could have declared itself neutral between the two blocks and should have done so by making India economically and militarily strong. Use of these three words by some ignorant people to distract the people at large have resulted in tragedy for India. It is about time that we stop this Nehruvian tradition for good.

In the wake of the collapse of the former Soviet Union, the two blocks have lost their futile hostility. China has made the world multi-polar. Now in the aftermath of the Pokharan II, India under the able leadership of Mr Atal Bihari Vajpayee has for the first time succeeded in its foreign policy under such a tremendous foreign pressure. Firstly, government could muster in only a slender majority in parliament and, secondly, there was pressure on India to sign the CTBT and when India did the Pokharan II, the hostile world trained its guns against India. Economic sanctions which were feared for long were finally imposed against us. India withstood such sanctions with ease and tact. Then came the Kargil crises, after the government had been destabilised. The Vajpayee government handled the whole thing brilliantly. The enemy was defeated and the land recovered. India stood tall for the first time in its history among the world community. Pakistan could find not a single country to support its misadventure. Therefore, it seems India attained an important position in the international affairs.

It is a matter of great satisfaction that the Indian army is still a volunteer army. But sadly enough we have sometime strange incidence taking place as a result of our negligence not only on our borders but in the recruitment as well. We have this cases of youths dying during recruitment in Patna in police firing and in Lucknow more than hundred youths falling into the septic tank and dying miserable death.

India is the most ancient living civilisation on this globe and it has the potential to attract people from the West towards its spiritual knowledge and way of life. It is here that the consumer capitalist culture feels threatened again. That is why they have to denigrate India and do their best to present a picture of India as poverty and disease infected country and keep it so by arming Pakistan because then India will have to spend more on defence and remain poor. This will have something for the West to talk about. But 50 years in the life of country is a small period and the future belongs to India if there is proper leadership in the country. This country has just to adopt the Jai Vigyan and Jai Iman slogan and develop the country on all fronts with a Swadeshi Plan guided by Navrang Marg.

India and World—Peace

India has always stood for world peace. Mahatma Gandhi's way of non-violence for the whole world and humanity has laid down the guidelines for India to achieve its goal of prosperity and progress, and peace is necessary for this. India also believed that the issues between the countries could be solved through negotiations and not by war. So when India started with its own government after 1947 it aimed at world peace. The decision to be non-aligned was keeping this in mind, because of the cold war going on between the two blocks. It was so stupid of the two blocks specially of the western block to have started the cold war whereas they just had defeated the Nazis jointly. The world was under threat of another war, because of the American anti-communist and anti-Russia policy and the Russian anti-imperialist capitalist policy. Luckily for the world, the threat of such a war diminished because of the nuclear power and the terror.

Unfortunately for India its neighbours like Pakistan and China never understood the importance of non-violence. So India's desire to contribute to world peace got a drubbing by the Chinese in 1962 and by the Pakistani attack on India in 1965 and the war of 1971. India learned the lesson that the world is not civilised yet to understand the non-violence principle of life. Not only her neighbours but the world at large, i.e., the governments around the world do not understand or appreciate peace. They appreciate balance of terror. So to be effective in the movement for world peace. India has to do two things. It has to get rid of the poverty and become a nuclear power if not a super power. But it has the capability of a super power. You do not have to go far to see that. India has vast stretches of land and a big population, a lot of natural resources, big fertile lands, and everything to grow as an economic power and moreover, big consumer market.

India being the chairman of the non-aligned movement at the time of Iran-Iraq war could not bring the two countries to peace for eight years. They are both the members of the non-aligned club. But both of them agreed to a ceasefire under the UN offices, because India and the non-aligned members do not matter in the case of wars because they do not have terror of the super powers. The two countries have been approached several times by so many people to stop the senseless war but they did not agree. Ultimately when they had killed about half a million people and made lot of destruction they agreed for a ceasefire without any gain on the ground. This world is full of such senseless people who start wars and it is a tragedy that such senseless people are allowed to get to power. India is a factor in the world peace just because of its size, but because of its poverty and lack of being major nuclear power it cannot play much role for world peace. It can preach non-violence and advocate for freedom and democracy round the world and share the movement of the conscious people and the countries of the world. Meanwhile, it needs to convince the world that our neighbours like China and Pakistan and others who do not have democracy and believe in violence should be criticised, exposed and denounced for being anti-freedom. It is because of them that India needs to develop its military power. It is not out of any desire to be a bully in the area. India should manage to settle its borders with its neighbours that have taken a large chunk of its territory by aggression. If they do not agree, we do not have to shed blood. We could only accept the line of actual control and make it a permanent boundary with the neighbours and infiltration into the country should be stopped, because we have so much population problem in this country. The neighbours could be convinced of the population problems in this country and in their own. Everybody in the country should be carrying an identity card so that the infiltration into the country could be checked. There are millions of unidentified people in India. We do not bother to check them but if there is a white tourist in India we all become curious. We put them in jail if they are without visa or deport them, but there are so many foreigners from our neighbourhood that are just going around unchecked.

India with its advancement in modern science and technology can help the less developed countries, because there are so many unemployed doctors and engineers in this country and we can produce more. We can send these people under programmes of development to other countries and help the Afro-Asian countries who do not have enough knowhow. We can help our neighbours also, like Bhutan, Nepal, Bangladesh, Burma and Afghanistan. India should encourage universal democracy,

India's foreign policy should be the propagation of democracy. It is no pride that we are the largest democracy of the world. Only effective advocacy of democracy around the world can stop the wars. We have experienced that whenever they have army dictatorship in Pakistan they have made wars with India and our problem with totalitarian China is because there is no democracy in China. The wars between democratic and non-democratic countries do take place and the tensions and war between the non democratic countries are always there. But a war between democratic states is rare. Though there is cold war sometimes like USA under the republicans supports a dictatorship like Pakistan against India. It is a shame that the American people do not see the stupidity of the foreign policy of their country. They are democrats at home or in the western countries of the white people but support the authoritarian regimes in the third world.

India's contribution to world peace has been considerable but its setbacks in wars of 1962, 65 and 71 have caused rumours against our possessed policy of peace. The 1962 Chinese aggression made the world feel that our policy of peace was from the point of being weak and the 1965 and 1971 wars with Pakistan gave opportunity to those that like to criticise India for their personal reasons, that the country goes to war very often. They do not realise that it is the others who impose wars on us. Sending troops to Sri Lanka to stop the Tamil militancy has shown that a stupid government can earn the whole country a bad name, in the world community and loss for the country in terms of men and money. India could avoid these kind of unnecessary involvements, and save its energies for the developmental programmes at home. India could have attained the Indo-Sri Lanka agreement without getting involved militarily. But who will advise the people who have no brains.

For India to help the world peace movement, it has to understand the world situations and our own situation, and conditions. The factors of wars are economical, racial, religious, geographical and political. For all these factors world gets divided easily into groups and blocks. When there is war between Israel and the others in west Asia, it is a Jehad time for the Muslims. A war between India and Pakistan also gets confused for the same reasons and colours. The racist regime of South Africa got criticised only by the black people and India, though the communist block also supported them. Had the South Africa regime been a minority of Indians or black people forcing a white majority, the response of the western block of white people could have been only a war. The tragedy of black Africa is that they are not united, and strength of unity would not come as long as there are dictatorships in that region. People have to get united on the principles of democracy and human rights, and not because of race, religions or ism. But these factors cannot be overlooked. The democratic government of Fiji was overthrown by an army coup recently. The world kept silent, because the people most affected were the people of Indian origin who constitute the majority. The Indian government and its foreign policy is more concerned about the non-issues that do not affect India directly, they are busy organising festivals of India but on issues like Fiji the government represented impotency. For the Americans and their block they had a friend in the dictator, for the Russians the people in Fiji are not communists, for the Chinese they are Indians and for the Islamic countries they are not Muslims, for the Africans they are too far away.

India has been a great champion of the world peace, a crusader against racism and a supporter of the third world, but because it being weak economically and militarily, even the people that India has supported do not support the Indians in the internationals forums when India needs their support. For example, India has been a great supporter of the Chinese case at the UN, courtesy Nehru's wonderful foreign policy, where China was represented by the Chang Kai government of Taiwan, as the Nationalist China. The western block led by the Americans never wanted to recognise the China of Mao, to represent China at the UNO. So its entry was always blocked by veto or other methods of the NATO block. For that support at the UN the Chinese gave India the friendly match of 1962, and then embraced the same Americans that have been opposed to the communist China. The USA gave more importance to China than to a democratic India, because India was not a nuclear power. India had been fighting against the South African racist regime who had offered the people of Indian origin a better deal than the blacks. What has India received from the black countries? The people of Indian origin from Uganda, Tanzania and Zambia were harassed, their property confiscated and looted and were made to flee those countries. The Mahatma Gandhi's Ashram in SA was attacked by a tribe of black people, looted and its buildings destroyed, because they did not know that Gandhi had been fighting for them as well as against the Racist regime. This is the fear of the White minority as well that when the power is given to the majority blacks, the minorities will suffer. India can do a lot for the peace in Africa but do the African people want peace and live peacefully? Recently when India was talking so much against apartheid, there was a decision to be taken about the venue of the next commonwealth games and India was a contender to host the event, the commonwealth club predominantly African voted for Canada. So if India wishes to promote world peace or the cause of the downtrodden it has to do that selflessly.

Now in Britain of Thatchers people from the Indian sub-continent need visa, most of the world is free but the Indians must get a visa and in many cases it is denied by the embassies around the world. The democratic countries like USA, Canada, UK and Germany, all are aware that the terrorists in Punjab have been using their places for terrorist activities against India, a democratic country, but would not take any action. The Reagan administration even asked Rajiv to take care of the narcotics going out of India for an exchange of the activities of the terrorists against India in the USA. India fought a bloody war in 1971 with Pakistan to help Bangladesh get freedom from Pakistan and same Bangladesh under an army dictator had declared itself an Islamic country. Democracy there have been strangulated and put behind the bars. Indian government watched it helplessly and the minority in Bangladesh suffers, because of Islamisation of that country. India's policy should be positive freedom and democracy throughout the world and it should help and even intervene in the neighbourhood for democracy. The government headed by one family and one party for so long had ceased to be a champion for democracy, and they intend to become totalitarian and how they can think of helping democracy outside if they support the dynastic rule in the country. The government once told the parliament that they might support the struggle for democracy in Pakistan, but soon we found Mrs Indira Gandhi assassinated and the trouble by the terrorists in

Punjab. We have not established yet that India could be consulted for peace in the region and the world. That was the failure of the foreign policy headed by a medicore government known for its foolishness very often. If Bangladesh returned back to democracy, Pakistan went back to army rule. Burma refuses to change and Nepal and Bhutan remain the same. Sri Lanka has terrorist problem like India and because of poverty and corruption we do not set a good example for others to appreciate democracy.

Indian foreign policy started to make amends from the days of V.P. Singh when we called back the troops from Sri Lanka but he presented Mandalisation to Nelson Mandela as if it was a movement against apartheid. Narasimha Rao moved towards the Americans probably under the influence of people like Chandraswami. He established diplomatic relations with Israel and started the so-called liberalisation of the economy. He even did not have a minister for external affairs and people have said that he did put brakes on the nuclear programme of the country. He expressed no opinion on the world situation of his time and tenure. India's silence on the world issues of war and turmoil have become a practice now. India has remained silent on the developments in former Yugoslavia, Iraq, Turkey, Israel and Palestine. India watched silently the atrocities perpetrated on the people of Serbia and Iraq by the NATO bombing and economic sanctions and even had to face the sanctions itself after the Pokhran II.

Lately under the Vajpayee government many good things have happened as far as the defence and foreign policy is concerned. India has asserted itself as a nuclear power though Pakistan has done the same. But good foreign policy decisions have been taken. We have become a nuclear power and have come out winners even after the economic sanction. There has been a considerable change in the American thinking and there has been a change of leadership in Russia. The whole family of president Clinton has visited India. Mr Clinton at the fag end of his term has visited India for five days and he stopped for just five hours in Pakistan on his way back. Prime Minister Vajpayee has been received very well in the USA on his tour of that country and both Russia and USA have and are consulting India on the terrorist menace posed by the Muslim fundamentalists. Recently, we have managed to neutralise USA's hostility towards India.

The Vajpayee government even under the economic sanctions did not develop anti-American policy but had a long dialogue with USA. I wonder if American cowboys could have thought of co-operating with India if the terrorist problem had not effected them. The two countries are moving closer possibly because we have befriended the Israelis and are buying weapons from them. With the collapse or say the disintegration of the former Soviet Union, the cold war has ended to a great extent but it is still not over and shall remain so as long as there is competition for gun running. The dimensions have changed, it has become a multi head chaos with the USA being a predominant super power. Now for sometime there is a statemate till the Russians overcome their economic difficulties or the Chinese emerge more stronger or the European Community developed into a federation under the new currency. It is premature and even arrogant that some people are quick to conclude that there is only one super power now and that is USA. This is also how the Americans want to allude the whole world. With this propaganda they want to conquer the world. Their plans are very visible that they expect the Russians who are white people to join the capitalist white west. It is for this reason that they want to help the Russians with 25 billion dollars of aid and more. On the other hand, where millions of people are starving in the third world countries there is almost no money for them because they are not white people. After the cold war with the Russians almost over the Americans must bully the third world countries. They must look for new targets now. Therefore, instead of talking to countries in west Asia they plan to hit them and subjugate them. There is no threat for the Americans from Africa yet militarily or economically.

The oil rich Arabs on the top in west Asia have to be managed, because of the Arab-Israel problems and the threat from the fundamentalist rich Muslim countries which bother the west and the east as well. A Muslim confederation from Libya to Pakistan could be a real threat for world peace. But that is very remote considering that the tussle between the Arabs and non-Arabs and the Shia and the Sunnis, but moreover in the Muslim world no man will ever be so strong to take over the other men positioned in different countries. Therefore, there is really no serious threat unless somebody like Osama Bin Laden gets his hands on nuclear bombs. It is a matter of introspection as to the strength of Osama after his daring attack on the World Trade Centre in September, 2001 which has shaken the whole world, more so, America. The dictators in different parts of the Muslim world are simply not educated enough to understand the world politics of the capitalist west. They even do not know how to use their new found economic prosperity to influence the world. Had there been some intelligent people in the Arab world and Iran, they could have fairly managed the balance in their favour. They always seem to suffer from inferiority complex like most of the third world. They have not learned from Japan and Germany how to use their money and where to invest it. The Arabs simply look towards the west for everything, who in return for the money just like to sell to them everything including the wars. The unsophisticated people in the Asian power centres simply prove themselves as hooligans. The Asian countries never had and could aim their guns against the west, but because of their small mind they let the gun runners from the west influence them and keep the parts of Asia militarily disturbed, partly destroyed and mostly poor. Look at how the west has managed to cool down the various battles in Eastern Europe but the Asian theatre is subject to American subjugation for two reasons that the Asian people who are such a chaotic mixture of races and religions do not even wish to be in peace with each other. They like to show the toys of the boys and exactly they behave like that. Look at the Pakistanis, Chinese, Afghanis, Iranians, Iraqis, Libyans, Israelis and even Indians and of course the Sri Lankans. Most of Asia is in trouble because of the gun idiots. The best thing for the Asian people of this region is to form a consultation committee and co-operate to make business with each other. The Arabs should invest their money into the Asian countries like the Indian sub-continent. The Arabs can gain lot of influence in the third world if they could invest their money here and they will be more wanted by the west also, because then they will need their money also. Till now they have been selling them wars only, to get back the money that they have paid for their oil.

A country like India consists of leaders who lack visions of the future as well as any understanding of the country's real problems and because they do not know the real problems, they cannot think to solve them as well While we cannot overcome our problems and remain a country of demoralised and directionless people, the country at its best can throw up hooligans as its leaders, and these hooligans are no match for the really wicked people that dominate the world scene today. Our hooligans can just match each other in the parliament or in the streets but should not poke their nose in international affairs while we cannot change the lot of the country itself. Our master has become the world bank or the IMF, a stage managed by the west. India is a potential world power both economically and militarily but to this day we have simply managed to be one of the most poor country of the world. With the collapse of USSR, India even cannot take a stand on International Affairs. At our best we can abstain ourselves. At stake is the ability of the country to manage itself, its sovereignty and integration. After USSR, India is the target of the US to balkanise it, what the British could not do in 1947 Indians could let the American and their friends in the west do in the very near future, if they are not careful. Indian democracy have kept the country together till now, but the economic backwardness could weaken the country into oblivion like the USSR. India only need a good leadership and work ethics, quality products and a 'zero' birth rate, national planning and definitely nuclear might if the Asian countries do not co-operate. India still can ask for world democracy, including at the UN. The United Nations is working like a mafia through its Security Council. Security council is quick to destroy Iraq, but there is no control on Israel. Two Libyan nationals could grant sanctions against Libya for the Lockerbie bomb blast, but no American could be tried for ordering to bomb the Libyan President's residence by the US airforce, that is the UNO.

The small countries of the world for whom India speaks sometime do like that but they sort out their problems with the Americans separately. Now in case of India at the moment as a result of the New York happenings, one thing has been accepted by the whole world that the terrorists who are tormenting India are connected and supported by Pakistan and that Pakistan is the midwife of Talibans. That the threat of terrorism in India is real, the world now understands it. That they now need support to wipe out the terrorists and the Americans have agreed to lift all the sanctions and are coming here to have strategic collaboration. Few years ago they were not even giving Indian Prime Minister any time to meet the American President or they were not giving India any attention. May be three years ago if India had decided to join the American block, they would have said, no we don't want you. Now suddenly India has become important. That does not mean they like us or our foreign policy has succeeded. India should be careful about every thing and stay within its limits. India should ask the world community to ask Pakistan to surrender its nuclear bombs and then ask for democracy, population control, education and abolition of poverty from the whole world. Only then we can achieve peace in the world. To say that religious terrorism is the new problem at the beginning of the new century is neither right nor enough. The problem is coming from injustice, population growth and illiteracy that should also include the sexual repression.

The bombing of world trade centre in New York by the (fidayeen) hijacked civil planes in a unique way has surprised people all over the world. The so called super power could not and cannot do anything to stop this disaster. It is for the first time that the enemies of USA could hit at such a high scale as good as war. The reaction of the people from all over the world except Israel is that they do not mind that somebody did hit the USA, but feel very sorry for the innocent people who are killed. This is because USA has double standards while dealing with the terrorists. If somebody attack the US or its citizens across the world, they naturally react against it but elsewhere they do not care, they even raise the issue of human rights where some countries are facing this terrorist problem initiated and supported by the Islamic *jehadis*. Whether it is India, Russia China or in the Balcan and former Russian provinces countries like Uzbekistan and others now USA and its agencies are actually connected with terrorists and anti-democracy groups in many countries. The NATO group also does not care for democracy in the rest-of-the-world. The present day terrorism is grown against the democracy and rule of law. USA the present day victim does not really care for democracy elsewhere in the world, it can have even its President elected through that Florida fraud.

The problem of terrorism and violence develops for few reasons. Where there is no democracy, when there is fraud and rigging of elections it is understandable. But when some enemies of democracy want to impose on the people, religious and other doctrines and cults through the guns it is unpardonable. The most dangerous form has emerged from the Muslim fanatics led by Bin Laden hiding and operating from Afghanistan. It is again the USA that was responsible for the growth of this Bin Laden—the Osama. USA has encouraged this religious fanaticism against communism and also against democracy, if they take a socialist programme. That is why USA has been supporting Pakistans against India. India is a democracy it had been talking about bringing in a socialist pattern of society under the Nehru family. Also because India is a big country and could have taken back Pakistan. The USA helped Pakistan militarily and during the Russian occupation of Afghanistan, the USA turned its eyes away from the nuclear programme of Pakistan. Now the nuclear weapons of Pakistan can go into the hands of these fanatics like Laden any time. Already some religious political leaders of Pakistan have said that a country like USA should be wiped out from the world. It is high time that the governments of the world unite to make Pakistan surrender its nuclear weapons and their factories to the UNO, otherwise much more dangerous things can happen any time anywhere in the world. The control of the military and its weapons can slip into the hands of these fanatics any time. The world should not wait and waste time because these fanatics are causing violence in Kashmir. India is hopeful that USA will learn some lessons from the terrorist attacks and join India against terrorism. The Indian governments have lacked courage to deal with terrorism, that is because we believe that there should not be unnecessary violence and also because we have unstable governments led by old aged men who naturally want to live and die peacefully after eating lots of rice pudding.

The terrorist attacks on USA have shocked the whole world. However, there are clear indications that there were people who could have known something like this would happen. In Germany there is a clear evidence that some people sold their shares stock markets just before the attack. There are also reports that Taliban already knew before the attacks that the

USA was planning to attack Osama and Afghanistan. What is more surprising is that the 30 billion dollar annual budget of the CIA could not anticipate an attack like that and they are still clueless as to who did it. The allusion of being in the super power or the super cop will cost them in future as well because of their mind-set. It is well known that USA is and has been responsible for many criminal acts of destruction around the world. It is only natural that they will pay for their *karma* today or tomorrow. There is instant *karma* and also distant *karma* but the wheel of time and *karma* is there. They must learn that from the war of Mahabharat that there is no mighty power that could defeat the allmighty. The Americans have no well-wisher elsewhere in the world, they get cooperation from others because they are either compelled to or have no other choice.

Coming back to the Indian scene, this attack has been condemned by most of the people, at the same time there is a strategic feeling in India that the USA that had ignored requests and callings from India against terrorists for the last 20 years have finally been compelled to change their mind. People are also surprised that the Pakistanis are getting away with the support they have extended or have been extracted from them. It is indeed Pakistan that is the real architect of terrorism. Osama does not have the resources, it could be that the pilots hitting the building in USA were either Pakistanis or were trained in Pakistan. There is a very big number of Pakistani army officers who are pro-fundamentalists.

Coming back to the terrorist problem and its solutions we have to have an international understanding of the problem and a joint effort has to be made to control it. USA should take a larger share of this problem because of their strategy of the past. Whether its gun running, selling of weapons of mass destruction and causing mass destruction themselves as well. Moreover, the drugs and narcotics mafia are also the partners of the CIA. The Americans must come out of their bad deeds and leave their ego and shed their arrogance. They can actually help the whole world to make it a safer and pleasant world. The politicians and their big money friends can make the money by spending on social security around the world instead of spending the money on star wars and such other negative projects. The US-led western world has ignored for a long time the growing population problem of the world. Even China has done its own birth control because most of the young people in countries like Pakistan, India and Bangladesh have nowhere to turn to for jobs. They easily get lured by the glamour of guns and sex and drugs. For lack of rock-n-roll life they turn to terrorism. This big army of fanatics in Pakistan.and Afghanistan is surely due to the population growth that has no parallel in the rest-of-world.

Indian population has gone up three times in the last 50 years but Pakistan has achieved 700 per cent population growth in the same span of time. There is simply no control in Pakistan. The Bangladeshis are infiltrating into India, already they are estimated at 30 millions. I do hope that world at large should come to grip with this problem of population growth and pollution, further that the USA should join the Kyoto convention and become a responsible and compassionate member of the world community. The UNO could be democratised and the Security Council could become more representative of the world community.

Indian foreign policy have been based on our Gandhian approach to life. Gandhi's practice of non-violence have been a big threat to barbaric, imperialist and communist forces around the world. Though civilised people have had great respect for Gandhi and his non-violence philosophy everywhere, but the people in power politics and the so-called powerful people to whom a civilised non-violent society is always a loss of opportunity to interfere and placate thereby not getting into the scence to become the VIPs. This kind of people who have an imperialist feudal mindset always create theatres of conflict so that they can destroy the peace. Once the peace of the people and the place is disturbed the potential for further trouble grows. Then it can be manipulated by reciting the history, ethnic, religious and regional factors. To come closure India did not have an enemy after the freedom. Specially when we had agreed for partition, yet some body in Pakistan thought of adventuring into Kashmir. And because of our beginning as a free country we had an open mind and the prime minister Nehru couldn't see the wisdom of clearing Kashmir when it was very much possible from that day onwards, India needed a foreign policy to protect itself. Instead of looking into the history, Nehru ignored defence and joined international politics only to draw a sad conclusion later on.

From the days of the American-Russian Cold War, these criminals have created theatres of conflicts in many places. They were joined by the Chinese. India became a victim for none of its faults Pakistan have remained a major cause of our sorrow because India lacks proper leadership and two superpowers America and China support Pakistan and its military establishment. No doubt, the present Vajpayee government have neutralised the American hostility towards India to some extent. And Osama-bin-Laden by the Tower attack have made America to realise that they need Indian help, still Pakistan remains American baby. They tell us to have dialogue. When we were actually holding dialogue we were handed Kargil because we did not include the Americans. Democracy in Pakistan was thrown out of the country and we are told to resume talks with the army dictator who is found of the freedom struggle in Kashmir where we have democracy like rest of the country and in Pak occupied part of Kashmir the terrorist are free to train and enter the other side of Kashmir to destroy democratic institutions and democracy like they very often do in Pakistan. India should only talk to an elected government in Pakistan and about the Kashmir issue we should ask the Pakistani leadership to declare what really they want to talk about and give our reply openly so that not only the people of the two countries know the truth but the whole world should get to know and we should not be afraid. For long, India have been and still is the supporter of the Palestine cause but Pakistan instead of supporting Palestine have managed to bring India and Israel closure by creating this terrorist proxy war against India for the last twenty years.

And recently the Chinese prime minister has asked India to raise the trade momentum and has asked for investments from Indian industrialists in China. No doubt our understanding with China has remained stable but its because we have not raised any serious contentions. It will be nice of China if they could acknowledge the presence of Tibetans in India and it should also make it easy for the Indian people to visit mount Kailash and Mansarovar our holy places of lord Shiva. There is no need to feel shy of talking to the Chinese on these issues. Till recently the trade the China was just two hundred million US dollars and it is now three billion dollars and Chinese want to raise it to ten billion dollars per year. Very welcome indeed, but we should not forget that the Pakistani bomb is Chinese made. However, the two countries should not think like rivals in the region or in the world. We are almost one half of the total world population. Therefore, we stand to benefit by friendship and cooperation but it cannot be on Chinese terms. However, we should avoid these so called think-tanks in India and in America who think that we can be used to balance the Chinese power. No doubt India should emerge as a great economic and military power on our own and should continue to pursue the case of peace and freedom and non violence regularly with pride. There is no need for India to provide military basis either in India or nearby places to America. We must accept friendship of all and reject and punish hostility from any quarter comprehensively. We also need not trust any body over limits because we are a unique country and we have to fight for our cause even against terrorists alone on our own because we are a predominantly a Hindu country. As we have seen, the American coalition against terrorist is free to take any action against the Taliban and the Al-Queda but India should have dialogues with Pakistan, the mid-wife of Taliban. This is typical western hypocracy. India should have strategy against Pakistan to neutralise it as a threat to India, there are many options. The advice of the leftist and the pseudo-secularists to handle Pakistan is really silly. They blocked the proceedings in the Parliament for over a week against POTO and at the same time the Indian Parliament was attacked by those five Pakistani mercenaries. We know neither those dead that day will wake up again nor these supporters of talks with Pakistan. Pakistan and India have population and poverty problems but both countries have done little about it. Pakistan have foreign mentors to make trouble to India and because no educated person (after Jinnah) have reached top position in Pakistan and because Pakistan is very illiterate country, it is very easy to talk about *jehad,* they still have to accept as a country what tragedy has taken place in Afghanistan. Probably they think India is not America. It is true but a war between India and Pakistan can go nuclear and that will be a great tragedy not only for India but Pakistan could disappear completely.

General Mussaraf sounds like a man who neither have moutaches, nor *sharafat,* should stop misleading Pakistan and alluding himself.

It is a great human tragedy that the Pakistanis have continued anti-India activities for too long. There may be few reasons for them like some foreign powers who encourage them, there is also a wishful thinking among some of the Pakistanis that they may succeed in getting Mughal empire back in India. I call it a human tragedy because it was poet Iqbal who have composed the most beautiful and evergreen national songs :

"sare jahan se achchha, hindostan hamara"

but later joined Muslim League and went to Pakistan, he never disowned the song. Similarly, these Pakistanis whenever they face pressure from India because of their own mistakes, they approach China and USA with whom they have no blood relations. With India they have blood and land relation yet love to hate us. Pakistan refuses to recognise that Bhārat and Pakistan have historical, geographical, religious, racial and cultural relationships which cannot be overturned into a hostile war of intrigue and hate on all these counts.

World and India

The UNO needs to be reorganised and democratised cannot be bossed and bulldozed by USA. India had developed a proper foreign policy, strategy recently. Growing relationships with USA and Russia in proper direction is a tribute to intelligent thinking. India will gain a lot economically and militarily by cooperating and developing new industrial relationships with Russia and Israel but same Mr Sharon is an embarrassment and awkward development for India like the Yeltsin years of Russia. At the same time India must restrain USA from having any adventure in countries like Iran and Irak.

Whether the human race came from the land, the sea or from the tree is still not final, it could be 2,50,000 years to three million or more. Some schools of thought say that all the people came from Africa. They moved to Asia some 100,000 years ago to Europe about 60,000 years ago and to Australia about 20,000 years ago and to Americas about 10,000 years ago. They became different races over all these years and then we have recent migration of the people as races. I doubt it as manipulation by the MNCs like they are doing with the beauty contests recently that we have so many Miss World and Miss Universe from India. There is a new colonialism in the garb of multinational companies. We all know they are out not to help but to make money. There is opposition to them in the underdeveloped countries because of poverty and the social concerns of different cultures. Probably they want us to accept that since everybody came from Africa, therefore, MNCs should be allowed to go every where believing in this new scientific discovery is great and could be helpful in promoting world peace and progress, but the MNC and the developed world should treat the whole world as its brother land and help people on the whole. The developed world does not even spend 1 per cent of their income on the third world or for the underdeveloped world economies. USA can give $3 billion help to one small country like Israel but is not ready to pay even $ 1 billion as its contribution to the UNO. That is where the fault lies with the developed world economies. They have limitless greed and they are still imperialists and arrogant on top of that.

No doubt we have made a lot of progress since 1947, we make everything in the country from a needle to a satellite, but we need quality. WTO would not help. Our IT section may have achieved some milestones but our roads are still dirty, bumpy, chaotic and full of accidents. Therefore, we need to improve in every field, every place and everybody, so that we can become and develop as proper human being. Last one hundred years have brought so much development and change that has not been done in the last five thousand of years or in the whole history. I say five thousand because of Mahabharat times when we assumed that time we were a developed lot. We should make progress properly in tune with nature and moral values. We can make India a Mahabharat by developing the country and the economy in a proper way. We have to control the population growth, remove poverty and pollution and make new, roads, villages and cities. We have to be prepared to face the natural calamities, we have to achieve the *yogic* high in every field. This is possible only if we adopt the proper system of programme and development as envisaged in these pages of Nav Rang Marg.

India has made mistakes in finding solutions to the Afghani and Pakistani problems that has caused India lot of sorrows. We should have always asked for democracy and in future we should again ask and recommend federal democracy for both countries. No doubt India has expressed the willingness of supporting and fighting the war against terrorism and are having a similar view like the Russians and the Iranians that we support and recognise the Northern Alliance. That the Russians and the Americans are supporting the alliance and are on the same side fighting against terrorism shows how the cold war has changed. Here we should appreciate the Russians that they have not entertained the sadistic attitude like the Americans do when the Russians or the Indians have suffered at the hands of terrorists and fundamentalists. The Americans were even ready to accord recognition to the Talibans on the recommendation of the Pakistanis but they say that there were two women who were opposed to that and they were nobody other than Ms. Hillary Clinton and secretary of state Ms Madeline Albright. Now it remains to be seen what reward Pakistan deserves for creating the Talibans. Democracy has to return to Pakistan and it should be adopted in Afghanistan. Only then we can have peace in our neighbourhood and in India as well. India's role for the attainment of world peace could become important only when—it achieves prosperity for itself and removes the scar of poverty from among the millions of its people; provides them basic human rights and practical fundamental rights, advocates universal democracy instead of non alignment. India has to go nuclear not only for peaceful purposes but for weapon systems, so that it could defend democracy not only in India but could intervene in situations like in Fiji, on its own, and restore democracy. We should advise our neighbours as well to democratise their systems. The threat to world peace is from the anti-freedom people. First step towards peace will be democracy and through democracy people can achieve anything they want. Even in the democratic country there are possibilities like in the USA when the forces of anti-freedom and anti-humanity take over the power in the leadership elections of the country and they can be as much anti-peace as the war mongers in the shapes of dictators. So we have to watch out for such offenders.

India has a great variety of cultural heritage of a global colour and dimension. Through cultural exchange and contact of people to people, India can help in achieving people to people friendship from around the world. Open India not for the multinational companies of exploitations and pollution but for the multinationals of culture, songs, dance and drama. People of travels and world consciousness and human rights activists. Sports is a big factor for promoting world peace. There should be more and more international sport activities. We have to develop a modern scientific and Yogic outlook for the world at large and avoid outdated and obstructionist attitudes. International trade of export and import with a balance is another factor in achieving people to people involvement to promote friendship and understanding among the different people of the world. Above them all, music groups from all over the world should be allowed to perform in India and we should make and encourage musical groups of international standards to perform at home and abroad.

Many ideas are there but the ideas with good *karma* can help in the cause of world peace. Peace in the individual, peace in the family and peace in the country can make a peaceful world. World peace is not possible just because of nuclear terror or balance of terror. There has to be a worldwide education against violence, that the violence is an old bullshit and people who think of doing violence are sick and uncivilised. Promotion of democracy and peace should be the rule of the world because that is the stage before you could achieve anarchy, a state of stateless and boundryless world full of the real freedom for the people and the individual. Absolute freedom for the individual and the society from the clutches of law and the state is the aim and for the attainment of such a civilised world we have to work and educate people. To be civilised in the true sense of the word, people have to know and learn to live in peace without violence in thinking, speaking and acting, having prejudice and malice against none.

India has been known for this philosophy from the day they discovered ॐ. That is the beginning of knowledge about this world and the life in this universe. The knowledge about the energy and life on this planet and the different creatures on earth. The ultimate knowledge has been achieved long time ago by some people about the human life and evolution through meditation and practice of yoga, but like always we declared those people saints or Sadhus, and nothing for the common man to follow in their own life but instead turn it into some rituals of worship and superstitions. Therefore, to make real progress towards a world of peace and enlightenment we have to start practising *yoga* and meditation on a mass scale, irrespective of our faiths and beliefs and prejudices and only then we will come to know that how futile it is to have negative ego and how useless and stupid all the violence and wars are ! Through democracy people will vote only for such people who have been and are practitioners of *yoga* and meditation and only then we can hope to stop the violence among people and against other animals in this world and make this world a home of love for everybody.

8

Pollution and Corruption

In the last one hundred years science has brought change in the evolution and development on this earth. In these one hundred years, tremendous progress and change has taken place not only in the human thinking but in the overall material life on this planet. We have developed so many things and technology that even human cloning is possible today. Just in the last ten years unbelievable and amazing progress in the field of computers and Internet has been made. It has brought the whole world very close in matters of communication. Yet in these hundred years we have destroyed the environment like never before. The chief culprit is the petroleum and coal energy. The petrol and diesel lobby has brought the whole globe to the verge of complete disaster. Hundred years ago there was a choice between present day scientific research and the other scientific research that could have developed an organic system from the very beginning in all the fields of science and technology but the petrol and allopathic lobbies prevailed over the organic lobby and, therefore, today we have this greatest danger of global warming and the planet is much more threatened due to global warming than even by nuclear war.

The nuclear war may destroy the life on the earth but the global warming will not only destroy the life on the land but the land itself will be merged in the water because of the rise in the sea level due to the melting of the snow mountains in the poles. It is estimated that the sea level would rise up to thirty metres that will mean one third of India would submerge into the sea. Cities like Mumbai and Kolkata and half of south India could be under water in 50 years or hundred years like the Dwarka of Krishna time submerged into the sea.

There are many kinds of pollution in the world. In the past

and even today, people have tried to keep the purity of their race, caste or tribe and religion. Social intermingling through marriage, sex and food was considered pollution. But we are not concerned about that today when we talk and think about pollution. Our challenge is from the industrial pollution, which is being generated by millions of tons every day and every year. Most of the industries in the non-organic field produce pollution, whether it is oil industry like the petroleum products, diesel and engine oil, factories producing metals, plastic and synthetic material, coal and tar, batteries and on top of that nuclear industry and power produces not only dangerous pollutants but is a serious threat. Noise pollution is another unattended problem in this country.

Indian cities are worst affected by pollution. Delhi and Mumbai are the top polluted cities of the world. The slums make them look worse. We have streams of factory waste running down to the rivers and finally to the sea, contaminating the land, water and the sea life. The rivers have got contaminated with factory waste, automobile oil, and open sewage. Birds, animals, humans, the land and the acquatic life all suffer due to this sort of pollution. We have become habitual offenders and it seems to be nobody's concern. Even the nature is suffering, we have cloud bursts, freak weather, early monsoon or no monsoon, record breaking temperatures and so many other strange things. The major effects of pollution on the general life, weather and the earth itself are really dangerous. Global warming is the most serious one. We all know that millions of years ago, there were the dinosaurs who were probably ruling this earth and they all disappeared in what is supposed to have been a big climatic change *mahapralaya* in Hindu philosophy. This global warming is going to cause that *mahapralaya*. In our daily life we face these problems caused by the various kinds of pollution, we smoke and our lungs get damaged, we inhale the dirty and polluted air. Our lungs suffer and we can have nervous breakdown. We drink and eat contaminated stuff. Our whole body can get paralysed. Our skin problems and many kinds of body aches are direct result of pollution. Similarly, all the birds and other animals are paying by their life due to pollution, many birds have become extinct. Pollution due to lead in petrol and food grains, fruit and vegetables contaminated by pesticides are causing major health problems. Pregnant women and their children are at great risk. Mentally retarded children with deformed bodies are born as a direct effect of pollution caused by lead and chemicals. Indian normal milk contains four times more DDT than is tolerated in Europe. The use of pesticides and chemical fertilizers is causing great harm to our body, many kinds of ailments from stomach gas, nervous breakdown and cancer are becoming increasingly unmanageable. We have these acid rains that spoil all the vegetation and crops. Due to these acid rains our output of crops get seriously low and there is always low output of fruits. This in the long run will create food problems in the world.

We can have an organic industrialisation in the country. For that we have to develop technology to have alternative energy, that of water, air and sun to replace the coal, diesel and petrol energy and we have to change automobile and factory engines that could run on the alternative organic energy that will mean an organic industry and organic economy, which will stop global warming and pollution. The biggest pollution of the air is being caused by the automobiles and aeroplanes. We have to change the energy use. We have to switch to solar energy or electric battery engines. Similarly we have to avoid coal energy. Should we succeed in replacing coal and petrol, diesel, kerosene, economics of the pollution by organic economy, we shall have done a great lot to contain global warming. We can even have motor vehicles on the wind propelled batteries and engines. So we should think of the organic economy, only that way we can save this earth from global warming and destruction and India can save a lot of money by not needing to import petroleum products. Pollution of air, water and the top soil by all kinds of pollutants is going to destroy all kinds of life on the earth. The forests turn yellow and the trees die slowly. The wild herbs all get contaminated and the medicine cannot be free from that. When people spray their fields with chemical pesticides, the bees die and there is no honey. If there are no bees, the problem of pollination comes and there are no crops of fruits. The friendly insects who eat the enemy pests also get killed by the poisonous spray. The ground turns infertile due to the chemicals and combined with acid rains, our output of fruits, vegetables and the foodgrains goes down. To promote organic farming it is important that we control pollution of the air and the soil. Organic vegetables and fruits are more tasty and healthy. They may not be attractive on the shelf but they are healthy. Similar is the case with polyester, which is very unhealthy, but people these days mix it with everything: cotton, wool and even silk. So it is very difficult these days to find anything like pure cotton, wool or silk. For a country that is over-populated and poor, synthetic economy may be a solution but it is an unhealthy way. Poor people have to buy synthetic shoes and clothes, plastic utensils, and so on, have to live in concrete houses. I remember in the 1960s and 1970s, it was the terene mixed cotton which was being sold as expensive, now it is pure cotton that is difficult to find and expensive. Pure cotton is being exported and rayon is being imported. The healthy cotton industry and its consumption in India is being ruined with the suicides by cotton growers, the state of cotton industry has become pathetic. With the population growth, more and more grazing fields and areas for the sheep are being grabbed by the people for cultivation which means less land and grazing fields for the sheep and other animals. That means less sheep or in some areas no more sheep. No sheep, no wool. So our clothing today is fully polluted by synthetic suiting and booting. Polluted air to breathe, polluted water to drink, contaminated land to grow food and broken ozone layer for sun. Are we trying to get sucked by the black hole as a whole meal with the whole earth. . . .

Many people may wonder that the petroleum and coal is coming out of the ground, why it should cause pollution outside on the ground and in the air after it is burned. It should be clear to everybody that this coal and petroleum we get under the sandy land and desert. The coal fields hardly produce anything and when we bring these products on the fertile good ground it destroys the goodness of the ground. The nature amazingly has kept it underground for the people to use it carefully when they could find the technology and it will not be out of place if I would recommend not to use these things at all because these two products have been the greatest cause of pollution. The earth kept those pollutants under the ground because they were bad but our greed which is itself pollution wants to use everything as if in the future there will be no user or the creatures on the earth would not need anything or we do not care.

It will also be interesting to understand the ecological balance of the nature. We all know that three-fourth of the earth is water, similarly our body is three-fourth water and as we have forest cover on the earth, our body has also hair cover. Therefore, we have to care about the ecological balance of the nature, we need to keep enough forest cover, we need to keep our water, air and land clean as it has been given to us by the nature. We all know that there are springs and streams and rivers of water on the surface of the earth coming from under the ground but the earth has kept its petroleum and kerosene all liquid hidden and controlled under the ground. Because the nature knows what is bad has to be controlled. But the need and the greed of the people was never satisfied and did not stay limited to the surface of the ground. So they started with digging wells for water. Later on found lot of precious minerals and metals. Soon they found petrol and today we are facing these pollution problems. The people then found nuclear stuff which is even more dangerous. So the misuse of science and technology is causing the downfall of the earth, so far the only planet known to have life. Science has provided us with so many things for our use and benefit, but the negative side of this development is what we are and should be seriously concerned that is, the pollution, which is causing global warming and ecological disaster. We are continuously doing things against the nature. We are building big dams on the rivers, making long tunnels, cutting forests and mining to satisfy our greed.

The four elements of life: air, water, earth and the sun, we must keep clean, but so far we are doing everything to make everything dirty. We have polluted the sea, the rivers and even the ground water. We have polluted the air, we have contaminated the land and we have destroyed the ozone. This has happened in last 100 years. It will be good if we could spend the next 100 years in restoring this ecological balance and make the nature clean again. There have been the earth meet where the European countries pressed on the United States to reduce its greenhouse effect by controlling the industrial pollution which is three tons per head annually whereas in India it is 200 kgs. But the United States came out with a funny scheme that they could buy the pollution quotas from other non-industrial countries. This is the way the United States, the leading power is concerned about the global warming. Research has to be done on the way of cleaning the atmosphere of the poisonous gases. The industrial countries should spend this money on the research. China is fast emerging as a pollution power. Its control on pollution is very bad. Because most of the industry is in public sectors. So the government agencies cannot go against the government industry. Hence the pollution controls hardly exist because they have to compete with the developed economies, the pollution control in China is neglected. When this state of pollution production in two super countries like China and United States is so bad, what the rest-of-the-world can do. It is also bad in Russia and India.

It is only in western Europe that the countries and their people have become aware of the pollution problem. It is because the people over there are more informed and educated and they have seen the industrial pollution. Because they have done population control, they have realised the need to live a better life, and better life is possible only if you can breathe better air and drink clean water. India need not go the full circle of polluting and then realising the need to come back when it will be too late. The low per sq. kilometre pollution in India does not make it a less polluted area because it is a country of one billion people five times more than in USA and further USA is three times bigger in size. So per person pollution in India is almost the same as in the US. Therefore, wisdom should tell us to develop our economy in an organic way, so that we can leave this world clean and safe for future generations.

Clean air and clean water, these are the two most important elements. Then we can also have clean earth and weather ozone layer. So this ancient knowledge about these four elements of life could be used to keep them clean, which some modern thinkers unfortunately ignored and missed due to the dazzling achievements of science and technology and the greed of consumerism. For thousands of years, people have used the spring water or the well water. They also used the streams and rivers, rivers have been polluted in the past, but not the way and so badly as we have done in the last hundred years. No doubt, the rivers have been used as transport for timber and boats but today they have been and are being polluted and contaminated by the sewage, industrial waste and chemicals, motor oil, metal and plastic waste. People have been throwing dead animals and even dead people in the rivers. Water is in everything in our body, in the body of animals, birds, vegetables, fruit and all the vegetation. Water is in the ground. It is in the rivers, in the sea and in the air. Water is everywhere, it is the greatest nectar of life. Indian legend had it this way that the nectar came out after the churning of the sea and both the gods and devils wanted to have it. So a dispute started between them. In their wisdom they decided that the nectar could be given to those who will take the poison first. In their scheme both sides tried to be clever. Whoever will take the poison shall die and the other party shall have the nectar anyway. But nobody was ready to take poison. Finally Lord Shiva offered to take the poison for the gods. As he was the greatest *yogi,* he took the poison and kept it inside his throat due to which his throat became blue and hence was called *neelkantha,* He received and won the nectar for the gods. So it is up to us whether we want to keep poison by contaminating the whole chain of water.

We go to the spring, we take the water, bring it in the house, drink it, or, wash with it. The water goes out through the drain. We pollute the water, if the pollution is organic like the urine, the ground can filter the water but if it is contaminated with chemicals, you can destroy the ground itself. This water also goes down into the river and then down to sea from where it comes back on the land in the form of clouds. The clouds are clean but get polluted by polluted air. It is here that the acid rains develop and rain on the ground. This acid rain spoil the crops and vegetation. The acid rain goes inside the ground and the ground water gets contaminated. We have no pure water either in the spring or the well. Similarly, we have contaminated the water by use or abuse through the industrial pollution by spraying chemicals and throwing things around on the ground and in the rivers. So we have polluted our whole chain of water. The river life is dying and the sea life is threatened. We might succeed in turning all the sea into dead sea. If the people on the earth think that it does not matter to them, they are mistaken and soon shall pay for their Karma. We have spilled lot of oil and other dangerous stuff on the sea. Some people have even conducted nuclear tests, all together we have been menacingly making the water dirty. Therefore, we shall pay. In India elsewhere the water has been considered as holy element, but we are even not ashamed of making holy river Ganga a sewage.

Similarly our important element of life, the air, has been polluted very badly by our industrial and automobile activities. Like water we have also an air chain. We cannot live without oxygen for a minute. Till now we used to get the carbon dioxide neutralised by the plants and trees that eat the carbon and let out the oxygen. But now our industrial pollution cannot be processed by the declining forest cover. When these poisonous gases cannot be consumed by the existing ecology, the gases form cloud like pollution layer and the ozone layer is broken over Australia and the hole is becoming bigger and bigger. In this polluted air, all the vegetation, animals, birds and people suffer. Because of the pollution, the weather is changing world-wide. Extreme weather conditions are likely in the near future and the behaviour and pattern of normal weather is changing. Moreover, this pollution of air is now a global warming term, which means weather change, the general increase of temperature on the planet by 5°C is likely in the near future which will result in the melting of snow mountains and that will raise the water level of the seas. This means more and more land will submerge under the water. That also means great problem for the world which is already over-populated. In the name of economic growth and prosperity we have forgotten to keep our air clean. Polluted air means polluted lungs and bad lungs mean untimely death.

With this industrial economy the earth is also loosing out to the land grab mentality and contamination. More and more land is going under the construction of factories and buildings and the cultivated land is being contaminated by the acid rain, chemical fertilizers and pesticides. The forest cover on the land is fast getting shaved off by the ignorant criminals. There is soil erosion, landslides and less oxygen and we talk about it sometimes but we have not bothered to think and start organic economy.

No doubt, earth might have split from the sun billions of years ago and it went that far and cooled itself to form an ozone layer to make it possible to have life on this planet. Does nature have some kind of ideas to do its business? It seams it does have its course. The earth is moving around the sun the whole year in a given space and discipline and also makes a full turn everyday itself. That is why we have the day and the night. It has been going on for countless years. There have been changes on the earth, mountains have come out of the sea, the earth plates have moved from one side to the other, and land has got submerged into the sea. The whole earth was like a fire ball of many gases like the sun when it split from the sun as is believed. It took its position where it is today and what it is today.

I have this answer to people that everything is gas, when they ask me if there is God? It appears that everything turns into gas and things form out of gas as well. The formation of things on the earth, like sea, rocks, mountains and the land all developed out of the hot gas ball that was the state of the earth at one point. All the seeds of life, vegetation, animals, acquatic life and the birds and human development come from those gases that have formed different forms. Even now we still have gases sitting inside the earth and this petroleum gas is one of them and we are using it today. For billion of years nobody could find it and when we burn it, it turns into a different gas. Similarly all the things on the earth can turn into different gases. You burn wood, even people and plastic, it turns into gas. There is water in wood and there is fire in wood, fire evaporates the water and water puts off the fire. It is so simple but this all come from that fire ball of gases. So everything is gas, whether you breath the gas or you have gastric trouble, it is all about gas. When you run out of gas you are dead. But even then your body can turn into any of the gases that make this water and land or rocks. Therefore, it is all about gas. Whether there is god or not it is not sure but definitely, this earth is gas.

The earth has had its destiny as well. It does have its activity and discipline, but after having been a part of this earth, we are today trying to break that discipline of the earth by polluting the system. No doubt what the people are doing today may be the part of the destiny of the earth but if we want to live on this earth as a human race for much longer, we must keep the environment that has evolved the human body. Otherwise we can disappear as human race and turn into the gas. Dinosaurs disappeared and so many other species of plants, animals and birds are disappearing due to the pollution or wrong arrangement of gases that we are doing in the moment and if we continue, the earth will definitely decide to get rid of the people and hand over the management to rats, a different form of gases. Among the Aryan race there have been a tradition of worshipping the objects of nature, like the sun, moon, earth, trees, animals and even mountains, rivers, lakes, springs, and the sea. All that was life giving and life saving. Today all the races of humans are competing to destroy the nature under the influence of the demon of consumerism. Therefore, we have to decide whether we want to continue with the life on the earth as it is, or we want to be part of this destructive race and change the gas. As I have said, gas has turned into things and things turn into gases the science can develop technology to turn the poisonous gases into material things. If we do succeed in doing so, we can suck the gases from the environment and make it clean. Help the nature to restore itself and make the life better for everybody. Until we find this technology and develop it, we have to stop polluting the nature. Also as a matter of policy we should not waste our time to make mistakes and suffer. If we have evolved as a super race of humans and developed our good brain, we must live like a super race and continue and we cannot allow some greedy and ignorant people to pollute and destroy this beautiful nature and life on the earth. All the four elements : water, air, land and fire are there for us to use, but we have to use them clean and keep them clean unless we all want to turn into gas. Pollution control have to be a part of our cultural reforms. We have to develop this discipline in our society to keep things in order. Discipline in our great country means to some people regimental discipline of the police or the army. Discipline should mean our everyday life, how we go about it and not to pollute our environment should be our top priority to keep our surrounding clean and tidy should be our culture. This will also enable us to keep our body clean and healthy. Therefore, we can also succeed in keeping away from the polluting and dangerous things like tobacco, alcohol and narcotics. These things and substances pollute our body and pollute us morally as well. It seems, therefore, we have to take care of pollution completely to keep this planet clean and lively.

Finally it can be said that for the continuity of life as we have it today, whether it is air, water, land and the ozone, or the natural life—that of plants, animals, birds and the human race, we have to keep the environment clean. Human greed or the greed of few among them is costing the whole natural life on the earth a great lot. These petro-chemical people alongwith the coal and tar have already destroyed a lot and they have made countless money, further they have made the economy dependent on them, that is why they can raise prices any time they like. Not only do they play havoc with the environment, they manipulate prices and influence the economics. They make people to pay the prices through their nose and make life miserable for the whole earth. In a country like India most of the people do not own cars, but they also pay for the pollution that the others make. They do not profit from the polluting industries but they are suffering from the pollution. These poverty-stricken people do not have even the basic human rights. They even live in slums next to these petro-chemical industries, but they have to pay by their lives, they do not have any access to free medical aid, these petro-chemical industries are causing the acid rains. The farmers and all other creatures suffer because of these acid rains, yet these perpetrators of misery on earth are the people who swag around like they own everything. Therefore, the right to free medical aid for everyone becomes necessary and the state should be compelled to meet the basic human rights of the people while it shares the blame with the petro-chemical people to destroy the environment. It is already overdue that these countries of the world start the organic system of alternative energies and develop organic economies, bring in total disarmament and save the world from spending its money and its resources on futile and dangerous projects that only make pollution and destruction.

Corruption

Corruption is actually the pollution of human moral values and is as bad and even worse than polluting water with dirty engine oil. To me corruption and pollution are the twins born to a mother called greed. Corruption and moral degradation is knocking at every door these days. The consumerism and the Panchayati Raj concept of a welfare state have furthered the cause of already well entrenched general corruption in the country. In today's consumerist society, materialism is knocking the spiritualism out. No doubt, religions have long time ago become the exploiting ways of the people but there have been some sort of restraint. Today, there are no restraints and limits about consumerism and this has started a race towards moral degradation and moral turpitude. People are becoming more and more greedy. The basis of relationship these days is not moral standard, education, knowledge or community but the material comforts that you could buy for your friends and relatives. The rich people are not interested in the spiritual or moral education. They have no time for their children, they have servants and child minders. They do not have proper contact with their children. In some cases many couples leave their homes at night leaving their children with attendants. They go to the night clubs or parties and get lost. In less rich middle class families the men do not return home before midnight and in most of such cases, the men get drunk. The poor children and the wife are forced to cope with the routine.

Not only India but whole of Indian sub-continent is sick with corruption and pollution. India and Pakistan are one of those top-most corrupt countries in the world that have very corrupt systems. The corruption is there at every level of government and society. Right from top to bottom India is deep down in the gutter of corruption up to its neck. Samples can be taken from each department of the government. From the peon to the prime minister, everybody is just either a spectator or a generator of corruption. The corruption in high places of power and in different centres of government and its exposure in media have created a bad social environment for everybody. A school student or a teacher, a farmer or a soldier, everybody is much affected by the stories of corruption in the media and in our day to day encounters that a general psychological deadlock has developed in the belief of the public that everybody is corrupt and who is not? What is there to be achieved by getting honest? This is the most helpless and serious downfall of the society and it is resulting in our social neglect and negative thinking of the general public. And how we can teach our children to be honest when they see and read stories of scandals and unscrupulus people everyday in the media, how can you expect a society to be just and caring while all this rubbish is being produced everyday. Therefore, it is the need and demand of the hour that we all decide to change the society for the better, that we insist on honesty and social development of a clean and prosperous society.

In every department of the country there is corruption at every level. Even if it is not the money there is a tendency to neglect work on the part of the employees and it is as if they do not work they are doing you a favour. Things do not move for the public without money or without the recommendation by the politicians in power. Daily wage workers on the roads are appointed with the recommendation of the MLA or even a minister. The appointments of fresh employees is always manipulated by the politicians and bureaucrats. Transfers are again done by the party in power, sometimes for political reasons and in lucrative sections it is done for monetary considerations. A minister of PWD can ask a sum of 50,000 rupees to transfer a junior engineer while a senior and higher officer can be transferred or promoted for more money. Therefore, many a time the corrupt officers have better chance of promotion while the honest man can wait for years or till he retires. The nature of corruption gets further institutionalised and accepted as a way of life to misappropriate the public funds. The daily wage worker of the PWD is even posted as the domestic help at the residences of the officers. The PWD worker knows the systems and even does not work efficiently on the projects, and if he is known to MLA, he can even threaten the officers. Then comes the supervisor, he can even have people on the muster roll who do not exist and in league with other officers and people he can even sell the construction materials of the department to private contractors in the public. It has been noticed that he makes these daily workers work for the private contractors and gets money for his pocket. There are those contractors who are awarded contracts for different construction on the roads and public buildings. Firstly, the contracts are awarded discriminately, tenders are a farce and manipulated by the politician and the bureaucrats. Once a contract is awarded a permanent commission system is at place. The contractor is supposed to pay about 10 per cent commission for his bills to be passed and cleared by the officials. Should an awkward situation arise where the contractor fails to pay, the contractor can wait all his life to get his dues.

Dr Ram Manohar Lohia, a great parliamentarian in the 1960s of the last century, used to say that the tax payer or the common man gets back only 25 per cent of what he pays as tax. 50 per cent of the tax money disappears on its way up to the final collection and 50 per cent of that collection is sucked on its way back to the general public. So the general public only gets 25 per cent of what they have paid and it is more than true. The shopkeeper who collects the sales tax from the consumers does not deposit even half of what he collects. The PWD and other non-productive departments lay their hands on the public funds. The PWD engineers are masters in misappropriating the public funds and most of them have made assets in real estates several times more than their known sources of incomes. But hardly anybody gets caught by the vigilance departments and it will be another wonder to see how do they work. The rampant corruption in this PWD department is in every section from appointments to transfers, from manipulating tenders and actual completion of work. Misusing of positions of office to use public places like rest houses and public vehicles and approving low quality of construction material for the department is a common practice. The PWD stands for public work department and this is where the public funds are allotted for most of the public roads, buildings, water supply and irrigation. So a lot of money through the traditional attitude of misappropriating public funds gets lost in the form of cash and material into the private pockets of some scoundrels. All over the country the PWD spends money on buildings like rest houses and on buildings for the housing of its employees at the cost of public funds.

The taxation departments like the excise, sales tax, customs and the income tax departments are all crowded with corrupt sharks. On a rough estimate, the shopkeepers who are supposed to deposit the sales tax just deposit one-third of the tax in the treasury. They have developed a system of fake bills and get consignments valued for less than the actual price. Next they corrupt the already corrupt officials of the tax department and get away with the loot. The owners of the factories do the same with the excise people and send out things by at least half the actual bills. The income tax department sends notices to income tax payers and then settles their dues after milking the tax payers or the tax evaders. They agree to settle down the dues for evading tax at least by 50 per cent, even though the income tax rates have been put at 30 per cent. The customs department is no different. They earn the same way as the other tax departments. They have like a mafia racket, similarly the exporters have to grease the palms of the bureaucrats in the department of exports to clear their consignments. Likewise, you can even import or smuggle in a factory or a plant lock stock and barrel without paying tax if you can bribe the customs or the minister. All we notice is that there is a mafia type corrupt tax system in the country where the tax payer and the people of India are regularly cheated by the bureaucrats. The customs and immigration departments are supposed to check international trade and travel. But they are not honest. The way Bangladeshis have been smuggled into the country has revealed that it is only money for which our bureaucracy is always worried about. The way the Kargil infiltration took place is nothing but negligence and part of that all pervasive corruption in the country in all the departments. One industrial house some years ago smuggled in one polyster plant lock stock and barrel and never paid the duty. There is lot of corruption in this department and many of these people after securing the jobs indulge in corrupt practices. They take money to clear the imports and exports. Its employees even take home things that somebody might have sent to children by parcels on their birthdays. They have even endorsement for their actions by the government who pays them commissions if they detect or derail some irregularity as if that was not their job. Most of the employees of these departments become millionaires in no time.

The income tax department is really a treat up to itself. Like the other tax departments they make lot of *Bakshish* actually through extortion by black mailing the possible tax payer or by making wrong assessments. The man in despair offers everything to the officials to get out of trouble and unlike the other departments, its officials are above tax assessments. Though 99 per cent of them accept money, not even 1 per cent of them get caught and punished.

The cases of public sector undertakings from banks, factories and corporations to include them all have always been the soft spots for feed for the morally weak chicken. At the banks the officials ask for money if they have to sanction a loan and in many cases they also grant loans that never get recovered. They rent buildings for the banks and for the use by the bank employees and for the holiday homes and they make money by taking regular commissions. Change of furniture and writing-off loans means money. At other public undertakings like factories, the officials buy raw materials and machinery on commission. The workers do not work properly and shirk duty. No doubt the factories run into losses. The corporations like transport similarly incur losses because of the corrupt practices in buying and selling and writing off things. In the transport sector, for example, somebody gets a bus conductor job by paying somebody or, he keeps some money and gives no ticket. On buses, planes and the trains people get free passes to travel and some people even travel without ticket. No doubt, the public sector undertakings become sick. The airline buys planes and the officials and the ministers gets a commission. The bus transport of any state government buys buses and they get commissions from the suppliers. From running a coffee shop on the airports to a canteen on a railway station all means bribes, even appointment of coolies on the railway station and booking of luggage all mean touts and traps laid out for the benefit of the bureaucrats. Food Corporation of India means buying grains even of unqualified quality, storing it badly and distributing it through the public distribution system through fair price ration card oriented shops which people get by unfair means and where at least 50 per cent of the ration cards are bogus. The sugar and other foodgrains all get misplaced and misappropriated by the traditional traitors. There is also a big scandalous cooking gas and petrol stations permit business. People pay to get petrol station and cooking gas agencies or they get through politicians if that should be considered free. Now the privatisation has been considered the only solution because it has become impossible for anybody to change the rot by education.

The educational institutions in the country are also a sad story. People have to pay donations and other things to get into professional vocational training institutions for various faculties. The state has failed to provide free education for everybody. Parents have to dole out money to get their children admitted into so-called high profile schools and colleges then into different vocational training institutions. Even after that they probably have to pay to get them a job. While this money business is known to the children during their education, you cannot expect them not to be corrupt when they do get government jobs. At government schools, first of all, there are not enough teachers. Secondly, the teachers in remote areas do not do their duty. We have an educational system that does not teach people to be honest and moreover our media brings in stories that youngsters read or hear about the people's representatives that such and such person has made money by unfair means or has done scams and scandals and people still vote for them, because certain party has nominated them. So corruption has become our *sanskar* and *sanskriti* and it will not be too much to say that it is the most popular religion. Because religions that have developed over the years have been the organised practices that have got established after the prophets of spiritualism and God have died long time ago.

Then we have this half-hearted and partially indifferent and distrusted health service in the country. Some countries in the world have great health insurance systems and some others have free health care of a reasonably good standard while countries like India do not have any health insurance or a proper health care free of cost. Though we do have hospitals and doctors at the government's expense and free of cost for the patients, but the level of care is neither enough nor proper. A proper health care system is suggested in the health assurance section of this book, but such public health care is prone to corruption and negligence like it usually happens with public funds. The doctors do not attend the hospitals or clinics. If they do, the surgeons recommend private hospitals or clinics where they are practising privately and charging money or they have got a commission system running. In the government hospitals the equipment for laboratories and the surgery is either outdated or is made redundant. So people must seek private service. There are not enough funds available for the maintenance of hospitals for medicines, equipment and beds. With the reservation in jobs, the quality of staff is further degraded by appointments through political and bureaucratic interference and recommendations. The medicines bought for the hospitals are resold in the market through private pharmacies and in many cases the medicines are bought only on paper and the bills are passed and entries made. In the process there is even no bandage available at the government free hospitals. The food that is provided free at the free food service for the patients is of poor quality and taste. No doubt the *massala* is not good for patients, but there have to be some taste and presentation. It is also possible that this free food is not free from some scandals. Therefore, if we have to run a free health care facility it has to be proper. In a welfare state we can produce drugs in public sector free from profits and of proper quality in red cross or red triangle packing and marks so that free of cost medicines are not sold in the market. State doctors should not be allowed to work privately because it affects their efficiency while on duty. All the staff at the state hospitals should be watched and monitored for their work and ability. Maintenance of hospitals and its equipment has to be up to the fixed standard. Schools and hospitals are the places which everybody is always in need. So we must develop and maintain a system. These days the doctors and nurses that are supposed to be on duty are very often seen in the bazar, and sometime they go on strike. Because there is corruption and no care at the government hospitals, some people are talking of privatisation of the health service, what will that mean for the people who have no money. Is not it the duty of a welfare state and a civilised society to at least provide its citizens basic health facilities in these days of basic human rights. Most of the health staff including nurses, doctors and technicians have been trained at government institutions at the public expense. Once they become good doctors after working for some years, the top breed among them try for green pastures in the private hospitals. Thus one hospital like Apollo in Delhi got its doctors from the AIIMS and high ups in the country accepted that as normal. This is just not a simple practice of corruption but a heinous treachery.

Soon after the independence the forest department has been very negligent about the preservation of forests. In the 1950s and 1960s large portions of forests have been cut down to lay down the railway line, the electricity lines and for timber and fire wood without replacing them with plantations. By the time some kind of sense prevailed on the political leadership, the smugglers and other mafia type people started fiddling and soon created an illegal prosperous business for themselves in league with the politicians and the bureaucrats and it is still going on. The case of Veerappan is but one among such cases with thousands of small Veerappans operating in every corner of the country where there are still some forests left. They all work in collaboration with politicians and officials. They have formed a nexus from the tree cutters up to the market place. The felling of trees illegally means double rates for the wood cutters, some money for the transporter, money for the forest guard and other officials and money for each forest check post till it arrives in the market. In some states illegal forest products are not illegal to sell because they come from other states. Thus, smuggling of forest timber from Himachal and Kashmir is ignored and tolerated in other states like Punjab, Haryana and Delhi. It is only illegal in the producer states if it is done illegally. It sells openly in other states which also receive timber from government run depots. Working of the forest department is such that they have been found more corrupt than the revenue department because a forest guard collects money from—shepherds, he collects money from the people who are given timber from the forests for local use, he collects money from the government contractors and from the illegal traders at all the places. There are these daily wage workers who work on the different forest department projects and there is lot of misappropriation. Construction of buildings and forest paths is all done by the department. So like PWD the forest officials all mint money.

India now needs a forest policy. All the encroachments on the forest should be made a criminal offence along with the illegal chopping down of trees. The government must protect forests and the forest land and raise more forests to enable the people breath better air and have better rain. The people will need timber all the time to build houses and get repairs. We also need timber for furniture, therefore we have to raise new forests and introduce new kinds of plants that could be grown up easily and at lower heights, and timber for railway lines has to be stopped and made illegal. People should also be trained how to treat and preserve the timber, how to build strong houses that do not need to be built again and again for every generation. People have to be provided cheap alternative fuel preferably solar energy so that people do not chop wood endlessly and most important to preserve the forests is to control our population figure immediately. Corruption can stop only if there is more supply than demand in the material market. So far there have been an over-production and supply of humans that have created a great stress on the land and the forests and no doubt the human life these days has become more cheaper. Coming back to the Veerappan episode, the Supreme Court of India commented that the two governments of Tamil Nadu and Karnataka should resign if they cannot handle the bandit who has abducted and killed many people. So far the two governments have not shown any moral courage to do so, nor have they cared about the adverse comment of the apex court of the land. As the Supreme Court has already chided the two state governments and advised them to resign, strangely no political party or politician has made an issue out of this comment, because the two Chief Ministers belong to both sides of the political divide, so all the political parties are quite. The ruling NDA government had their partner in Karunanidhi and also the so-called Third Front is hoping on him similarly, the Congress party and its allies has their chief minister in Karnataka. So nobody has ears for the Supreme Court, even the media is silent.

It is not only the forests but the wildlife as well that have to be protected as well. Many species of wild animals and birds have disappeared and are threatened. They have disappeared because of pollution and wild hunters. The balance of nature has been disturbed by the greed of the human race. No doubt in the beginning when man was dependent on the wild and sea food out of necessity, we could understand the hunters who used to lay traps for the animals. But in the process man developed agriculture and civilisations. The nature on its own has a system where some carnivorous animals are solely dependent for food on other animals and herbivorous animals make a living on plants and grass. Some birds are similarly divided by their nature of birth. And like humans there are some animals like dogs who could eat both vegetarian and non-vegetarian food. In the wildlife, the nature has maintained its own balance but the man has been very adventurous and greedy since they invented the guns and, therefore, the balance in the nature has got unbalanced. Man should not interfere in the Jungle Raj since we have inherited civilisations. There would have been no hardships for Sita and Ram, if Sita had not asked for the skin of that wild deer of maya. There are lot of more beautiful wild animals and birds in the nature including the honey bees that are becoming rare and extinct because there are few uneducated people who prey on them and the society thereby has to spend a lot of money to protect the wild animals and birds and even breed them. We must show restraint and responsibility and not invade into the Jungle Raj territory. No doubt our Hindu scriptures have recommended "Van Prastha" meaning thereby to go to the forests and live in the wild in your old age but are not supposed to live on the wild animals as Van Prastha is a stage after Sanyas. Van Prastha must live on wild fruit and grass. In simple words, it means to live a frugal life and relate to mother nature and God and leave *Prana* after you have made your glorious innings. Walking into the calm forests and watching the wild birds and listening to their songs brings great peace to anybody. Van Prastha actually means to be at peace with yourself. It surely does not mean that you carry your old aged parents or grandparents into the forests and leave them there. I have heard a folklore about, somebody who brought his old father in a basket to the forests and dropped him on a hill and started to go back. Before he could leave, his father asked him to take back the basket. When the son asked why? The old man said that his grandson might need that basket to bring his father to the forest. Realising his mistake and crime, the man asked for forgiveness and since then in that area those people stopped carrying their old aged people into the forests. Now we have these people who carry their old aged into the homes for old aged and yet use and share belongings of their old aged parents and grandparents. Many people in the country complain sometime that we have Jungle Raj because of corruption and because we have this organised chaos or the chaotic Raj because we do not have leaders but hooligans and cheaters.

Dealing in coal turns your face black too, this is an old saying in this country but it is not limited to coal alone. Now all the mining industry that includes all the minerals, stones, metals, precious stones and so many other things has become a scandalous industry associated with mafia, politicians and bureaucrats. The demand of a separate Jharkhand state is not entirely a demand of the tribes, it is more to do with the mines of minerals in south Bihar. Whether it is Jharkhand, Madhya Pradesh, Tamil Nadu, Rajasthan or Himachal, the people dealing in stone mines and mineral industries all have formed gangs and syndicates. The famous Dhanbad coal mafia is one of them. The big industrial houses in the country dealing with coal, iron, cement, stones and other things are in a very big business. They do provide funds as tax and royalty to the government but more than double that amount is squandered away by the government and its servants because they are part of this great loot. Till recently we had this quota, licence and permit system that had become very corrupt. The whole economics and industrial system had become very corrupt and that is why we lacked in producing quality products. So many bureaucrats and politicians became rich because of the licence and Permits Raj. Even now the same old system exists, though they have done some reforms but the old corrupt system continues to operate in the country. Flagrant disobedience of the industrial regulations regarding pollution and quality continue because of the tradition of fixing *babus* by money.

Employment in India has been arranged mostly by the government agencies if you take out the rural employment as farm labour, which is in the private small-scale sector. Due to trade union black mailing and the so-called socialist policies of the government in the 1960s and 1970s the employees of different wings of government and public sector undertakings were doled out concessions and favours. All the departments of the government pay to their employees what the pay-scales are. But there are some departments who dole out favours, not only to the employees but to their relatives as well. Some of the notorious departments are railways and other transport departments including the buses and airlines as well as the department of telephones. The erstwhile minister Mr Paswan doled out free telephone connections to its employees on the public expense. This is clearly favourism and discrimination in a democracy. There are millions of poor and millions of unemployed people in the country. They do not get anything, not even social security of basic human rights. But employees of the railways and other transport agencies and companies must get free passes to travel, the police and the armymen travel free. The public representatives of assemblies and members of parliament must travel free, not only the employees but their relatives also get free travel passes. Departmental rest houses, holiday homes, vehicles and funds for medical treatments are provided not only to the employees but to their children as well. These government departments are public properties and are run by public funds. Majority of the public is poor and you have a system that these government *babus* should be favoured to have concessions on top of the jobs they are holding. No wonder why there are so many departments complaining and trying to compete with other departments in doling out favours. The customs are rewarded if they bust any smuggling or tax evasion. The police is also getting rewarded if they catch people with narcotics as if these activities are not part of their job for which they are paid. The army runs tax free shops and almost in all the departments people get their retirement prematurely and the replacement is allotted to the son or the daughter.

Global tenders are being given to make motorways, airports and even railway lines, though we have the cheapest labour in the world. Soon it will be dams, tunnels, canals and the hydroelectric projects. The cooking gas and petroleum products all should slip into the hands of multinational companies alongwith the insurance companies. That is because of the corruption and inefficiency in our country. Should building of new cities become our plan and programme in the country, the outside companies will come with offers and cheaper. Now the multinational companies with their globalisation song will definitely become a threat not only to our economic progress but to our national security as well and this is because we are lazy and corrupt. We recommend people on the basis of caste and creeds to be our leaders and government servants and we shut our eyes to their misdeeds because they happen to belong to our caste, religion or region and you have some people even defending them saying that the man stands for the development of their region, does not matter if he has misappropriated funds of the central government. This is because illiterate and ignorant and selfish people have right to abuse their rights to elect their representative, that is why I have said that the corruption is knocking at every door these days of Panchayati Raj which has been introduced from above by dividing the people on the caste and gender basis without quality and corrupting them by doling out money on the so-called social development funds which they habitually misappropriate.

From few major departments of the states that I have reported above, it will seem there is no need to discuss them all and everybody. The crux of the matter is that corruption is the most popular religion in the country. Therefore it will be very difficult to sort out this disease. Computers and direct elections of the executive may help retrieve the situation but ultimately it will be the people themselves who have to call a spade a spade and get out of the different shades and colours of corruption. A simple way to reduce corruption will be a rule and tradition to put a sign board on the project sights whether it is making a road, a canal, a tunnel, a building or a complex, laying out an electric line or telephone line, it should be written in details about all such projects so as to ensure transparency so that the common man in the streets must know the amount of the money to be spent and the way and completion period of such projects. Similarly, the funds that get to the Panchayats and the members of parliament and members of state assemblies for different projects should be all detailed and printed and should remain displayed on the notice boards of the Panchayats and in constituency headquarter of the MLA and MPs, so the transparency has to be achieved in every sphere and at every level of administrations.

In the rural areas and also in the urban areas there is one creature called Patwari whom almost everybody must know. All the properties lands, houses, factories and shops are recorded and registered with the revenue department. The Patwari is attached to all the villages, towns and cities and to the whole country. This all pervasive creature is the 'be-all-end-all' figure for almost all the people. So Bakshish starts from this point. The disputes and court cases start because of the property. Where property is involved money is needed. The Patwari does not sit in his office everyday nor his presence in his office is fixed by a routine. If you want a record copy of your land and property, he tells you to come next time and the next time he is not there. Finally one day you do manage to get a copy it is not free. In many cases of land disputes, it is the Patwari with whose negligence or participation there emerges change of records that finally leads to land disputes and even murder. When the Patwari goes out for demarcation of land, it is always different from the previous demarcation, because there is scope for mistakes. For the inheritance of property the Patwari is involved followed by his superiors up to the Tehsildar, they all take money to manipulate the people. It will also be appropriate to highlight the functioning of court in civil suits, it takes years and years to go through the courts to settle the cases or find justice and on an estimate by many lawyers there is no proper justice given to 95 per cent cases. Some time back, in Himachal Pradesh, there is move by the Dhumal government to issue Kisan Patra and institute revenue courts where all the records of land and property shall be made simple and time bound by the Tehsildar and only the people from the revenue officials shall form the land courts that will decide in fixed time the disputes arising out of land and property inheritance. This is a welcome move but only time will show if the otherwise general corrupt mentality will allow it to help the farmers and the people.

Generally people mean by the word security, that if you walk in the dark, nothing will attack you, no snake, no animal and no bandit or the so-called hooligans. Nobody attacks or breaks in your house or abducts your children and wife. This is security from the criminals, the others being security from the nature for which we have clothes and house and then there is the economic security. Here we need to discuss the security from the criminals. In the old times people had formed community life by making villages. Then they made the kings to rule and protect the people. The king in turn appointed some of the army men as policemen to establish the administration and law and order. So we have this police force. The Indian police is still under the Police Act of 1861. The British colonial mentality together with our feudal traditions have further degenerated and turned the police into an oppressive, corrupt and mafia linked force. Moreover, the Evidence Act is another disadvantage for the police to prove cases of criminal activities and offences. The working conditions of normal policemen are far below the present level in the developed countries. One third of the police force has psychological disorders, due to the stress and general functioning. The general wrong doing on the part of the police results in guilty consciousness and the society does not love or respect the police. This is tolerated by the society as a nuisance force and not appreciated as a public friend. The mentality of a normal person changes very fast when he joins the police force. The life of a policeman can be a personal tragedy if an honest man joins the police force and continues to be honest. It is for two reasons: his colleagues may not be honest but corrupt, hence do not work with integrity and honesty. Second, in criminal cases where the police generally fails to prove the cases due to the Evidence Act or hostile witnesses, the general moral of the policeman suffers and becomes a part and parcel of this almost false justice system in the country. For long we have these untrained and less educated policemen who are bossed by their bosses in the force and by the politicians and their friends in the underworld. This has made not only the police force an inefficient and corrupt force but has earned an impression of being a nuisance and the personal honour of every policemen suffers. In everyday life, you see policemen on duty like checking traffic, and luggage, etc., they take bribes publicly, you see somebody murdered, the case never gets properly investigated or the murderers get away with that. You file a complaint of theft or assault, you have to pay the police to get going otherwise the police forgets about it or refers it to the Panchayats.

Not only police is partner in many crimes but it is one of the most corrupt agencies of the government. Like the other services of the government there is no honest procedure in the selection of policemen for the job. There is discrimination in their postings, transfers and promotions. Political pressures and financial considerations are the main ingredients to be a successful progressive policeman. To start with, the traffic police, the *Havaldar* and *Thanedar* all get posted by the superintendent after they have promised to return regularly the *Haphta bakshish.* It is the not so clever policemen who get posted on the management at the crossings. The *bakshish walahs* on the motor cycles prey on the *truckwalahs,* it does not matter whether the illiterate drivers have proper papers or not, they must part with some money. They take on the private bus operators, three wheelers and two wheelers. No doubt, there are some people who do not carry proper papers with them about their vehicles, but most of the time the police in their hearts waits for this to happen so that they could make some money. It is only those people who cannot pay or do not pay the police on the spot that their vehicles are taken to the police stations. In the big cities there are these contract vehicle lifters as there is no proper parking facilities in the cities. People try to find a parking place for their cars and other vehicles. These contract vehicle lifters come and tow away the motorcycles and cars. These people are paid by the police, because when the people will go to release the vehicles the police will get paid. So it is business as usual. Apart from this traffic police there are these vehicle robbers who run their nets in collaboration with police. The prostitution, bootlegging, begging and drug trafficking all are done with the knowledge of police. Cases of dacoity and murder all get coloured by the police. The vigilance department that is supposed to look after corruption of all types get involved in the corrupt practice of making money. People even pay police to have some body murdered. From petty criminals to mafia dons, all share the loot and the crimes with the police. You see policemen even involved in extortion rackets and abductions, dacoity and stealing. To say the least, the police guards of Indira Gandhi even killed her while she was the prime minister.

Indian police shall behave like the colonial police, even worse specially in areas that are backward. You cannot expect any help from the police. You file an FIR, it is never investigated properly. Recently the supreme court has ruled that there should be no arrests in bailable offences, because the police harasses lot of people mostly poor who cannot pay or are victims of somebody's conspiracy who must have paid the police to harass or arrest somebody. People's human rights and fundamental rights have been abused and violated by the police countless times. People are tortured and loose their limbs and lives in police custody. The Bhagalpur blindings and so many rapes and deaths in police custody and staged false encounters and disappearance of people after they have been picked up by the police are such serious crimes that are done by the police force which is supposed to protect the people from the criminals and maintain law and order.

In the hey days of militancy in Punjab there have been all kinds of crimes perpetrated by the police. Same is the case with so many other terrorists infested areas. There is this so-called CBI which is very often called upon to make investigation in serious crimes and in such cases that are otherwise supposed to be not being investigated and pursued honestly by the police for one reason or the other. But the record of this agency is very poor as well. The agency fails to prove its cases like the police do in the courts. And this agency is not free from the style of the normal police. They make expensive foreign tours, make money while investigating and even plant evidence. Many times they go out to other countries, because they like it very much on the public expenses, to arrest somebody in such countries where they have no chance because there is no extradition treaty with that country. The case of Italian Quatorochi to remember is one of such cases. This agency is not free from corruption and political influence. To sum it up in few words it will be appropriate to say that should a progressive policeman or an officer of the police be tried for the offences that he has done during his career in the uniform, seven lives in jail will be just complementary. So we all know what is police like, but at the same time we have to sit down to discuss the problems and decide on the general code of conduct for the police which is already there but not practised. Now that there is more awareness of human rights and some Preventive Detention Acts have been abolished or the so-called TADA, is gone but it has been replaced now by POTA and a lot needs to be improved. First, we have to make the job easy for the police to establish the identity of the person, then we have to computerise the whole country and make every police station accessible through internet. We have to make changes in the Police Act of 1861 and make the service conditions more human.

The selection and training should be done with a standard and there should be periodical tests of the mental and physical state of the personnel and a tab should be put on the record and behaviour of all the policemen. If the police arrests a person, he should be medically examined before going in the lock up and two witnesses should be informed about it alongwith his family and in case the person is released he should be brought to the place from where he was picked up. During his arrest and in the lock up or in the prison, a person should be able to receive all kinds of medical and legal help that he needs. Third rate of physical torture or any form of physical assault on the detained person should be banned and all kinds of physical torture instruments should be removed from the police station and lockups. There should be separate police women to handle the cases of women law offenders and victims of rape, etc. Somebody from the police has made a comment in the past, when people criticised the police, that the police force only reflects the society. No doubt, there is little bit of truth in it, because our society has not complained much about it. Otherwise the police force could have been reformed by now or we could have reformed the whole country by having a cultural reform.

Next we should discuss the para military forces and the total defence setup. India is spending a lot of money on the defence of the country and out of this money lot of it is pocketed by the wheelers and dealers or some of it is wasted. No doubt there are agents of gun dealers and their connection in the defence circles. Irrespective of what the government says or does about the transparency, the hard fact is plain truth that people make money out of such deals. The men in uniform, the bureaucrats, the politicians, and of course the dealers take the cream out of all the deals.

Further down the *nallah* the colonel and his jonga is famous among the armymen for his misappropriation of ration and other goodies that the armymen are supposed to get. Some even sell ration, petrol, diesel and kerosene to the public. The cheap army canteens are misused by civilians. In the construction of buildings and border roads, there is lot of corruption. The men are involved in selling cement, concrete and iron and even roof sheets. The border roads where there are flooding rivers that wash away road and buildings, are never fixed properly. They make temporary jobs like crate wiring of stones to make retaining walls that get washed away in the next flood. This is a very big scam. Further tarring of roads, is done manually when they have got the machines further proves their guilt. There is a big *bakshish* involved now to get into the army. To be enrolled as a soldier people pay money like Rs. 20,000 onwards and to be an officer either you have to be the son of an officer or you may be coming out of school run by the army where you pay a lot to be regimented or you pay over Rs. 1,00,000 to get an officer rank if you could qualify. The physical fitness takes a back seat. Now more serious crimes are being done by the men in uniform outside their camps and they are shown present inside the camps. They even sell ammunition, etc., and allow terrorists to enter and escape. The recent Bharatpur ammunition depot fire has been covered up so easily. The MIGs of the Indian Air Force crash regularly and misuse of helicopters goes on, what kind of armed forces we are going to have. The Kargil intrusion has proved our negligence once again. They even complain being put on duty in the disturbed areas that are terrorist infected who are supported by foreign sponsors of terrorism and proxy war. All is not good with the defence forces of India. In the changed atmosphere of security and the lapses of the past, there is much to be desired and improved in the whole setup of the defence and its command. The only good thing about the Indian armed forces has been their remarkable restraint to be tempted to make coups to rest power like the armies of other countries.

The government of India or for that reason the people of India want to have a permanent place at the Security Council but it is not able to manage security for its citizens at home. First, there is no social security from want and hunger. There is no security that you will not be intimidated by anybody, or that you will not be attacked, looted or raped in the streets. The government is unable to stop the terrorists, it succumbs to the abductors and releases the criminals for the hostages. There are crime syndicates and the mafia tormenting the people every day but the government of India and the provincial governments has no idea how to stop it and make the life of the people safe and secure. Yet it has the face to ask at the Security Council a permanent place because talking is very easy and if you can get something for talking it is great.

The election process and the democratic decentralisation of powers from the President of India down to the president of a Gram Panchayat or the election of a ward member that of *Nagar Panchayat,* municipality or a councilor of metropolitan city all involve spending of money. The elections of members of state assemblies and that of the Lok Sabha have become very expensive. Once you get elected, the donators and contributors expect you to do favours for them. This is our general system because we have given financial powers to our representatives who elect the executive which is dependent on the public representatives for confidence vote. So with the financial powers given to the *Panchayats* and the grants that the local bodies receive to spend on the development projects, corruption is knocking at every door from the day of election till the end of the term. Today the Panchayat members and its President alongwith the secretary find extra money and lay their hands on it. The state assemblies are full of people with limitless greed. So is the parliament of India. The indirect election of the executive and its dependence for continuation on the legislature have caused great corruption. As already discussed in the chapter on direct election of the executive, that the parliamentary form of democracy and government have become very corrupt, it will be more important to say that the Panchayat system is effecting everybody now. With the reservation for various birds in the wards and for the *Pradhans,* there is no quality. Many illiterate people like women and Scheduled Castes get elected as *pradhans,* then they do not know what to do. They get allured by the galore of the office. They easily get trapped by the traditional crooks and many end up in causing harm to the Panchayats and the people. Some Panchayat women are even causing grief to their husbands by flirting around with the crook public servants of block development department and other public services because they have to see them for the projects and surely this is a new development. In the past may be some male *pradhans* must have been corrupt and not loyal to their wives, but with reservation for women in *Panchayats* and more allocation of money for development through *Panchayats* the public servants are now using these women as instruments of pleasure because it is the bureaucrats who will release the funds allocated to the *Panchayats* and mis-appropriation of funds is becoming more glamorous as is the general habit with most of the country's people not to be honest with the public funds. Corruption and moral degradation has reached every village and street. However, it is not my intention at all to put down the illiterates, the women or the other reserved sections of our society but we need to talk about it.

The provincial assemblies have already dirty stories to tell in the past, at present and for the future as well. The MLAs, the ministers and the chief ministers break all records in the Indian Olympic of corruption. Appointments of people in the government jobs, transfers and allocation of work all is done by the recommendation of MLAs and the ministers and they take bribes and commissions and sexual favours where public funds are involved in any projects. Same is the case with members of parliament and the central government if there are big projects like dams, canals, hydroelectric works or national highways. Some people are regularly milking money through corrupt practices. Under the central government and members of parliament and the ministers there are not only projects but policies as well. Permits and licences and contracts are awarded by the ministers and most of them stink of corruption. When some people in the provinces ask about more power for the states it is this aspect that hovers over their heads. The telephone scandals, the sugar scandals, the gun deals, the petrol pump and gas agencies, the import and export licences, and so many contracts awarded by the central government and its agencies are not free from illegal and corrupt practices. Out of the last fifty years or more in the last 30 years we have known so many scandals that have gone unpunished and unhindered. With the change of taxation policies, the political parties get lot of money from *Bania* lobbies and industrial houses in the country and with globalisation and inviting foreign investments by selection they also do the same. The policy changes are influenced by vested interests.

Finally at least one former prime minister of India has been found guilty of corruption. No doubt he will go in appeals against the judgement but it is great day for the country. Though previously Indira Gandhi's election has been set aside due to corrupt practice, but she refused to resign and imposed emergency in the country and changed the law that she had broken with retrospective effect. Strangely enough, the Supreme Court did not object and allowed the change. The country has had 13 prime ministers as yet and out of these five prime ministers that the Congress has produced two have been found guilty of corruption and a third one is named in Bofors gun deal. None of the others from the non-Congress parties have been charged with corruption. No doubt, Mr. Narasimha Rao by buying the Jharkhandies kept the government stable and saved the country lot of trouble and money but corruption is corruption and it needs to be wiped out and punished. In the same case, strangely enough the Supreme Court had given a judgement, that taking money was not corruption while giving was. This kind of judgement has to be reviewed one day. These corrupt people have a great saying, 'who is not corrupt', to save their skin. They even forged signatures and opened one account in the name of V.P. Singh's son known as the Saint Kitts Case to defame him. Because it was V.P. Singh who had staged a revolt against Rajiv Gandhi for supporting corruption. However, there are at least three former prime ministers namely Chandra Shekhar, Mr. Deve Gowda and Mr. Rao whom the government of India is asking to pay their bills of helicopters and air planes running into crores of rupees. The Supreme Court have said recently that the punishments awarded to the corrupt politicians should not be reduced and the high-courts have acquitted Jailalitha and Rao.

There is hardly any place left where there is no corruption, except places where people have no choice and no power and no opportunity to do so, are holding onto old fashioned values that the others laugh about. Now in this country of more than one billion people where there is so much poverty, unemployment and no basic human rights the things have to be set right by the people at large and specially the unemployed youth have to get organised and demand their due from this good-for-nothing-society that has become a helpless spectator and approver of corruption. We have to rise from our low moral stagnation and wipe out reservation, the corrupt parliamentary form of government and the low grade general mentality of the people. The youth have to act now and in total solidarity because the corrupt politicians and the parties have divided the youth on the party lines so that they do not challenge the corrupt system because this corrupt system is being run by the common bosses of these political parties that happen to be the corrupt and morally defunct money *wallahs* who are sucking this country and its people everyday. These people have created a class of drones of vested interests right from the village up to the national level. Let us get rid of this corrupt system once and for all times to come. Truth and transparency in our action and service of not only the mankind and our motherland but of all the creatures and this planet have to be the sacred religion of the citizens of India. We have to take on the path of truth.

There are books on, secrets of knowledge and secrets of truth. Something can be kept secret, it may be unknown like an event to the people but definitely there is no such thing as secret of truth. Truth is scientific, all that science is discovering through research and development of technology is to discover the truth what is already there. Research literally and practically means to search something which is already there. That is why probably Mahatma Gandhi said that truth and non-violence is as old as the hills. Truth is open and transparency is another coined phrase to explain truth. Transparency is plain truth, but it cannot be always good, whereas truth has to be good as well. It is like this that if someone kills a man and says that he has done it, that is transparency and it may be true that he has killed somebody, but it cannot be described as truth. The truth is that he has committed a crime. Similarly, in the pursuit of privatisation and democracy of the country, the present government can claim transparency but the truth whether it is good or not is another thing. Therefore, to eliminate corruption plain transparency is not enough, it has to be the ultimate truth.

Corruption follows untruth, when people indulge in untruthful activities or try to cover up truth, it becomes corruption. Mahatma Gandhi had developed this great virtue of truth from his childhood, whereas in these days most of the parents teach their children tricks of cheating. For example, when somebody you do not want to see knocks at your door and you tell your children to say that you are not at home instead of saying that you do not want to see the fellow. So from very small things like this, consciously or unconsciously we do things in front of the children that they learn how to be a liar and mixed with the general social environment, we all learn to indulge in practising falsehood to prove how smart you are. This develops further into full corruption and some people become masters in this art of cheating. They practise cheating on their children by not doing their duty towards the children, the parental duty to look after the material needs and moral education of their children; cheating on their spouse by keeping their partner in dark about the status of matters and marriage between them. cheating by not doing your job properly as what is expected of you, it all culminates in making a person corrupt and so many corrupt persons make the whole society corrupt. Corrupt people are very weak and such a society becomes morally weak. One example of Indian morals is the participation in the Olympic games at Sydney. 72 athletes and 80 officials including officials of such organisation as well whose players did not take part in the events like *kabaddi*. If you take the hockey team out then we have 50 athletes and 80 officials. In the great pursuits of *kootnities,* our business, administration and politics have all become examples of our moral turpitude and we have become a weak society and a weak state. Winning one bronze medal at the Olympic proved our weakness, the whole exercise of dealing with Pakistani proxy war of terrorism against India is nothing but our weakness, our moral defeat is due to corruption. Our police is corrupt, our army is corrupt and our politicians are corrupt who have no guts to live a life of truth.

For too long India suffered the agony of slavery that created a great confusion among the people who were Hindus. Whether to follow the Indian concept of living and following the orders of the kings and the religion. When alien rulers by religion, race and place tried to rule the masses or parts of this country, the people got confused in the absence of education and self-rule either by kings or the people who lived like confused people and this confusion further resulted in the development of not doing our duty. After the great hour of our freedom from the alien rulers, we did not develop a foundation for the moral and spiritual education of the people. Mahatma Gandhi has said, "truth and non-violence are as old as the hills" but soon after independence we forgot him. First we managed to kill him what the British did not do in thirty years we did that in five months and after he was dead our leaders made it a practice to confine the principle of truth and non-violence to the *Raj Ghat* and visit it once a year on his birthday.

We cannot just isolate corruption and close our eyes. It has to be cultural reform. In the last fifty four years we as a society have become corrupt, partly because of democracy and mostly because our general ignorance due to illiteracy. Our politicians who were to lead the free India had become addicted to anti-imperialist and anti-British movement. While we framed our constitution and borrowed rules and forms of the constitution from other systems in the world, we did not adopt norms of behaviour like the citizens in the developed democracies do, we learned about democracy from the British system and demanded Swaraj in India too. But conditions in India were totally different. It is one thing to be educated or brought up in England even now and altogether a different story to be living in India. Development of democracy in England has been a long process and it did not come overnight like it happened in India. Though we had these provincial assemblies after 1935, but it was nothing like democracy. There were acts of British parliament of 1909, 1919 where public representation were allowed. Soon after independence unfortunately we started to loose the leaders one after the other. Most of the leaders had become old. Mahatma Gandhi was assassinated at 79, Netaji Subhash died or disappeared at the end of the second world war. Sardar Patel died soon after we adopted the new constitution. Before the independence it was the freedom fighters and after independence the same people turned into politicians. Instead of really imparting education about democracy, we started to follow demagogy of Nehru and later on till today the dynasty that according to Indian culture should have ended with the death of Indira Gandhi. We refuse to learn anything about democracy the type that we have copied or adopted. The media in the country has no intentions of developing democracy due to which they have come to exist and live. No doubt some of them do criticise or report the bad stories and scandals but the basic education about democracy and moral standard is never channeled to the people who are still illiterate either because of no schooling or because they have not been to a proper school yet because some school dropouts can become politicians and leaders. Even great leaders and dear leaders. So not many people attach importance to being educated. Now with the disgusting situation of employment for the so-called degreeholders, the concept of education is getting further retarded and defeated.

No doubt, some people call India the biggest democracy because of the population, but we are a developing democracy and with the present level of corruption and chaos we have become an organised chaotic democracy led by hooligans and pushed around by hoodlums and terrorists. So where does the education about democracy and morality have to start from. It has to start from the top because there are some natural rules that we must follow. It always rains from the sky on top of our heads, on top of the mountains and on top of the soil that rain is necessary for the growth of life and vegetation. The sun always rises above our head and when it disappears, it is night of darkness. Similarly the air above our head. So everything that we need comes from the top of our head, but that we have to stay on the ground on our feet is another reality. To make this democracy work we have to develop a proper system. As I have advocated the direct election of the executive from Panchayat level to the highest in the land for a fixed term not exceeding two terms. It is only because the present system has brought us where we are today. No doubt, what Nehru the first prime minister of India said about President Rajendra Prasad that he should not exceed two terms as President, was a right advice. But he should have followed himself the same principle as prime minister. Had he done so, a proper healthy tradition could have come to live. But alas the rules are always for others to follow, that is where we have developed this chaotic system. Further we have to stop the reservation system. We have to give people full choice to develop quality in the country. Backwards cannot be brought forward by putting the forwards in the backyard. It is like the front door of your house, one day at the bathroom the next day at the back door. Replacing of doors and experimenting the change in the house is not wise. It has to be like furniture that you go to the market and buy a chair, after four years you could change the covers and after eight years you can replace the chair itself. But here also you cannot replace the furniture every week or year, it is costly. Similarly electing your representatives should not be a regular exercise or a habit of buying second hand cars every week. So we have to appreciate political stability as a system that does not become stagnant. Similarly we have our moral education or *dharma* but we have to be careful that it does not stink.

Coming back to the theory from the top, we have also an old saying of wisdom in this country *Yatha Raja Tatha Praja*. So if the highest political authority in the land is corrupt, so shall be the public. Once the public becomes corrupt they shall elect the corrupt as their leader. Now these kinds of trends are actually there. The people vote for people of their caste and creeds because in return they think they will profit. Now this is a corruption of the principle of the democracy. Today this is a major consideration in the election process. But the country has a very big constituency where the election of the chief executive has to be above these considerations of present political factors in the country. The person should have a national appeal and acceptance. He cannot be a person to be posted from nowhere because some political and vested interests find it easy to manipulate such a person. Secondly, he cannot be also an autocratic organisational man. The person to be the chief executive has to be a person that the people have known and liked. Further with the fixed term of office, there is no possibility that it will become like the terms of Nehru and Indira Gandhi who wanted to establish personal rule or dynastic rule or it cannot be like the bunch of others whose term could not last more than a year. This top of the authority has to be discussed here again because it surely is the factor that has influenced the factor of corruption in this country. So to describe it briefly the direct election will save the situation of horse trading in the aftermath of elections. The prime minister or the president shall get elected directly, the chief minister or the governor shall get elected directly so you cannot have the wife of a former chief minister imposed on the legislators. The village *Pradhan* shall get elected directly, and they shall carry with them 50 per cent plus votes, so a sectarian person does not get elected. Once this is done the sectarianism has to stop, because this is a great factor and source of corruption.

There is no need to name those who have become sectarian leaders in different parts of the country and who plan to arrogate to themselves the dynastic right of the king makers by all kinds of manipulations. It is not only the Congress party that has indulged in corruption, the regional parties have done it more than anybody and in a state like West Bengal the left parties totally changed the system by giving the government jobs to its cadres. In Assam, the north east, Kashmir, Punjab, Haryana, Tamil Nadu and other provinces, the regional bosses have all done a remarkable job in the field of corruption.

It has been simply illustrated in our heritage scriptures that *kama, krodha, moha, lobh* and *ahankar* are your enemies that try to block your path towards the ultimate truth. It is important to relate these factors in our daily and everybody's life. *Kama* here stands for lust, that is physical and material lust which people with money and other means try to satisfy and when things do not go your own way you become angry that is *Krodha*. You may now become angry with others because they are doing things that are morally and legally wrong, you may get agitated with others because they are not accepting or allowing you to do wrong. But this anger is a negative development and it destroys a lot of things in your body and in the society. *Kama* and *krodha* are very fast to appear on your body. Next is subtle and stagnant *moha* and *lobha* literally meaning attachment and greed. Attachment to life is natural and good. It is good to be a loving person who loves all that is good, who loves his wife and children and good food but if you apply discrimination to have these things and get allured by *maya* it becomes *mohmaya,* this *mohmaya* is morally and legally wrong. Like the attachment to your public office. The famous Kissa Kursi Ka, that you will try to hold or get the seat or throne of a public office by all means. Next comes this mean fellow who is under the influence of greed. This greed is a very big world and limitless. You have these beggars, you give them one rupee and they want more. You give your children one toy and they want more. You have one son and you want more. People make you an MLA and you want to be a minister. The company has printed a price on a consumer item and the shopkeeper prints his own. He makes 1000 rupees a day and he wants to make 10,000 a day, the government appoints you as public servant and gives you pay and you want to get more by unfair and illegal means. People go to a temple and make offerings and most of them ask the deity to give more in return. Then all these greedy people go to a Brahmin or a Tantrik who satisfies his greed by telling you to do this or that to achieve this or that thing. Now this greed joins the kama and moha elements and you become an abusive person. You must have seen so many foul mouths around you. Then you have these people with money, with bureaucratic and political power who abuse their status to water and harvest their plants of kama, moha and lobh and if they fail in their pursuit they become angry and if they continue to succeed they develop *ahankar,* the final block of vanity that leads them in the domain of arrogance.

In simple words you can describe this system of corruption like this, that the business man wants to have his secretary or receptionist a beautiful woman whom he can abuse and misuse to satisfy his lust of *kama, krodha, moha, lobha* and *ahankar*. He has got the money, he can think of wine, women and wealth. He visits prostitutes, he appoints a secretary or an extra marital relation on the side and if he does not get what he wants, he becomes angry and his appointed person gets sacked. But if he manages it all very well then he has lot of things to come, more money and more arrogance. He can put money in the coffers of politicians and pursue his ambition of greed and arrogance. Similarly you have these bureaucrats and politicians who misuse their position of powers to appoint people in service. If a beautiful woman qualifies for a job they would like to have her in the bed with them before appointing her on the job. If she refused their advance they can get annoyed. In the case of the businessman who can sack his servants, the bureaucrats or the politicians can only transfer the women. This is the *kama* factor and the greed factor is limitless. The appointment through money, the transfer and promotion, the licences and permits and the work through tenders are all part of that limitless greed of money that we already discussed. Then these bureaucrats and politicians and the businessmen want their children to get up the ladder like them, that is the *Moha* and when they do not get it they get upset, so they demand no confidence motion in the assembly or in parliament. If they can influence that or if they manage to continue their corrupt practices they become so arrogant. In this arrogance they have lost sight of truth, whether you are a businessman, a bureaucrat or a politician, most of them have got blinded by the historically known vice and I doubt if ever they think of living a life of virtue because *in the vainful sleep of vanity and in the false pursuit of arrogance there is nothing to be achieved.* The present level of corruption in the country is because of the fast breeding of the elements of *kama, krodha, moha, lobha* and *ahankar* in our genes. But alas this knowledge of our scriptures that has been gained and achieved after so much penance has been washed away. It is like somebody saying after Socrates the famous Greek had been assassinated, "Alas! the world could not stand by a great man while he was alive."

Finally, will the Lok Pals succeed in taming the tail of this monstrous corruption. It all depends on the political will of the people and the leadership. It depends also whether we can switch on to the system of direct election of the executive. As we have seen the anti-corruption department which is called vigilance department has so far been very much invisible. The appointment of the Lok Pals and that of their staff have to be free from political interference. The appointment of the Lok Pals should be done by board that will consist of top officials of any state and the central government. For example, the Lok Pal of a province should be appointed by a board consisting of the Director General of police, the chief auditor general, the chief secretary and the chief justice of the high court, they should select the Lok Pal and his staff. Further on, it should develop into an autonomous body that should take its salary from the governor. The vigilance department should be merged into the Lok Pal institution and they shall train their own cadres. The Lok Pals shall operate independently and they should be able to keep details of all the projects of development and should reply and investigate any complaint of wrong doing by the bureaucrats and the politicians. Similarly, at the centre there has to be a central command to prove all the cases of possible corruption by anybody. The appointment of the chief Lok Pal should be presided over by the chief justice of the Supreme Court, the Board of appointment shall consist of the cabinet secretary, director general of the CBI, the attorney general and the auditor general of India and in the end there has to develop an All India service with its own cadre free from political interference. Only then it can help the country otherwise the lip service to have Lok Pals will end up like the CBI and the vigilance departments. There has to be an all round development on the lines of this *Nav Rang Marg*. Because we need a complete system that makes it simple and easy for everybody to participate and understand the system of administration and justice and development and where only quality is the basis of success. This department should be free from all kinds of reservation. It is possible that the habitual corrupt and lazy and truant type of government servants may join or slip into this service but soon we need to develop this into an all India cadre based service that will be of such devoted fresh young people who shall have only one aim and that is to free this country from corruption.

At this time of going into print, a news have ticked in that a very huge ice rock of the size of 3000 sq. kms. weighing billions of tons has just broken off in the south pole. The study groups on the global warming had warned way back in 1998 of such an eventuality. Because in the south pole the temperature has increased by 2°C. Yet you have some monkeys claiming recently in England that the global warming is not really a threat, toying the line of president Bush who is opposed to Kyoto Declaration.

9

Making of a New India

It shall mean making a prosperous country for everybody where poverty is under control and basic human rights are guaranteed to everybody, where the law and order is maintained and the state is helpful instead of being oppressive. It is a state where corruption, nepotism, pollution and all sorts of hooliganism are absent by education and severely punished by law. It is a society where people are not indifferent towards the social cause. It is an awakened commune where people use the public funds properly and are not misappropriated by the so-called leaders and their henchmen. It is going to be a stable system of progress and development. It is the self-dignity of the people and that of the country, which is going to matter in the international new order. We have not only to sort out internal problems but the external security and economic threats. Violence and terrorism of all kinds have to be controlled and eliminated. Politics of caste, creeds and religion has to go. Hypocrisy that is rooted in our culture from the days of *Mahabharat* has to go. We have to develop a scientific culture that should be free from prejudice and honest just like the computers. We shall use our brains and science to develop this country and overcome our problems of poverty, population and pollution. We shall also fight starvation, hunger and disease and make life good for everybody.

It is going to be a great country in the near future if the country adopts a proper programme and system, otherwise things can go really bad because we have already plenty of problems, from poverty, disease, unemployment, regional terrorism, external and many internal threats that could cause real chaos and problem and could cause the disintegration of the country. All the right thinking people in the country are concerned about these serious problems but the capitalists and the communists are hardly bothered about it. The people are so divided on party lines that it becomes difficult to start a proper movement for the development of the country and free it from the hegemony of corrupt politicians of both the left and the right. There are about five or six major political forces in the country. First is the Congress party and its culture which has got overtaken by the Sangh Parivar and this Sangh Parivar has become the number one political force. The third political force in the country is the regional parties who have a narrow-minded agenda to sensationalise the issues at local regional level and stay in power. The fourth political force is the left block, which still believes in Marxism. This force unfortunately has not been able to convince the majority of the people about its bonafides. There is also the fifth block of the so-called secularists and socialists who still believe that there have to be a third force. However the sixth force in the country is the terrorists that believe in violence and are a frustrated lot. These include the religius fanatics, communist renegades and separatist tribal forces. On the whole all these political forces believe in advancing their own cause. The cause of the common man and that of the country is never the aim of these forces, all they believe in is how to emerge as leaders of sectarian politics and enjoy the power and pelf through corrupt means.

It is this development in the country of political chaos that ensures the survival of the corrupt and negligence of the poor that freedom has brought about. This organised corruption and chaos is harmful for the people and dangerous to the country. Harmful for the people in the sense that the basic human rights of the people take a back seat, and dangerous for the country because when the state does not deliver and take care, it is going to loose out to the forces who are alien and hostile to India. The greed of these forces can make India loose its freedom and culture, economy and power. Therefore, we have to realise what is good for us in the long run. We have to establish a system, a proper system that stands up to the problems and challenges of modern times. It will not be out of place to say that all the religions when they came to existence were the social systems established in the past as per the demands of those times and the possible solutions to social problems faced by the folks of that time. Similarly in the post-second world war a new system of social welfare and human rights has emerged and is being developed in the developed countries of the west. Soon after independence our great country has tried to develop this sort of new social status but we have not succeeded yet and even have strayed from the right path. To be honest we have become very dishonest in pursuing the cause and the direction and we are either standing helpless or have become indifferent to the social cause and our responsibility as citizens and have failed miserably to develop this country into a vibrant society where everybody could feel the glow of freedom. But it is also not too late to leave the matters for the nature to sort out. We can do it and develop a proper modern system. As discussed earlier, we have to start with a basic approach on a road where traffic rules are for everybody and the rules are the same and everybody has to follow the rules to avoid accidents and harm to all the people on this path of development and destiny.

To develop a modern social system we have to start from the very beginning and basic rules of birth control with limited two children family. Every family has to be registered and monitored for health by the primary health centre. Everybody shall have a health card from birth. The pregnancy has to be registered and the child has to be cared from pregnancy. This should be called the new health order in which a person shall have the right to be looked after all his life in a national health system. To put it simply, the child in pregnancy should be attended through ultrasound scan and after the birth all the innoculations and vaccinations should be done and how the child is looked after and grown up, the society or the state has to take care about that. The system has to be complete from parents to the state to provide the complete health care for a child, to provide free school education, with fully equipped schools with basic facilities for a balanced growth of the children. The state shall make it sure that all the children are saved from all sorts of exploitation and abuse. That all the children are provided facilities for play, painting, swimming and cycling. That there is cultural development with art, music and yoga. It has to be a state undertaking the responsibility to prepare a child for the growth of a society with social justice and development without discrimination. After school, there have to be a one-year social service mandatory for everybody and the youths should be given education about sex, family planning and employment. They should work in this one-year on social projects, like, building of schools and hospitals, laying down water, electricity and road lines. Only then they should be allowed to go for higher education and all those rights of citizens of India. Punishment should be awarded for those who will not present themselves for this social service.

The next step is the identity card for everybody. This identity card should be given to everybody at the age of fourteen after the birth health card and the school card. This identity card has to be compulsory and computerised by the local authorities. Everybody should carry the identity card or school card with them so that they could be identified, even if the children go missing or are abandoned, during travelling or at crowded festivals. Parents should be punished for such offences that will fail to do their duty towards their children. This identity card should be treated as the most important document and should be the basic document in the identification of everybody, in relation to law and order, travelling, business and in matters of administration and health related activities. It should be an all pervasive document. It should be mandatory for every citizen to produce his/her identity card in every situation whenever it is necessary to know the identity. All matters related to the individuals should be registered and attended on the basis of this card. Therefore in all business work, constitutional and administrative procedures this identity card number has to be mentioned. In the matters of property, income and tax and bank accounts there have to be a single account. The whole country has to be integrated on computer for identity, crimes and business information, so detection of everything becomes easy. This will help everybody, including individual and the state to make a more easy, safe and secure system in the country.

The job, property and income card should have the details of everybody, therefore the tax and income details are recorded and in all the deals related to transfer of property, it becomes easy for the authorities to assess and detect tax evasion and corruption. Therefore, to deal with the shady deals of corruption and cover-ups, it will be easy to detect the transfers of money and property. It will also become easy to handle information regarding the gifts, etc., and to develop a truthful and straight tax system. These cards shall be helpful for the state to put things in order. First, there will be a regular national census, because everybody is registered. Secondly, it will improve the law and order situation and then everybody will benefit from this system, if we have to provide basic human rights to the people. Moreover, it will become easy to detect immigrants, lawful and unlawful, specially when we have a population problem in this country. The multi-purpose identity card should be good for voting and any other official purposes.

To make a proper system in the country we have to decide the basic needs of the people. For example, we must make a census of total population, registration of all the people and families and families below the poverty line. People need to be provided basic human rights at the state expense. The housing situation, the school and hospital and many other agencies are needed for the functioning of the state and for the welfare of the people. For example, we need one billion bedrooms, one bedroom for everybody. So for a family of four we need a house or a flat, so we need 250 million of houses or flats to provide housing for this population of one billion people. Likewise, we need classrooms, hospital beds, doctors and teachers. Therefore, we have to know how much more construction work we need to do to accommodate this population properly. Hence we have to do a lot of construction work. All construction work should be done with quality material.

We have to make new cities and villages with modern facilities. At least half of the population should be transferred to the new modern cities. We cannot have slums in the cities. For the migrant labour we have to make shift camps with proper amenities. Begging has to be abolished by social security. Cities are good for caring about the people. It will cost less for the state to look after its needy citizens in a city than to do that in the scattered villages. In the cities people have more opportunities of work, business and social care from the public funds of state. Therefore, we should have atleast 30 new modern cities newly constructed, with proper rules and architect, properly planned with modern facilities of roads, streets, markets, hospitals, universities, stadia, *yoga* and meditation centres, public health clubs with swimming pools and public gardens. In such cities there should be no illegal construction.

Construction of houses in the countryside should be planned as small villages with modern facilities. It is no use or achievement to stretch a line of one kilometre of electricity to provide electricity to a remote house on public expenses. We have to make regulation about the house construction in the cities and villages, so that some sort of architectural decorum is maintained in different parts of the country that will also reflect the cultural heritage of the areas and its people. Once we have achieved zero population level by law, we have to plan the construction of villages and cities with a concern for social welfare. Therefore, the access to public care of water, electricity, health and education could reach everybody easily and cheaply.

Construction of public buildings, like schools, hospitals, bus stations, railway station, airports, universities, courts, civil offices and police stations, military academies and headquarters, ministry and secretariat buildings and above all the private housing and social care and security houses of all the people should be done with architectural beauty. We should really avoid making ugly concrete boxes while we can do better for the same price. All kinds of temporary construction should be avoided and people should not be allowed to break municipal laws and no construction of kiosks even in the countryside should be allowed and it should be punished. Because of our negligence, greed and poverty. We have slums present all over, they have no sanitation and cleanliness and are a threat to the health and environment.

Construction dangerous to public safety and ugly to public view should be stopped. Every house, public or private, shall have a beautiful garden. Every school compound, public office compound, hospital or even a railway station should have enough space for gardens and proper sanitation and garbage collection system in place. Every household, shop, street, village or market shall have total sanitation and garbage disposal system. The garbage has to be separated from organic to non-organic and kitchen wastage should be properly recycled, we can have stuff to produce manure from our eatables, we can recycle plastic, paper, metal and glass. So we have to put everything separately in proper garbage bags. Our efficiency in disposing and treating the waste should be the test of our culture.

In the reconstruction and rebuilding of the country we have to make organic system of development, production and living. The natural energy system of water, solar and wind have to be developed and we have to take care that we do not make a concrete chaos. Should we make the solar energy work we shall solve the power problem in the country. Most of India is hot and sunny round the year. We can put solar energy system on top of every roof that will provide power to light, cooling and warming of the whole building. We can have tube wells in every village and city to take ground water for the vegetables and gardens and the people.

We have to make new roads, motor ways, railway lines and ports and airports. We have vast scope and potential and need for proper development and we can make a dreamland out of this country by making new water canals, electricity centres and putting to best use of what we have. These matters I have discussed in the interest of economic development of the country as we need a proper system to make a state work properly and to make this dream come true, everybody has to do his best. Doing our best does not mean that we should work 20 hours a day, it only means that we should work properly. To create this feeling to do our best and to bring this awareness in everybody, we have to ask everybody to present themselves for compulsory social work for one year at the age of 17 or 18 when they finish school. In this one year of social service, everybody can contribute to the society and the state. We can quickly make new schools, hospitals, water lines, electricity lines and many other things including garbage disposal system in no time. So we have to do it soon, only then we can turn this rot in the country into useful fertilizers to grow beautiful organic crops, trees and people. This one year of social work by everybody will definitely bring that social awareness of our *Karma* towards the creation on this earth and towards all creatures including the human race and thereby shall improve upon the general character of the country and our people. Rich or poor everybody must contribute physically to the well being of everybody because we all take what we need from this society. We cannot go on with this mentality of just take and grab and hold on to it. We have to give also.

How this one-year of social service shall work? People in India come from many backgrounds. There are poor people who are afraid even to talk to authorities and the rich people. They must talk like beggars and even worse so that in our feudal mindset they do not offend anybody. There are these rich people for whom 80 per cent of the people really do not matter. They can buy everything that is all they know. Now there is this disparity and clash. The middle class in the country is getting pro-rich these days and the mindset is changing. More and more people are becoming money minded. The only purpose of life it seems to them is to make money, does not matter whether the means are good or bad. Money can buy everything. It can buy you any authority, it can buy you friends and supporters, it can buy wine and women, it can buy you all luxuries of life from cars to planes and it can buy you law and justice. Now it can buy not only contract killers but also you can buy, children, human spare parts and anything that you can think of including God. On the other hand, the poor people cannot even think for themselves. They live in slums and shacks, they do not have any basic human rights and many of them work as bonded labour, they die without care. Both these classes of poor and the extra rich either are not capable of thinking for the country or the poor because of their miserable plight and the rich because of their indifference and the middle class which is the backbone of society is drifting apart under the pressure of materialism. Few of them are running to join the rich and many more are becoming depressed because they are also joining the poor. They also feel depressed because the social values they cherish are being trampled upon by the ignorant and indifferent rich, the ruling class. Now when we think and talk about building a new India, we have to take everybody with us and just not only we talk and think about it but act and act collectively to establish a system in the country that provides basic human rights for everybody and everybody owes their security to the state. Hence everybody must contribute to the state and society that they belong to.

This one-year social service from everybody will bring that necessary push that this country needs like overdue. This will be part of education for the whole country. In countries like Israel everybody has to go to the army for three years. Because that is what they need in face of the threats that the country has. In USA everybody can be enrolled for the army and it is mandatory otherwise not many people will join the army. Similarly in India we need everybody to join the social service because not many people are interested in it and the country is in a mess. We do not have the social awareness that you need to develop to make progress with social justice. In this one year of social service everybody rich or poor shall work for the country under social construction work. That will make everybody realise his or her duties towards the country and its people. It will also educate people on equality of sex and class. It will also enable the young people to have a fresh brainwash of their prejudices and make people understand that they need to have a social outlook that of commitment towards our fellow human beings and our duty as citizens of free India towards the country. Thus, a daughter of the richest man may work as a nurse and health worker for one year and that a son of poor man may also see that the rich can work also on the social projects. Everybody will be able to open up their eyes and see the disgusting situation and conditions that we have.

When you will work on the social projects like building of schools, hospitals, water pipelines and electricity poles, everybody will realise their duties. It should be possible to join any walk of life later on for everybody only after they have done a social work. This one year social work cannot be an assault on the freedom of anybody, this should be treated as part of our overall education. There are many people who do nothing for the country, yet they want to be leaders of the country because their parents are or were politicians or industrialists. This one-year social work should educate people about how to plan a village, a city and a country. The local bodies should be treated as a village secretariat like the Panchayat. The primary health Centre should be the beginning for the national health assurance. There have to be a *patwari, gram sevak,* and a health worker associated with the Panchayat who will monitor the population, health and education of the children in the area. There have to be a social worker who will also monitor the child abuse. The local bodies have to work to provide basic human rights under the national level. It is possible that there will be resentment to this one-year social work by some people, but this will start with one year for those people only who are at 18 and soon people will accept and appreciate it.

Model villages should be made with 500 families and there will be a village secretariat for 10,000 people. That should be the Panchayat and public servant concerned with the local departments. Each family and village should be registered with the local body and the primary health centre. There have to be a computer in the Panchayat and the national election commission should be associated with population control and identification of the people. The family homes should be inherited by one family only. There cannot be two families for one family home. The whole village should be planned and designed to look appropriate and beautiful. There have to be proper planning, lay out and construction. The villages should be fully accessible to people by road, and the villagers should have access to everything they need. Similarly the cities have to be planned, designed and built with architectural beauty. You have to lay out street roads, pipelines, etc. properly, so that you do not need to do that every year.

The work force to lay out the cities should be the first to get accommodated properly so that there are no slums growth and sanitation problems from the very beginning. Now people will naturally say that there is not enough money to build new cities, new villages and a new India. Even the major airports are being handed over to the private sector. So where will the money come from? Handing over airports to private sectors is the failure of these airport authorities and the bureaucrats who are corrupt and indifferent towards their duty. Misappropriation of funds and negligence on duty is the normal practice in the country that does not mean that these airports cannot be managed anymore. Moreover, there are these poets in the country who want to buy every public undertaking for a song. Our great politicians share the loot with them, hence the call for privatising. This call for privatising will not stop until the people realise that there are these sharks that want to eat everything. However, it is not true that this country does not have the money to build itself. There is this old Keynesian theory of economics that says if the state puts one rupee in circulation on development projects, it attracts four times private funds. Because to take this one rupee the private sectors have to sell something four times of the value. That will do in the employment sector as well. If the state employes 10 people to construct a school building they will spend that money which they earn and the material that will be sold will generate employment in other sectors. But if the government spends its money to buy guns and ammunition from outside the country or its politicians and bureaucrats spend the money outside the country and deposit money in foreign banks this shortage of money in the country shall continue. In the last fifty years not only has there been brain drain but money flight. This money flight has also been responsible for the downfall of the rupee. Many people continuously manage to take their money outside the country, then become NRIs and later on ask for concessions to take the money back as NRIs white money to invest in the country and loot more. For long we have heard in this country people blaming the high caste people for the exploitation of the poor people. But till this day the *Banias* (business class) have managed it so well that even they suck the whole country, rich and the poor, high caste and the low caste and all the religious sections are being looted and have been looted for centuries by these *Banias* but our political parties as they are paid by this business class have never raised any eyebrow. Now in the name of globalisation and liberalisation, this *Bania* class is ready to Americanise themselves even if some of them want the Ayodhya temple. You cannot just have the whole country working for one class of *Banias*. They are even fixing the cricket matches. If in India everything has to be decided by money, it can be very dangerous. People like the communists can also say that power comes from the barrel of the gun. The Bania would say that he could actually buy the guns that will further complicate the matters, when everybody in the street would say that he is the government himself. In a democracy like India money is playing a very big part.

Money has corrupted everybody. The *bania* class has emerged as the ruling class by corrupting everybody. Though you cannot blame them entirely for this situation, the fact is that these mentalities have been encouraged by moneybags playing a big role during the elections for the parliament and assemblies. Later on, because these moneybags put money on all horses. They get obliged by whoever comes to power. It is here that the Banias has emerged as the ruling class.

The politicians after getting into power have made it a game to mint money. The public money that is looted by the three classes, the *Banias,* the bureaucrats and the politicians to keep in their stranglehold on the poor masses. They have developed this divide and rule concept on the basis of reservation for the people. They divide the people on the slogans of secularism, Hinduism, customs, and so on. In the beginning, Nehru targeted the former princes and feudalism but never dared to say anything against the people who think of buying a village with a brass pot, his daughter Indira Gandhi even went further and in league with her son Sanjay started to threaten everybody. The *Bania* learned the art of paying and being safe. Ever since then it has become the religious system in the country. Because the politicians are simply incapable of solving the problems of the people and the country, they only divide them by offering reservation in jobs and legislature.

It had been declared in the constitution that after the coming into force of the constitution there will be reservation of jobs for the backward and Scheduled Castes and Tribes and that there will be reservation of seats for the membership of state assemblies and the Lok Sabha under the constitution for ten years. It is now more than 50 years that the same reservations are continuing in all these fields and are being pursued vigorously. There are people who had been opposing these reservations, but are now saying that not only these reservations will continue, but there will be reservations for women and that in the case of government jobs it should be above fifty per cent, the limit laid down by the supreme court after the Mandal Commission reports implementation by V.P. Singh government. That made total reservation up to 49 per cent. There was agitation and even immolation against this policy. The V.P. Singh government was pulled down, but the same people who opposed V.P. Singh for Mandal had in their manifestoes accepted the Mandal report and now they want and are supporting the reservations for political reasons.

At the beginning of free India, there were only 4 per cent people that could be called or counted as literate or semi-literate. So it is simply clear that 96 per cent of the people were hardly eligible for the government jobs. So where such a high percentage was already backward there was hardly any proof of forward classes or castes in the country for the government jobs. Now the national averages of literacy has gone up over 50 per cent. So there has to be a greater demand for jobs. Because most of the people still think that the ultimate goal of education is to get government jobs, not that everybody have to be literate and educated. This system of reservation has been used as a political card for too long now and a vested interest group has emerged. It is always aimed at getting to the vote bank of the backward classes and castes, which the politicians presume, goes en block. This system is also called positive discrimination, thereby implying that though it is already a discriminating system, it is used for the upliftment of the downtrodden and for the progress of these people that have been poor and backward as a class and caste for much too long. Not only reservation in jobs and legislature but special concession and subsidies are being given in the various economic policies of the government to these backward people and castes.

Since a lot of people are unemployed in the country, a lot of people think that this reservation in jobs must go and not only that, the system of promotion on the basis of castes should also be stopped. Looking practically at the whole issue, this reservation system should have been stopped by now or at least the benefit should have been given to one generation in the family. If the first generation had got the benefits of reservation in jobs, their children should have been able to do better than the others. Hence they should not have been given such benefits. Many first class jobs have been secured due to the reservation system yet their children also qualify for reservation, while the children of the other illiterate reserved class or so-called high castes but poor have to compete with this privileged class. The result is that a vested interest creamy layer has emerged among the backward castes and tribes. Moreover, efficiency of the working class has been suffering due to the reservation. Many incompetent people have jobs from a peon to a minister just because they have been selected or elected because of reservation. The case of Mr Jagjivan Ram who stayed around power centre for about 30 years is an example to remember. Being a cabinet minister at the centre he forgot to pay income tax for 14 years, it was only after so much discussion inside and outside parliament that he had to make a statement that he forgot. Again his case can also be cited as an example of caste dislike and discrimination by the high castes towards the lower. That though he was even promised prime ministership when he defected from the Congress to the Janata Party, he was sidelined and later on when Morarji Desai government fell, Desai refused to resign as parliamentary leader. Jagjivan Ram had chances of becoming prime minister at that moment more than anybody else. But the Brahmin President of the day and the Congress party denied him the opportunity. So the chance of a Scheduled Caste to become PM was aborted. Till this day no leader of his stature has come up from this class of people. Again his case is further example of the creamy layer that his daughter is contesting elections on the reserved seats.

As far as the bad effects of this reservation are concerned, the Mandal Commission had generated a lot of bad blood in the country and if it goes beyond the 49 per cent limit a civil war like situation can develop in the country. The country will be a great looser if such a situation develops because many people think enough is enough and also society cannot be divided in the name of caste, class and religion. The Mandal Commission report is pregnant with partisan attitude and distorted sectarian conflict and in its acceptance the government has sown the seeds of a civil war with these consequences. A responsible government and parliament should make introspection and drop the reservation system on such a high scale. At the most, it can be given on the ratio of population and it should be one time exception for one generation and it should not be given for all the generations. Also it could be given on population ratio only when the parliament has passed the two children family law for everybody, because most of the people do not worry for family planning. Secondly, the reservation should be for economically backward only and 50 per cent of this reservation should be for women only. In that way it would become acceptable. We have to give jobs to more qualified and efficient people to improve the efficiency of the administration. Also you cannot have a system where the son of a Minister or an IAS officer or an income tax payer Harijan can be given reservation opportunity over the son of an illiterate poor villager of an upper caste. Therefore there is no need to carry on the old style of caste based reservation system, as the 40 per cent of the people are under the poverty line. The reservation could only be given for the economically backward people. The country has to evolve a system where no poverty and economic backwardness remains, only then there will be no need for economic reservation. The caste factor is a disgusting factor in this country. There is also some weight in the argument that the high castes that are well entrenched in the bureaucracy in the country will choose the new members for the jobs from their castes and community. Therefore, a time does not come when the backward classes will get an opportunity to have their members reach the decision making bureaucracy and the result is obvious that they will remain backward and without jobs.

To highlight the present corruption in the administrative system of the country, you could see it how deeply the system has degenerated. People sit in the competition examinations (IAS or the state ASI. Some people have approach to the centres where the examination papers are marked. So they go there and get the papers marked of their candidates into merit list. When the merit list is prepared, the favourite candidates get already an upper hand for being called for the interviews. It is here that the fate of the deserving and non-deserving candidates is decided. People are paying who can and have the channels of payments and contacts through the establishment. A right candidate who could have faired very well is thus pushed to the back seat. So a serious question arises, what is meritocracy? Is it genuine? When the merit list has already been prepared through the back door, what remains is the personality test. That means again whether you know a minister or a bureaucrat who could intervene for your selection. Some people know that the examinations for the selections of government jobs are done at many centres and the answer sheets are even written with pencils so that the answer sheets could be written again. The anti-reservation people do not know this. All they know that the backward people without the sources of money and corrupt officials should stay backward while they should remain in power generation after generation. Now even the army recruitment should be discussed. It is no secret that the recruitment in the army is thoroughly corrupt. The sons or relatives of army officers either in service or retired find their ways into officials cadres. The recruitment of the soldier grade is also done through money and intervention of officers and relations in the army.

The whole degenerated corrupt recruitment system in all the forces has amazingly remained hidden from the people and nobody has complained. Our media is so innocent that they have never bothered to go and investigate and report. All they do is what bad news they can report and print on the front page, negative reporting and statements by the good for nothing politicians.

Before people can bring in the country a genuine system of employment, reservation cannot be stopped but it has to be for the economically backward people and 70 per cent of the total jobs should go to the rural areas. This should not be applied for the private sector. As far as the efficiency and availability is concerned, there is no security. So a general consensus has to be arrived at. It can for instance be like this that of the total jobs 70 per cent have to go to the villages. The reservation for economically backward people can stay at 50 per cent, of this 50 per cent should be reserved for women. Only then can we assert that some social justice has been done. To all these government servants it should be binding that they do not have more than two children or they loose their job, that they will make proper sanitary arrangement in their living and shall not be corrupt and lazy and habitual to strikes.

No doubt the right to have strikes at work is reasonable for the redressal of the reasonable demands of the workers. But to resort to it very often is not necessary. Some people just look for excuses to have strikes just to get to the leadership of some unions. It is a pity that the public sector and government departments are the most likely resorts of the striking employees. Since the strikes harm a great lot of the economy of such companies and departments, there should be a minimum way of sorting out the disputes and demands. Strikes may be tolerated in some non-essential spheres of public activity and services, but for the very essential services like transport, power, water, communication, banks and hospitals it should be banned and made illegal for all times to come. There should be a statutory board to sort out the matters and decisions of such boards should be legally binding on the government and private institutions. At present these departments go to strikes very often without any social responsibility, causing lot of trouble, problems and inconvenience for millions of people. On top of that, many times people on agitation resort to destruction of public property, ransacking of public systems and blocking of roads and railway lines, causing even death to innocent people. This is the biggest hooliganism that any civilised society can tolerate. But India is still waiting to grow out of this hooliganism. Resort to hooliganism and violence is considered like an act of bravery or a gold medal.

All the essential services should be declared above strikes and blocking of roads and railways should be made illegal with some punishments. Police should have powers and the responsibility to observe law and order in such areas. Any such strikes should be declared a war against the state and dealt with accordingly. No politics should be allowed to compromise the interests of the state and the society. Everybody knows that such blockades and strikes in the essential services make life difficult for people who get stranded, incurring heavy losses, even children and women are put in great difficulty, injured, sick and needing emergency treatments get stuck on the roads asking for mercy from the hooligans who with political support even become goondas and ask for money and even beat innocent people who argue with them and even extort money. This nonsense has to be stopped. Lots of perishable goods meant for markets get destroyed in the trucks or on the streets because a bunch of crazy people are allowed to play with the life and property of the people in the name of strikes and Bandhs. It is not only the roads and railway but electricity, water and especially the hospitals get badly effected. Nowhere in a civilised country people would resort to strikes in hospitals. But look at the hospitals in India. The staff and the doctors resort to strikes without any regard for the patients that may need the medical care either outside the hospitals or inside. Therefore, it is still not too late and is high time to make an introspection if the country has to grow into a civilised society, the need of the hour is to mend our ways and sort out these matters for the future. Strikes have done great harm in the past. The system very often bends before the government employees because they have become very big interest groups to be ignored or antagonised especially when we have unstable governments that goes to polls very often. This country has seen all sorts of *hartals* (strikes) by all kinds of people. There is only one *hartal* that has not taken place yet and that is the housewives *hartal* or the children *hartal!* It is possible that soon some people will also get this idea and form unions and go to strike. No doubt the workers need better ways and there have to be a national wage board or a commission that will have this job to make an annual report and recommendations that should be binding on the government and private sector and the wage boards should take into account the inflation in the country and the planning commission has to work in such a way that it does not make inflation and should promote growth.

Water Management

The pressure of increasing population on the land can be seen everywhere. There is scarcity of water; the water table is going down. There is no drinking water in many parts of the country and what to speak about irrigation and swimming pools in the country there is not even enough water to wash clothes and most of the water is not even safe for drinking and then we have droughts in many parts of the country and most of the time there is no rain; most of south India or half of India has rains only for about four months and the rest of the year remains dry, while in the north there is more rain and snow. There is, however, lot of rain during the monsoons, there are even floods in many parts of the country. There are many rivers and lakes in the country but the water management in the country is very poor. We have very long coastline on eastern and western side and on the southern coast, yet we have drought conditions or scarcity of ground water in most of the country. Now there is technology to turn the seawater into useful and potable water. Atleast we can make canals throughout the southern part from Gujarat to Tamil Nadu and to Orissa with lift irrigation and to lift this water you can even make electricity by the ocean water. But nothing much has been done or planned by the central as well as the provincial governments. After a very long time the Kaveri water dispute has been solved but with a change of government in Karnataka, the Congress party led government is opposing the accord. There are lot of rivers in the north, some even going through Pakistan and Bangladesh and also coming from Nepal and Tibet. But we do not have proper planning and management of these rivers. We have to sit with our neighbours and reach some agreement. It is not only the hydroelectric potential that we should look into but we have to think about the total use of water from the rivers. These rivers cause floods during the monsoons. States like Uttar Pradesh, Bihar and Assam get flooded and there is no action to control these floods and when there are no floods, the rivers have become totally polluted. These rivers have become open sewage mixed with the industrial waste. With this pollution of the rivers the water is contaminated and hence dangerous and unfit for use either for drinking washing or irrigation. We are continuously destroying the nature During Rajiv Gandhi's tenure a Ganga Water Pollution Control Authority was constituted but to this day there is no sign of progress and in the late 1970s during Desai's term one Mr Dastur had presented a two Canal garlands for the country where he had proposed to join all the rivers through two garland like schemes. That was to avoid the floods, because he had noticed that the floods take place in some areas due to one river or the other and if the flood water could be diverted to other rivers, there will be no floods on the scale that they take place. Now this whole water management has to be done on the sub continent. We cannot use the water of the rivers that run from Himachal Pradesh and Kashmir into Pakistan. So is the case with rivers from Nepal and Tibet. Every year Brahmaputra River causes floods in Assam. Now there has to be an inter state and international planning and agreement for this water management. But until now we have been either polluting the water or suffering from the floods.

So to put the water to its maximum use and the rising demand and scarcity of water due to population problem we have to do a proper planning and execute national schemes in agreements within the country and with our neighbours. We have managed and diverted few rivers in Himachal Pradesh to benefit Punjab and Haryana, but there is no progress on the Rajasthan canal. There can be a parallel river Ganga canal. There can be a diversion on the river Brahmaputra and there can be agreements with China because it has taken over Tibet. Nepal can also become our partner in water management. We have to do a great job and we should start soon. There have been wars for land until now and there can be wars for water in the future.

Transport and Communications

The next steps towards progress are surely the transport and telecommunications. The need for making new roads and railway lines is also because of the population growth. We need motorways and we have to build them properly, we even need a motorway from Iran and Iraq to Far East in Vietnam. We also need a railway line through Burma, Thailand and Bangladesh. Similarly we have to develop the sea transport because the air transport is very expensive and limited. When we talk about transport, we can talk about this transport industry as well. As I have said earlier that India could make its transport planes in collaboration with other companies and countries in Asia.

Air India could become the biggest airline of the world, just now the government has announced its privatisation by 60 per cent. No doubt it was overdue because of mismanagement of PSUs as usual. But it will be a foolish plan to sell its shares to multinationals. Air India has been an expensive airline to travel with and even then it has increased losses. It has become sick because of the corrupt bureaucrats and politicians. It is a shame that very small international airlines are making profit out of India and they run regular flights out and in but the Air India authorities are looking for strategic partners, it is simply because of our good for nothing bureaucrats and politicians. India has the cheapest workforce if we go for the hard currency rates. But since the planes are bought in dollars, and the international prices of plane tickets are not in rupees, we can say that we have cheap workforce as far as the Air India is concerned but we have failed to compete. People should know that the other airlines also buy their planes for the same price as India. That they also pay the same money for using the international airports as India and on top of that all the workforce employed by Air India is the cheapest and even then it is in the red. If you count the passengers that go out and come into India, more than 90 per cent of them are Indians. Why is it then that Air India does not have 90 per cent of the travellers. The simple answer is our bureaucratic syphilis and our good for nothing political leaders who have no qualifications even to be managers but happen to be leaders, who in their desperation will not only sell the public sector undertakings but sell the whole country and put their money into Swiss Banks or NRIs multinationals. The way the Indians have been thrown out of north Africa and now the treatment of Mahendra Choudhary in Fiji is perhaps no lesson for the leaders and probably for most of the Indians who want to go to the west. The English medium schooling in India has created a class of neo-elite who neither think of India nor of Indians, they want to ape the west, no doubt the Sangh Pariwar is concerned about the cultural colonisation of the country but its economic and education policies are similar to the west and even worse because it does not speak about the basic human rights nor it does anything to remove poverty.

Like Air India we have also failed to improve on the railways and surface transport. The money meant for public works is pocketed by the bureaucrats and hardly any one of them gets caught and punished, because you can buy even the judges. But should the people realise their responsibility and decide to improve, it is not too late and we can make everything better.

Energy Change

The third very important thing that this country has to change is the energy system. But the way more and more car makers are being allowed in to make petrol cars, it seems we do not attach much importance for a change of energy system, especially the petrol alternative. India does not produce more than one-third petrol of its total consumption and most of our foreign currency is spent on the importation of petrol. Moreover in a situation of war with Pakistan, the petrol supply could be doubtful. We should develop an alternative to petrol and Engines that can run on alcohol, solar and wind energy. If we had spent some money on research in these fields like we have spent on the nuclear field, India could have developed an alternative system of energy and engines. Not only these alternative systems will make Indian rupee strong and fully convertible, it will save the environment and it will be good for our security as well. The petrol and diesel consumption in automobile and factories has caused the pollution not only in India but it has caused global warming which is very dangerous for the whole world.

Population growth has put lot of pressure on our forests. We need to have forest cover on atleast one-third of the country because more and more forest areas are being destroyed every day. The poverty in the country still makes people dependent on forest fuel in the rural areas and that is 70 per cent of India. People in the rural side depend on firewood and therefore lot of forests get destroyed. The petroleum gas is being made available to the rural areas as well. This is a help but it is not good for the long time strategy because India has to import gas that will and is costing India a lot of dollars and is also not safe because the supplies are not reliable in time of war with Pakistan. It is necessary to develop the solar energy system for every household and also we can have electric supplies from different sources, but the solar system could be developed as most reliable.

We have to develop new forest lands and save the existing ones. Also we have to plant trees that will grow fast and are useful as timber and moreover we have to bring timber treatment technology to the villages and cities so that valuable timber could be saved from termites. Forests are needed to have ecological balance specially this day when the pollution is on the increase.

But the politicians in our country are doing nothing to save the forests or for developing new forest lands. The forest departments are there, they are also funded to develop new forest land, but the desperate rural people tend to encroach on the forest lands and the department of forests do not take any action, because there is no political will. So we shall pay for neglecting to develop new forest as there have been wastelands in the country which were distributed among the landless people, the lands that could not be developed for cultivation should be developed as forest land, but we are not serious, and we have seen that the forest department uses lot of wooden poles to fence the areas where plantations have been done. The plantations do not survive because there is no care and the poles disappear because some people use them for fire. If the department uses the steel poles, they also disappear. So it seems the department should develop concrete poles for fencing. Moreover, the forest mafia has political connections and forest officers are as corrupt as the others are. The forest guards take money for illicit felling of trees for letting people to smuggle out the timber. The checkposts on various roads open the barrier if they get paid in the middle of the night. Though the controls have increased and there are heavy punishments but it is not enough because more and more forest lands are getting encroached. Lots of funds meant to save and develop forests get misappropriated and some of the money is even spent on checkdams on Nallahs which is useless and non-productive. The explanation is that it is done to save the soil erosion but it is like throwing the money into the river. Soil erosion can be avoided by forest cover alone and if you block a nallah or a gorge, the checkdam either gets washed away or the water spreads to the other side. This has been a foolish exercise and misuse of public funds. We have also seen that at many places forests are set on fire by miscreants and no body is punished. There are new plantations being grown and the people set such areas on fire because they want to have grass for the cows. Many people set forests on fire when there is drought, thinking that it will make clouds that will bring rains. That is the height of ignorance because there is lack of education and awareness and the indifference on the part of the government agencies and the people as well. So we have to make a proper national forest and timber policy. We have to develop fuel technology and bring to every household and save the forest from the poachers. The case of the famous sandalwood smuggler Veerappan in south India whom the police of two states Karnataka and Tamil Nadu have failed to catch is an example of the forest mafia problem. Forests are not only important for good environment, but for Jungle life as well which means wildlife. The population growth is also destroying the wildlife. People are making houses of concrete, which are very unhealthy. The use of timber in construction of proper houses is becoming rare.

People have lost the intelligence of making proper houses. The provinces that have proper timber have destroyed lot of forests in the first two decades after independence. The priceless timber has been used to lay down the railway lines. Moreover many people have used the timber as firewood. On the whole it is the overpopulation of the country that has destroyed the forests and again it is this population that needs more forests to keep the ecological balance.

India has to develop the organic farming as, petrol, chemicals and fertilizers are very dangerous. They are causing lot of harm to the general health of the people and the soil. So are the allopathic medicines. India has an ancient Ayurvedic school of medical science but we have neglected its development. The growing pollution in the country is damaging the wild flora and fauna. Spraying of pesticides is causing lot of harm to the wild plantation as well. Our ground water is getting contaminated, the milk in India has four times more DDT than in the western world. Therefore it is more likely that the Indians will soon have four times more cancer cases and other diseases than the rest-of-the-world. It will be the health policy of India not to create new diseases and should treat the old ones. There is a new technique now which has raised a storm of protest in the west that is genetically modified food. With genetic engineering they can produce more foodstuff that could be dangerous. It has not been tested on mass scale yet, so people are apprehensive about the results of eating such foodstuff. Genetically modified vegetable plants and foodgrains could be developed that could be immune to many plant diseases and could grow a bumper crop even on rocks. But effects on human health of eating such stuff are not known yet. However, we have noticed that the average height of people in countries like Holland has increased. Because the cows could be given such food that could change the hormones of the cows and consuming of milk products and beef could change the hormones of such eaters.

There is also talk on medical science that could be used in cloning and change of genes that could also save the people from about 400 diseases and can increase the age of the people. But this genetic engineering is a matter of dispute and has not been approved of yet. To provide basic human rights that of national health assurance we have to put in the place a health system and Ayurvedic and allopathic system has to be developed side by side. Post graduate or medical colleges should be attached to district level hospitals. Advanced technology should be available at district hospitals and all medical aid including medicines, doctors and total facilities should be there at district level. People should not have to go hundreds of miles away to institutes like Institute of All India Medical Sciences at Delhi, which is so crowded that not many people get a chance to be checked and treated. Same way, we have to develop and advance the Ayurvedic system. At the hospitals we should have all things available that are needed. We should have dentists, surgeons, midwives and all such instruments and equipment that is required by the modern systems of world standard.

Once we establish a system of national health insurance we have to develop a culture of physical fitness through sports, Yoga and meditation. Yoga should be the religion of everybody, majority of the people neither look healthy nor they are. Many people in the cities do not have any physical work so they develop unhealthy bodies. The best and the cheapest way to keep your body and mind fit is the Hatha Yoga. And then if you are good at Hatha Yoga, you can be good at meditation as well. Once we develop the culture of yoga and meditation you will have a totally different society and culture which should include physical exercises, sports and proper diet. The traditional mindset of the people has to change. For example, some people think weight lifting, wrestling or building muscles is healthy or to be a boxer like a heavy weight champion is sign of good health. This is an illusion, because this type of bodybuilding starts to crack after you become 40 and then onwards the body develops more disorders and complications. Whereas if you continue with light exercises, long walks and Hatha Yoga you stay fit and relaxed. Yoga and meditation should be a part of education and continuity by the employees of government should be compulsory which will improve the behaviour of the people at public places and offices.

When we think of a healthy country inhabited by healthy people we have to develop a system where atleast it should be compulsory for people to get checked for contagious diseases before they could marry. We know that AIDS is fast spreading in the country. Already we have an estimated four million infected people and it is going up everyday. Because of lack of sex education in the country and reckless sex behaviour of many people, the danger and risk is too high to be ignored. Because there is so much pressure on the people to get married or to marry off their daughter to some stranger, it is very likely that in these days of dangerous contagious diseases like TB, Hepatitis and AIDS, many innocent people can contact and suffer from such diseases and their children can inherit the same. People cannot ask for the medical certificates from the possible partners as a matter of courtesy. Therefore, it is the duty of the government to pass a legislation to make it compulsory for everybody to go for a medical check before compromising on a matter like marriage This is not to say that people carrying such dangerous viruses should be disqualified for marriage, but it should be the right of a person to ask and know the medical status of their possible partners specially when the families arrange the marriages. There is even a risk that somebody may even cheat by giving in samples of healthy friends, as there are no identity cards. To this day this country has not woken up to this problem. Many men, who contact these diseases while working in cities and by having unsafe sex pass on the same to unsuspecting or helpless innocent wives and after infecting the women, their families abandon them. This has to stop. This neo-sati development has to be stopped.

How to Manage the Finances to Build A New India

As we all know that our cities have become slums and there is big chaos. There are no parking places for the vehicles and in most parts of the cities the streets are so narrow that it is either difficult or not possible to drive through. Many cities have been built when there were no cars, electricity poles, telephone poles and sewage and water supply lines. Now those narrow lanes have become chicken boxes. But because these lanes are still used as market places and doing any thing new, like new street or buildings has become difficult because there are so many owners of every square metre that there is no decision or plans that could be made about making something new. Therefore, we have to make new markets, cities and villages. Now many people will ask from where the money will come. In a country of more than one billion people there is as much money as there are people. The countless poverty is not the reflection of the wealth of the country, nor the number of rich people. We simply have to make a plan and a system. For example, in the cities where we have those crowded and narrow lanes we can simply pull down the old buildings, make multi-story buildings and markets and parking-places. If they resist then we have to make alternative markets and cities. There is so much black money in the country and people with white money or even banks hesitate to put their money in real estate because there are no proper laws in the country. For instance, if you make a shop or market to rent, it is more likely that you will never get that place back because there are no rules and laws to evict the occupants and tenants. Whoever gets hold of any premises stays there with the place that is in their possession. The rent and lease laws are so bad and complicated that nobody is encouraged to invest in real estate to rent out the shops and buildings for housing. Unless we change and make proper laws, the chaos and dishonesty and blackmailing and crimes related to possession of properties shall remain. For example, some people made shops in Connaught Place in Delhi in the 1940s. In those days when a daily wage worker was paid 25 paise a day, the people rented their shops for fifty rupees a month, now with our distorted socialistic laws, some people like the tenants continue to pay as much the same rent even daily wage worker gets Rs

100 a day. Same way nobody in future will think of making investments in making markets or housing because they don't want the risk of having difficulty in evicting tenants or getting market price rents and loose peaceful sleep on that account. Similarly, banks will also not invest money on such projects where there is no guarantee.

So to lay out new cities all over the country we have to find out the natural and economic viability Natural viability means sources of water, land and people and economic considerations means the likely industrial and business support and the possible suitable situation for all communication and transport purposes. Once these factors are sorted out you can plan beautiful modern cities that should be good enough for next 300 years. Where there shall be proper housing, markets, industry and places of work there shall be beautiful schools, colleges, universities and hospitals. Playgrounds and lovely gardens, health clubs, clean bus stations, parking places and railway stations and airports. All this is possible because we have a developing economy, because we have poverty and there is scope to invest because people need all the basic things. You cannot invest in cars, because there is no buyer; because there are so many cars, you will have to change the petrol cars because there will be no petrol very soon. So we can announce new modern cities for each province and we have to do reorganisation of some states. For example, Punjab and Haryana have been agitating for the possession of Chandigarh. We can plan one new city for each of them. We can plan a new city for Uttaranchal, Chhattisgarh or Jharkhand. Similarly, we can have new port cities on both sides of our sea line but must take care that the new cities are atleast fifty metres high from the sea level because the sea level will go high as expected.

And in the rural area we can make new modern villages with five hundred families for each village. There should be a village secretariat for few villages where there have to be schools, Panchayats and all such departments that are concerned with the rural administration and development. There have to be proper sanitation that will include the sheds for animals and control of stray dogs and animals. All basic amenities like water, electricity, roads, playgrounds primary health centers have to be in place. Once we make these model villages and implement population control, people will stop migrating to the cities. People will love to live in the villages that will be the real development of the country. When we plan these new villages and cities we must take care that they stay away from the main roads and railway lines. It is also relevant to say that apart from making new cities and villages we have to make proper rent and lease laws. We have to make a law about maintenance of buildings as well. Most of the people just do not bother to complete their building and move in. There are unfinished buildings all over the country, in all the villages and cities which makes it so ugly. There is no architect and the sanitation is very bad. Moreover, the shacks and kiosks spread like wild fire, turning every place into slums.

So it is about time that we give it attention and not only make laws but actually take care about it. Every town and city is fast turning into great mess and we do not seem to care about it. Many people even go out of the country to see life and culture in the west, but when they come back to India they do not seem to learn anything as if Indian way is the greatest way and style of living. Many Indians go out as snobs to feel better that there are these people in the country on whom they can look down. Some people may feel genuinely like helping the rest but they become helpless, as there is no system. So whenever a new city is being planned one should make it sure that you do make houses for the working class before you start to make a city. At the same time, we have to see also that people from across the borders get identified. To control the population growth in the country, we have to ask our neighbours to make laws as well to control the population and people of countries like Nepal and Bangladesh have to be identified and birth control laws have to be implemented on them as well, migration to this country has to be controlled. It is hard to believe that India has just 1 per cent of the total global land but we have 17 per cent of the total world population.

It is possible that when we make new cities, market complexes and public and private buildings we shall forget to make them beautiful and just end up making ugly concrete jungle as is the mentality. Because beauty in this country for most of the people means staring at yourself in the mirror staring at others in the street and looking for beautiful faces in the movies. We do not care that our bedroom and the house and its surroundings look beautiful, we do not care that our shops, streets and roads look beautiful or even proper. We simply push ourselves or get pushed by the others, whether, you are on bus or a train, or you are getting a ticket or a biscuit, its always pushing, which goes on in offices and in market places. Shopkeepers have a tendency to put out their things for sale on the streets. Many people start selling things on the pavements; few mechanics can be seen doing their job on any space they can grab. On the national highways or other roads you can see motor vehicles standing on the main road causing problems. People open restaurants on the side of the roads and the traffic just becomes more chaotic. So we have to make not only proper roads but the services on the side of the roads have to be properly in place.

Now this cannot be the trend for the future it has to stop. To sum it up, it has to be said that we cannot make a new prosperous India by just saying that we have to increase the total gross product by 8 or 10 per cent. We must see that we work on a plan to eradicate poverty and disease. That we provide basic human rights, that we improve on the social justice and destroy corruption and control pollution. That we bring in reforms in administration, judicial system and the political set up by having direct elections of the executive. Therefore, to make this country prosperous for everybody, to make all its citizens proud to be Indians, to make all the people safe from all the dangers of attacks from disease, social insecurity and criminals we have to adopt the path of this 'Nav Rang Marg.' We cannot go out halfway on one point and leave the other point. Our whole body has to be in order, when we take a glass of water or glucose it goes to the whole body. Similarly we have to take a whole treatment to make the body better. So this country of ours needs this treatment now, we cannot leave it for the nature to take care of the mess, we cannot leave it for god to intervene and we have to stop having wishful thinking that by the year 2050 the country will learn to overcome its problems, we have heard from our good for nothing politicians in the past, and in the present that in the next ten years we shall overcome our difficulties. This is the time pass mentality, it has to be checked and stopped and we have to move forward and take a decision today. We have to start this all India development revolution and within 20 years you will see a new India

Employment and Social Security

India has been a feudal society for too long. We have avoided communism and not adopted the capitalism in its American form, instead we went for mixed economy. Mahatma Gandhi's concept of Ram Rajya is the concept of a welfare state. It is not a concept of Hindu fascist state. Though I have wondered why a preacher of non-violence like Gandhi should find solace in the company of *Bhagavat Geeta*. Probably all the Mantras and *Shalokas* are not aimed at making Mahabharat the war. Still a practitioner of non-violence and sanity should not glorify *Geeta* because it was used to prepare Arjuna to make war, the Dharam Yudh. Ram Rajya has to be a social welfare state, free from violence, exploitation, starvation and corruption even pollution. To achieve a state of development where the state becomes unnecessary and people live like communes in border-less habitats. But we have not been able to visualise this Gandhian dream. We have all that poverty and it is associated problems intact. Unemployment and crimes have created social insecurity and it is increasing everyday. What is social security? It could be explained in simple words. There is this saying that man is a social animal. Animal but social, since man is supposed to have developed and involved out of the animal kingdom and with the cultivation of land has become social. Cultivation of land developed into civilisations. People formed social security rings, in the form of families, villages and kingdoms. The family, the village and the kingdom all live to defend themselves. They feel secure only if they could defend from attacks from the other. Similarly, an individual will also feel secure if he can defend himself from disease, hunger and violence from others. This is the basis of social security—that when you are living in a society, you have to feel socially secure. It is not just the security behind your walls. A person must feel secure on the street in broad day-light and at midnight as well. A poor man feels insecure all the time. First, he does not have enough to eat, he does not have enough clothes and a proper house to live in, and similar is the case of families and villages. Where there are no schools and hospitals and on top of that we have terrorists all over the country, who are terrorising and killing people and the police everyday. On the whole, the country is pretty insecure from all sides. This is the environment of social security in India. Whether it is Kashmir, Tripura, Bihar or Andhra Pradesh, there is non-stop violence and the people under attack constantly are insecure.

Same is the case with unemployment. People send their children to school and college to educate them and hope that they will get a job or be employed, but the job situation in the country is becoming worse. The increasing unemployment has made people insecure when you cannot find a proper job, there is no money and without money you cannot look after yourself and there is no family future for you, this is the social insecurity and this social insecurity makes life miserable for you. People turn anti-social and few of them even become Babas because it is a case of finding security. People are afraid of darkness, because you cannot see. When you cannot see and you go out, you can have accident, that is why people are afraid of darkness. Darkness is good for anti-socials. So there is insecurity in darkness. When people see their future as dark without proper employment the social insecurity hounds them. The way of a civilised society is to guarantee social security to its citizens and they put in place a department of social security. This department of social security looks after needs of the helpless people, who are poor and who do not have employment. It looks after the children who are either abandoned or have lost their parents. It protects children from abuse, from parents or from children and protects children from social assault and abuse from the sexually perverted criminals and this social security department runs homes for children care and destitute people, victims of domestic violence, mentally retarded and the handicapped people. The social security department looks after the old helpless people and provides free education to those who cannot afford. The national health assurance is part of the social security system. The social security department also provides funds for the unemployed people on a weekly basis. To say it all in few words, simply and straight, is that the social security department shall look after the basic human rights of' the people and provide them justice and security. Therefore, we have to create this new ministry of social security and the human resource development ministry should stop this hypocritical approach. The ministry of social security shall mean the recognition of the basic human rights of the people and the right to work.

Coming to the issue of right to work, we have to sort out the general employment situation in the country. Soon after the independence, the government started with five-year plans. Education was given priority and many projects started. Anybody who was going out of school was getting employed either by the government agencies or in the private sector. Things started getting cool in the 1960's and then onwards it started becoming difficult for the graduates to get jobs and today we are living in the worst of all times as far as the employment is concerned. Today we have only crossed the 50 per cent mark as far as the percentage of educated people is accounted for. Think about the time when there will be 100 per cent literacy in the country. Few things have gone wrong: (1) Many people long for the non-productive government jobs; (2) the private sector does not pay well; (3) the education lacks professional courses for people, it only produces graduates that go for degrees in arts, the clerical people. Now how many clerks the country can have. Moreover the government has put brakes on the social development projects. In the 1960's there was 1 teacher to 30 or 40 students in one class, now it is one teacher for over 80 students. It is the case with other institutions like hospitals. The only department that has got crowded is the police. Their ratio has tripled even more in relation to population growth. There are over 10 crore that is 100 million child labourers in the country. If we put them in school we need at least 2,50,000 teachers. Moreover, to put down the teacher student ratio to proper level of 40 students a teacher, we shall need another 25,00,000 teachers, i.e., 5 million jobs. Another five million jobs can be created in the health sector where we have to provide full health assurance. Half a million jobs for gardeners and another half a million jobs for garbage handlers. One million jobs for population control and health work. One million jobs for the social security department that shall be responsible for providing basic human rights to the people and there will be 10 million new jobs for construction workers who could be involved in construction of roads and canals and another 10 million people should be involved in the construction of new villages and cities, i.e., to create about fifty million new jobs. Where we do create these jobs, the purchasing power of the people shall put another fifty million people in employment to make the consumer goods and construction material. The whole country can have an economic growth like the developed countries had in the 1950s and 1960s.

Naturally many people will again ask the familiar question about the funds that the state has to raise to embark on a plan and programme like this. As I have said earlier that we have to put a new tax structure in place, all the people can be asked to pay five to ten per cent of their total income as social development tax. That will make the people aware also about the use of public money. Till this day we have known only one way of misappropriating of public funds by the corrupt people from bureaucrats, politicians and the contractors. To make India a developed, cultured and civilised society we have to do this restructuring of our whole system. For long, the human race has been brought up on examples. People give examples, some great men set examples and some countries set examples. That is probably the reason that we talk about those people who have made progress. We talk about those countries that have developed, because we still remain a poverty-stricken backward lot. It is not only us who talk about others, the others also talk about us, but not the same way.

We all know that Japan and Germany lost the Second World War. But after the war they developed their industry very fast. Even though they are still under the American control. Japan is the country that does not have national resources like India; they import the raw material and make goodies that the whole world loves to buy. If Japan had remained a useless backward feudal lot; they could have been in a much worse situation like India. But they have excelled in technology and workmanship, that is why they are economic super power. Israel is another country to look for example. The Jews were killed in the gas chambers by Hitler, they had no country. After the war they grouped up in Israel, the Anglo-American block decided that the Jewish people must have a country or the Jewish people demanded it. What is important to note is that this small country of six million people is standing on its feet today like a tiger? It has hostile neighbours like India has but it survived. We are going there to look for technology to fight terrorism in Kashmir. India is a country of more than one billion people and if it has to ask for help to fight terrorism and poverty, from small countries like Israel, then it is a national shame. We even loose in cricket to very small countries, it must be the match fixing. The facts are that we are a very corrupt and lazy people and we have been under the foreign rulers for very long. That is why we are looking foreign wards to have help. We are asking for foreign investment, we are asking for recognition, we have developed and adopted this foreign language English, and the Congress party even wants a foreign leader for this country. I wonder what could have been our state of mind if we did not have our beloved *sanskriti* to fall back on. Some people even blame our Sanskriti for our present day plight while others want to go back into the history. Let us not waste our time on such futile bickering and develop our *sanskriti* with educated *sanskars*.

Gold cannot be purified with water. Though water can determine how impure the gold is, gold is purified by fire. Similarly, a country can be purified by a revolution, revolution does not have to be a violent one, especially in a democracy. The election results of 1977 were a revolution, but it had no leader and no programme. It ended up in counter evolution. Now we can have a plan and programme with this Nav Rang Marg for the development of a reasonable revolution in the country that will improve on our misplaced *Sanskriti* of distrust and cheating. We need immediate action on all fronts, population control, basic human rights, defence of the country corruption and pollution, economic reforms and justice and all the problems of unemployment and poverty have to be fixed with a quick action and a steady revolution.

The country at present is being torn apart by the separatist calls of regional, religious and caste maniacs. This has become the politics of the day because the politicians have found these issues as easy handles to open the gates for their political careers. That is why we have so many problems in the country due to these kinds of politicians who play on the sentiments and general ignorance of the people. There are calls for separate homelands, state autonomy, and so on, but there is no call for the basic human rights, because once the basic human rights get prominence, these sectarian politicians and the criminals will loose their business and jobs. There is a need for people to understand how stupid they are when they think and discriminate in terms of religion. Just look at a man who is not recognisable by his appearance as to which religion he belongs. In his case you will not form any first hand impression about his religion, then the next step you will ask for his name and then you will think about his religion and form an opinion about him. Man is known by his dress and address, but cannot be accept a man as a man, a part of this human race without fighting with him. We should know which is already known that all the alphabets from A to Z look different yet they have no confrontation with each other. Together they make a language and on their own they are just letters. The humanity could very well take also a lesson from the universe that the stars and planets have such a discipline that they hardly strike against each other, had they been doing so there would have been total chaos and nobody could have survived. So we should see that the human society would work in discipline and without premonition and in harmony. We must respect and give space to everybody and nobody should think of special privilege.

National Sports Policy

With the development of media, the world is becoming smaller. You can watch on TV any sports event from anywhere of the world. You can have information about all sports and you can also know what is the state and standing of sports in India. If you can ignore few rare cases of some individuals, our sports scene is as poor as the general poverty in the country. It is because of our attitude and poverty and general mismanagement of the sports bodies. In the old times, hunting wild animals was considered a sport, it was indulged in by people who could have bow and arrows and later on guns. The general folks were playing *kabaddi, kho-kho* or *gulli danda.* Wrestling and bull cart races were done is some village festivals. Now the major sports has got introduced in the country in the last century or 100 years. We had attained excellence in field hockey and are still a good side. There was a time when India won a gold medal in every Olympic till 1964. And there came also a time when India and Pakistan fought for the last spot. Now we have this cricket which has dominated the last twenty years, thanks to the match fixing, many people have withdrawn from this cricket fever. Otherwise this good for nothing sport which was an obsession of the English aristocrats had paralysed the Indian subcontinent. Football is top sport in the world, because of its popularity but Indian subcontinent in still not charged with the passion for football. Apart from few names in tennis and badminton or chess we have not produced any sportsperson of world class. This is because of our attitude as a developing country. Because of poverty and illiteracy caused by the colonial occupation of the country, sports was only the privilege of the princes or the rich. Rest of the country could afford playing cards. After independence we had open schools everywhere and like always we do not have enough funds, so the sports action cannot be supported. Because the children were supposed to be learning writing and reading, and passing examinations to get into government jobs, the general public was not geared up to enjoy sports, so the government did not provide funds for sports. The funds for sports are generally misappropriated and there is lack of promotion for all sports.

Cricket has emerged as a dominant force, because there is not much competition outside the subcontinent and the media and business have created this publicity for the sport. Also Indian teams have achieved a lot and especially with personal world records of few players. The cricketers and the sport are making lot of money. It is the funds that create players. During the cold war we have seen how Russia and East Germany got away with most of the medals at the Olympics. The sports were organised by the state funds like an army. Now these major sportpersons all over the world have lot of money spent on them in providing facilities and training and when they win they make lot of money and get name and fame that it becomes a craze. The day is not far when India can produce world class sportspersons. It is only a matter of funds and craze for sports. The bureaucratic corruption has to go, we have to make sports bodies that are to be handled by the sportspersons. We cannot have a selection body of bureaucrats who have hardly played any sport in their school days. It is this bungling of bureaucrats and politicians who want an all India representation in the national team that represent India that we end up with a team which lacks quality and co-ordination and that does not win. We have ministers of sports, we have managers and heads of sports organisations, who have never been sportspersons in their times. How they can produce results in sports. The little money that is allotted to the sport activities also gets misappropriated by the habitual corrupt.

We have to develop sports in the country as part of our culture and physical fitness. Therefore, we have to organise it properly. If anything needs globalisation it is sports. I am sure that a country of one billion people can produce world class sports persons in many sports. This is necessary not only for the sake of sports but to raise the national psychology and fitness. If the teams represent the country in any national or international event, there have to be a national federation of such sports which shall have a management board and selection committee. Majority and heads of such boards and committees should be sportspersons who have represented the country, captains, champions or senior players. Similarly on the provincial level, the same rules shall apply to all sports bodies. Most of the sports should be professionalised, so that the people can get and find money to support the sports and advance the cause of sports. However, at school level the state has to put and provide money for the promotion of sports.

Administrative Reforms

Administration in a democracy is to serve the people and not to rule. Since India has been a feudal country for too long, the bureaucrats have become the new feudal lords. It starts from the village *patwari,* the forest guard, the policeman and the excise inspector. Then upwards, the *tehsildar* and his *babus,* the SDM and the deputy commissioner. The *thanedar* and his *munshi,* the DSP and superintendent of Police. All these people in the administration have to be approached by the general public for office work and complaints. There are other departments and officers that the public has to see as well. The block development officer (BDO), the forest range officer, the JE and SDO of the PWD are some of the public servants that have become public masters. The electricity and water supply departments are a permanent headache. To help and serve the general public, there has to be a code of conduct for all these people that are supposed to be public servants. The *patwari* should have his weekly timetable fixed. He should be available for the first three days of the week in his office. The rest of the week he can be on field duties, he can be seeing his superiors or can be on a holiday. But the public should be sure that he is available in his office on the first three days of the week, so that if a man of the public has to see him, he has to be assured of the proper functioning of the *patwari.* On the way up the dates of the visit of the Kanoongo and Tehsildar in the Patwari office has to be fixed and practiced as per the timetable. If the people find these officers not doing their duty according to the timetable, the concerned officers should be punished. On their days the officers have to be in time and not to come just before 5 o'clock. The Patwari office shall display a timetable so that the public knows when to come. The high rank officers of the revenue department cannot take a Patwari out of his office on the first three days nor can he be absent. Similarly on all the other public offices we have to fix the time table, so that the general public does not suffer because of the autocratic behaviour of the public servants. As mentioned already in the previous chapter on judicial reforms there has to be a bench system in all the courts from the district level so that when a common man has to see the courts, he has to be attended and not told to come on some other dates, we have to reform the whole bureaucratic set up, make the public servants responsible and fix the responsibility and assure the public that there is responsible system in the country that they can trust and be proud of.

Fighting the Natural Calamities

Our great Bharat is the land of the limitless miseries apart from illiteracy, poverty and disease. We have lot of natural calamities to contend with every year in one part of the country or the other. We had the great food problems in the 1960s then we have floods every year in one part of the country or the other. Almost every year we have floods in the Brahmaputra belt, Bihar, U.P. and Andhra Pradesh beyond control. Our neighbour Bangladesh gets flooded every year and then we have floods in many other areas in the country. As if this is not enough, we have droughts in many parts of the country and the people and the animals suffer. We have cloud bursts in the mountain areas that cause flash floods and wiping out many bridges, roads and villages. We have lots of landslides causing lots of deaths and damage to the roads, vehicles and the property of the people. We have these cyclones that wipe out villages like it happened in Orissa. We have had devastating earthquakes in different parts of the country from time to time. In the last hundred years the famous Kangra earthquake in 1905 that lasted for nine days when almost all the buildings perished in Himachal Pradesh. Since then we have seen many more earthquakes again in U.P. Uttaranchal, Maharashtra, in the north east and now in Gujarat which is the worst so far. We have not bothered to sort out these calamities like floods and droughts and have no choice in the case of the earthquakes. The whole country has been divided into five minor earthquake zones. Yet there have been no building regulations in view of the threat from the earthquakes. In Delhi there have been a fire brigade rule about buildings that the fire brigade cannot handle the problems beyond ninth floor but there are so many buildings that have violated these regulations and what about the earthquake. Our cities are being built in a chaotic manner and full of slums. Here is no safety either from construction side or from environmental side. There has to be a proper distance between streets and buildings that should be safe in cases of earthquake.

Now to make an emergency authority for help in the event of natural disasters is not enough. It is a good idea that there have to be one national natural calamity help centre with one command. It could be called the national guards and this national guards should also include the readyness for a possible nuclear attack. First, let us start with the threat of earthquake. It has been known since time immemorial that this happens in different parts of India from time to time. It is not like the earthquakes in Japan or the volcanic disasters in the Philippines. The Indian earthquakes are severe sometime and cause destruction of buildings and loss of life. Even then we have not bothered about making the buildings safe. We forget within months of an earthquake and with our careless and chaotic mentality we build markets, buildings and bridges that are not safe. First, we are not honest and we do not use the materials for construction that should be according to prescription. We have sand which is full of clay and soil. This sand mixed with dust and dirt does not hold the cement and concrete. This is the beginning of the foul construction. We have builders who for the sake of profits and with usual sickness of being careless and chaotic make bad mixtures of sand, cement and concrete. In place of cement they put more sand and in place of sand they use sand full of soil that comes down with rivers. At no place you can see people separating the sand from the soil by washing the sand. That is why we have so many buildings collapsing. Also the cement needs curing and about that we also do not bother. Therefore, we see lot of buildings having damp and leakages, the iron gets rusted and the buildings loose their life span. In the last 20 years people have become more dishonest and careless as they have developed this illusion that they are more educated now than their previous generations who were backward but honest.

Similarly we have destruction from floods. Again people are responsible for this. First, we cut the trees in the mountains with criminal greed. Then there are these heavy concentrated rains due to pollution. But moreover, even when we did not have so much pollution the country had been prone to floods. As mentioned in the water management chapter that we have to divert rivers when there are floods. We have to develop the technology to avoid the heavy concentration of clouds and even to make rains when there is none. We have seen that people, as chaotic and careless as we are do not bother to make a proper habitat which is safe from the possible floods. There is a saying that do not make a house near a river or under a hill. But we ignore and if you do care about it there are others and the government does not care that people do not endanger their lives by making homes in the river-basins and nallahas. The politicians think that this is really a good vote bank on the sides of the river banks. Now people have died in thousands in the Orissa cyclones and the Gujarat earthquakes. We are thinking of a national natural calamities authority that could help people in times of such disasters. No doubt, the contours on such an authority should be drawn soon and such a centre should be established with all that is needed in times of such disasters like proper tents with sanitation, blankets, medicines, doctors, field hospitals and emergency lights and water and food system. It should be totally a mobile national service with national funds, and be a part of the defence line that is why I called it a National Guards. Again we should also have droughts management under the same authority that could help people and their livestocks in case of droughts. Few thousands people dead in one area makes a big news and alarms the whole world but India is land where about 30 thousand people die everyday from old age, accidents, starvation, malnourishment and so many natural diseases and epidemics. We run so much help for the victims of these natural disasters, but have remained silent about the disease and poverty. We have news that some miscreants have been stealing and looting in the trouble torn situations like these earthquakes and floods and we do not care about the general law and order in the country. We do not care about the disastrous and dangerous growth of population and we do not care about AIDS that has infected about four million people by now in the country. They will all die, but there is no concern yet. Soon it will be half the populations, as we have seen in the Saharan region of Africa that in some countries about 80 per cent of the population has got the HIV virus that causes AIDS.

Talking about the management and help for these natural disasters, there is a very shameful aspect of such help as well. No doubt there is genuine concern of many people to help such people in need but there are not only few people that steal and loot in such cases, but there are others who are supposed to bring help to the sufferers, but they steal it and stash it in their stores and pockets. The bureaucracy of the *babu*cracy eats most of the help that is supposed to be delivered to the sufferers. This is the truth and this truth has never been exposed and punished.

From food packets, blankets, rations and cement that is supposed to reach the sufferers things disappear on their way and monetary help is also pocketed by the *Babus* and other unscrupulous people. For example, if the government is supposed to have given 5000 rupees to each family it so happens that the family gets only Rs. 500 and their signatures are obtained. In many cases there are bogus entries as well. So we have to think and plan and establish the organisation for fighting the natural calamities and providing proper help to the sufferers.

The Talk of More Autonomy for the Provinces

This talk has been generated by some vested interests in some parts of the country who simply cannot say openly that they resent being in the Indian federation. This idea has got circulated among some regional parties who find it easy to talk about it in their constituencies to survive politically as they have created political parties on regional, linguistic and religious basis. The ignorant public gets manipulated by these vested interest groups, some of them even have their mentors outside the country. Let us discuss this issue regionwise. To start with Kashmir, it was the former state of Jammu & Kashmir that had a princely ruler who was absolute in his power. Though he accepted the British Monarchy as his King of kings, he did not allow them any land even to buy. The British had to build the house boats on the Dal Lake if any one of them wanted to stay in Kashmir. The Kashmiri people had no say and were subjects of the king of Jammu & Kashmir of the Dogra dynasty. After India became free the ruler decided not to merge with any country, but Pakistan soon attacked Kashmir in collaboration with some tribes like Afridi to avoid international criticism. Because Pakistan knew that the majority of Kashmiris were Muslims and adjacent to Pak, therefore they could finally grab Kashmir. The Maharaja Hari Singh of J & K sent his Prime Minister for the talks to Delhi with a request for help and had signed a blank paper because he needed help. But Nehru was enjoying the company of Sheikh Abdullah and both of them were anti-Maharaja. None of them had any legitimacy as far as Jammu and Kashmir was concerned. Because the Pakistanis had attacked Kashmir therefore they got this importance to be contacted as Nehru having Kashmiri ancestral links had become the prime minister of India. Both of these men wanted to humiliate the Maharaja forgetting their own duty towards the country, i.e., India. It was this relationship between Nehru and Abdullah that created this Kashmir problem for which the country is paying till today. The Kashmiri Muslims are migrants from Central Asia and even Greece. They do not deserve special treatment, as the whole country has hundreds of such tribes who are diverse in their situation. The merger of Jammu and Kashmir with India is final like the rest of the country and we should not waste our time on explaining this merger and talk of autonomy, this is an old Abdullah trap that has no takers The Maharaja of Jammu & Kashmir had signed a blank paper for the merger of his state with India. It was prime minister Nehru and Sheikh Abdullah who had conspired to create the Kashmiriat. The Kashmiri Pandit under Nehru had joined this plan to keep Kashmir as a distinct province. Even the refugees from Pakistan in 1947 were not allowed to settle in Kashmir. Today, the Kashmiri Pandits are paying for Kashmiriat and junior Abdullah will make the whole country to pay soon if his demand of autonomy is not crushed. Indira Gandhi had done well by controlling Sheikh Abdullah but Rajiv Gandhi brought Farukh Abdullah back and it is this junior Abdullah who needs autonomy who cannot attend office, he has to fly in helicopter from his residence to the office. It is for this kind of public service that these regional chieftains want to become absolute rulers. Recently at the Indira Gandhi Airport at Delhi people had to wait to get out of the airport because the daughter in law of the Punjab chief minister Mr Badal had come from Germany and black cat commandos were seen carrying and loading her suitcases through the green channel, this must be the financial autonomy for the Akali Dal. It is these regional parties whose chief minister like Jayalalita and Laloo Prasad Yadav and some others who have not been named yet or charged with enormous corruption and in this era of coalition governments, it is difficult to deal with them. The Kashmiris have to be told publicly that they benefit from being a part of India because their business prosper in India, it is the Indian people who are tourists, their products sell in India and on top of that they depend on India for financial support that has been given to them in the last fifty years. The Pakistanis are only interested to grab their land and the women and make a bigger connection with China. And this Arabic terrorist Osama not only wants Kashmir but also Himachal and part of Nepal even and that is to grow narcotics and sell that to the rest-of-the-world. The Islamic card is useless for the people of Kashmir as they have seen it in Bangladesh. The Pakistanis killed three million Bangladeshis who were its own citizens to subjugate them. It was only the democrat India that saved them and now they are a free country. But Islamic fundamentalism tries to placate them against India, The advocates of autonomy should explain to the people as how they plan to run such states without help from the centre.

The other party that speaks for more powers for the provinces is the Akali Dal in Punjab another sectarian outfit. It was this ideology of the Akali Dal that has produced people like Bhindranwale and the demand for Khalistan. Punjab is a prosperous state and the rest of the country buys the food-grains from it. No doubt, it is a great contribution on the part of Punjabis that they produce so much foodgrain. But then the market is also the rest of the country. Himachal Pradesh is producing lot of apples and the market is rest of India. It also is producing electricity and again the market and finance are coming from rest of the country. That also does not create a demand for autonomy in Himachal.

There is some oil coming from Assam and some coal as well and we have this regional trouble there as well. As if the ULFA was not enough, there is this Bodoland problem. In other eastern states like Manipur, Tripura and Nagaland we have similar separatist outfits that have their parties who ask for greater financial autonomies these are also regional outfits like the DMK's and Desams. These greater autonomy demands are their political survival tactics otherwise they hardly do anything for the basic problems of the people, they only want to enjoy the power and pelf at the cost of the whole country. They do not have any agenda or plan to provide the people basic human rights. Many of these outfits are supported by the enemies of India. This is a fact and their regional outbursts against the country will not succeed because the people know that greater the country the better for everybody. As we see the progressive countries are uniting as common market and global market and the backward thinking is reflected by the division of the countries, the Germans have united and the Koreans are thinking because they want progress. It is only those ignorant people who think of separating people. So that they can grab some pockets for their shirts. There is a movement for a borderless world so that we could move freely across the world and that will be good for everybody, but there are these feudal interests that want to keep their fiefdoms and create more so that they keep the world divided by borders and make wars and live from wars.

However, we should proceed with reorganisation of the provinces. This has to be done if we want to have progress. The smaller states of Punjab, Haryana, Himachal and Goa have made progress in the sense that the life standard of the common man is better than in the bigger provinces. Karnataka and Kerala are other progressive states. But the bigger states like UP, Bihar, Maharashtra, Andhra, Madhya Pradesh and Rajasthan are badly managed and very backward. The life of the common man is very poor and suffer from all that is associated with poverty. These bigger states are also lacking in family planning. They are backward in every field but forward in crimes. The making of new India shall not entertain any talk of autonomy and separate homeland because that will make more mess in the country and we have to supervise the whole country towards the Nava Rang Marg and bring in a revolution that is going to bring the whole country on a par with the developed world, that is going to help every individual, every family and the whole country.

The Kashmir assembly had passed a resolution for autonomy, for restoring the pre-1953 status few years back. Tomorrow somebody in Hyderabad or Junagarh can pass a resolution to restore the pre-1947 status. And somebody in Pakistan can pass a resolution to restore in India pre-Aurangzeb status. It remains to be seen how the Abdullah BJP alliance will use this new handle to stay in politics. Today we see lot of activity on the part of the central government to woo support for India to get a permanent seat at the Security Council and fighting Pakistan sponsored terrorism. We are continuously asking for foreign direct investment in the country and for this we have half the cabinet running around Europe. This is typical Indian approach not winning a medal at the national level but wishing to win an Olympic medal at the expense of the national exchequer. Ridiculous approach, isn't it? The home minister visited Israel and was shown the border management with Lebanon. It is like Choudhary Devi Lal visiting Australia where he was shown the tallest building as a piece of development. Mr L.K. Advani probably wanted to demonstrate his intentions to please his constituency in his party. Otherwise it is a national shame that we have to be told by a small country like Israel how to manage a border and Mr Advani took such a pride in telling the whole world that he saw how even a bird cannot cross the border in Israel.

Back home Mr Abdullah, his party's ally is behaving like the senior Abdullah did with Nehru. As usual the communist party has declared its support to Abdullah's autonomy resolution. The prime minister Mr Vajpayee has found it compelling to declare that his government will deal firmly with the freak violent attacks on the Christians at the time of his visit to Italy and Portugal and meeting with Pope John Paul. The people who do not show any concern for the Pakistanis sponsored terrorism in India that has cost in India thousands of lives should be concerned at the murder of few Christian missionaries who have an agenda of creating so many East Timore in India through conversion by unethical means. Countries like Portugal and Italy have racist past and we are asking for their support to get in the UN security council or in European common market. We do not do any homework, yet we want to pass school examination with fake certificates. As I have discussed in the economic reforms chapter earlier, that we need to improve quality of our products and produce cheaply only then we can compete. The market forces operate on this basis, you cannot ask countries and the governments like we deal with Russia to buy things from India. No doubt there is protectionism and discrimination in the Europe common market and USA but should make it a point to make our business and products attractive. Only then we can succeed. Otherwise the foreign direct investments are coming only to take money and wealth, they do not come here to help us.

No doubt our foreign policy has made some improvement but success again depends on our performance, if we cannot solve the terrorists problem then we can have only some supporters of Indian disintegration who will ask us to agree to autonomy of separatist forces. Our dependence on foreign weapons is the most harmful situation. To have strategic relationship because of the weapons is not an intelligent policy. India must buy technology and must spend money on research. We cannot be safe with foreign weapons, foreign weapons make wars. This you can see everywhere. As long as we are dependent on foreign weapons we shall have insecurity and border problems. If we can develop software of world class we can also produce weapon systems of world class, we have to privatise the defence industry especially for new technology. But our defence establishment finds it easy to go out for shopping. Though there has been little improvement in the general functioning of the system in India at the policy level, the bureaucratic syphilis remains to be cured as ever and the traditional thinking and functioning founded by the Congress party remains intact as if it is our national tradition. The BJP government has not shown yet in four years that it is different from the Congress and that it can change things for the better. So it is time that the people of the country that is the one billion Indians take to the path of *Nav Rang Marg* and make India a better place for living. It is neither the golden bird of the Firangy nor the golden Lanka of Ravana. It is naturally a prosperous country and civilisation. We have to restore the links of development, one billion Indians have to find synchronism for its two billion hands and stand on their feet, walk, play, win, enjoy and live with honour. *Nav Rang Marg* is a never-ending *Marg*.

Index